sex

and

unisex

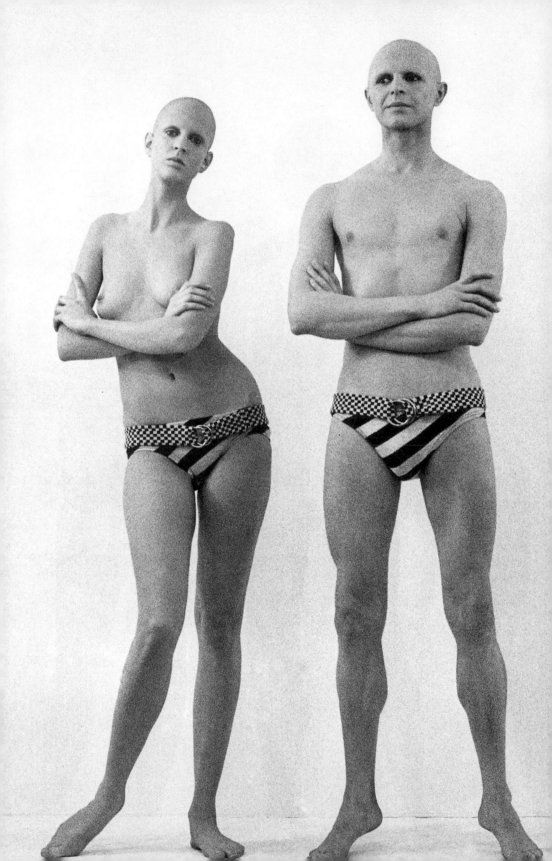

Jo B. Paoletti

Sex and Unisex

Fashion, Feminism, and the Sexual Revolution

INDIANA UNIVERSITY PRESS
Bloomington and Indianapolis

This book is a publication of

INDIANA UNIVERSITY PRESS
Office of Scholarly Publishing
Herman B Wells Library 350
1320 East 10th Street
Bloomington, Indiana 47405 USA

iupress.indiana.edu

♾ The paper used in this publication meets the minimum requirements of the American National Standard for Information Sciences—Permanence of Paper for Printed Library Materials, ANSI Z39.48–1992.

Manufactured in the United States of America

Cataloging information is available from the Library of Congress.

ISBN 978-0-253-01596-9 (cloth)
ISBN 978-0-253-01602-7 (ebook)

1 2 3 4 5   20 19 18 17 16 15

*For the men in my life, especially
Bob, Danny, Jacob, and Jim.*

contents...

Acknowledgments

Acknowledgments   ix

Introduction   1

1 Movers, Shakers, and Boomers   16

2 Feminism and Femininity   35

3 The Peacock Revolution   59

4 Nature and/or Nurture?   92

5 Litigating the Revolution   123

6 The Culture Wars, Then and Now   150

Notes   173
Bibliography   181
Index   191

 *Acknowledgments*

Writing a book can be hard, lonely work. Fortunately, I had help and support throughout the process, appearing as if by magic precisely in the form required at the moment. Indiana University Press encouraged me to build on my first book, *Pink and Blue: Telling the Boys from the Girls in America,* and continues to be a wonderful partner. Karin Bohleke, director of the Fashion Archives and Museum at Shippensburg University, was generous with her time and energy, providing access to their marvelous collection and assistance with many of the images for the book. Philip Cohen, Susan Kaiser, and Eliza Buchakjian-Tweedy commented on the project at various stages in ways that were both constructive and encouraging. I am enormously grateful to the College of Arts and Humanities and the Department of American Studies at the University of Maryland for a grant that reduced my financial burden.

I wish to express my love and thanks to all the communities that sustain me. My students challenge and teach me every day, and my colleagues across campus and around the world have been good listeners and excellent advisers. My spiritual community, the Unitarian Universalist Church of Silver Spring, truly gave me roots and wings as needed. Every writer needs a break, and mine usually came courtesy of the "regulars" at Franklin's Restaurant, Brewery, and General Store—my Friday evening retreat for excellent conversation, on- and off-topic. Finally, my family deserves special thanks for their patience and forbearance over the last two years, for all the times I had to say "later" instead of "yes."

sex

and

unisex

Introduction

ho knew that the 2012 presidential campaign would turn into a 1960s flashback? For many of us, the moment of awakening was when Republican candidate Rick Santorum seemingly stepped out of a time machine and proclaimed his opposition not just to abortion rights but to birth control as well. The controversy began when columnist Charles Blow rediscovered Santorum's 2008 speech to the Oxford Center for Religion and Public Life in Washington, including this comment the senator made during the question-and-answer period:

> You're a liberal or a conservative in America if you think the '60s were a good thing or not. If the '60s was a good thing, you're left. If you think it was a bad thing, you're right. And the confusing thing for a lot of people that gets a lot of Americans is, when they think of the '60s, they don't think of just the sexual revolution. But somehow or other—and they've been very, very, clever at doing this—they've been able to link, I think absolutely incorrectly, the sexual revolution with civil rights.[1]

With all due respect to Senator Santorum, I do see connections between the sexual revolution and the civil rights movement, and his comments suggest that he does too, even if he believes they have been linked erroneously. In fact I venture to say that many of the issues in today's culture wars—gay and transgender rights, gender equality, reproductive choice—center on the disputed territory of sexual norms and are argued in terms of civil rights and government authority to dictate morality. As a means of expressing sexual and gender identity, the fashions of the time revealed the cultural shifts set in motion by the women's liberation movement and the sexual revolution. The countermovements and controversies over these changes are likewise visible, particularly in the scores of legal cases involving long hair on men: cases that explicitly enlisted the language of civil rights.

This book began as an exploration of gender expression in unisex clothing from the 1960s and 1970s. The culture of that era is a puzzle, even to those of us who lived through it. Was it the "Me Decade," characterized by narcissism and self-indulgence? Or was it a time of social activism and experiments with communal economies? Did we discover our environmental conscience or dig ourselves even deeper into consumerism? The question originally animating this research was this: Was unisex fashion simply a playful poke at gender stereotypes, or was it a deeper movement to become our "true," unessentialized selves? Over the past thirty years the '60s and '70s have been reduced to a laughable era of loud clothes and crazy hairstyles, just another ride in the pop culture theme park. It is easy to dismiss dress history as a superficial topic, meaningful only to fashionistas and industry insiders. Most of the popular works on '70s fashion are image-heavy exercises in nostalgia, often with a touch of humor. Those crazy people and their wacky clothes! The problem with popular images of fashion is that they tend to erect a trivial facade over real cultural change.

As I went more deeply into the subject, nostalgia was replaced by déjà vu. Even before Senator Santorum made his revealing remarks, it was obvious to me that we are still wrestling with controversies about sex, gender, and sexuality that manifested themselves in the fashions of fifty years ago. Sometimes the argument was loud and public and fought in the courtroom, as with the question of long hair for men. Sometimes it was an inner, personal conflict between the tug of deeply ingrained feminine expressions and the ambition to succeed in a male-dominated profession. Exploring the rich cultural setting of unisex fashion not only contributes to our understanding of history but also helps us comprehend the current culture wars. It is not hyperbole to say that the lives of today's children are still being shaped by the unresolved controversies rooted in the social and cultural upheavals of the 1960s and embodied in fashions of the '60s and '70s.

I study gender because it is what I must untangle in order to understand my own life. For others the puzzle may be race, death, or something else, but my deepest questions have always been about this paradoxical thing we call gender. I call it "paradoxical" because the term was invented

Gendered clothes for a formal portrait, 1952.

in the 1950s to describe the social and cultural expressions of biological sex. Yet in everyday usage the concepts of sex and gender are almost always conflated, inseparable in many peoples' minds. Because my relationship to the subject is, and has always been, personal, I include my reflections as part of the body of evidence. Not that my experiences were more authentic than anyone else's. Rick Santorum also lived through the '60s and '70s, though as a man born in 1958, not a woman born in 1949. It is important that our histories incorporate diverse voices, and I include mine as one of millions.

You see me here in three very different childhood pictures. The formal portrait is me at about three and a half, in a velvet-trimmed dress I still remember fondly. My mother's red houndstooth check dress was also trimmed with velvet, and my father and brother wear nearly identical warm gray suits. We look like the very model of a gender-appropriate family in 1952. The snapshot of my brother and me was taken around 1953 on a family vacation. My hair is in its natural unruly state, and I am wearing my brother's old T-shirt and jeans. This was my world in the 1950s: dresses and pin curls for school, church, and parties, but jeans for play. I wanted to be a cowboy when I grew up, and one Christmas my parents humored me with a cowboy outfit with a two-gun holster. I adore all of these pictures, because they are all so very me.

I got my first period the year after the Pill was approved by the FDA. In 1963, when Betty Friedan's *The Feminine Mystique* was published, I was just starting high school. Like so many young women who were swept along in the sexual revolution and the cultural shifts of the 1960s, I was promised much and given, well, not little, but less than the word "revolution" implied. The more I pursued the idea of "gender," the more it got tangled up in sex. This became ever clearer as I explored unisex and gendered clothing from the 1960s and 1970s. There were so many dead ends, so much confusion, and so very much unfinished business! Researchers

Neutral styles for leisure, 1953.

thrive on open questions; gender is mine, because it is the aspect of my own life that puzzles me most.

The project also became broader, more complicated, and its scope widened. Enlarging the time frame was easy: while unisex fashions peaked in the early 1970s, they first appeared in the 1960s and did not shift out of the foreground until around 1980. When I realized that designer Rudi Gernreich had created both unisex fashions and the topless bathing suit, it was clear that the sexual contradictions of the period demanded attention. Reflecting the revised scope of the project before me, the working title for this book went from "Unisex: The Unfinished Business of the 1970s" to "Sex and Unisex: Fashion, Feminism, and the Sexual Revolution." "Feminism" dropped in and out of the title as I pondered the constrained and loaded meanings of that term. Finally it stayed in, because the feminist movement for gender equality was an important factor in the linkage between the sexual revolution and civil rights, and because as I completed this book in 2014, feminists were being blamed for all sorts of ills, from poverty to the decline of toughness in our foreign policy.[2]

Jo Barraclough, cowboy, 1956.

The actual timeline addressed in this book is complex. It includes the early 1960s, with teens and young adults imitating popular musicians, and with young designers producing clothing for a new generation inspired by the civil rights movements and the sexual revolution. Designers from Paris (Pierre Cardin) to Hollywood (the uniforms in *Star Trek*) imagined a future of equality and androgyny—within the limits of their own worldviews, of course. The movement of women into male-dominated professions, facilitated by the equal employment opportunity portion of the Civil Rights Act, coincided with the rise of professional clothing for women. The history of the Equal Rights Amendment (ERA) to the U.S. Constitution, which was reintroduced to the public discussion in the late 1960s, parallels the popularity of unisex clothing for both men and women. Passed by Congress in 1972 when unisex trends began to peak, the ERA ultimately failed state ratification, vanishing from the nation's agenda at the same time more stereotypically gendered styles were enjoying a revival.

The unisex movement affected all ages, in part simply because adult fashions trickled down to school-age children. Beyond the usual influence of fads and fashions, public discussion about the origins and desirability of traditional sex roles fueled changes in clothing for babies and toddlers beginning in the early 1970s. Between 1965 and 1975, girls started wearing pants to school, just as their mothers wore them to work. Boys as well as men enjoyed a brief "peacock revolution," when bold colors and patterns brightened their wardrobes. Legal battles were fought over hair, beginning with lawsuits over school dress codes but eventually extending to the military, police and firefighters, and white-collar workers. These sartorial changes occurred against a backdrop of intense popular and public policy discourse on issues ranging from access to contraception in the 1960s to girls' participation in organized sports, following the passage of Title IX in 1972. The pendulum started to swing back toward more traditionally feminine clothing in the mid-1970s with designer Diane Von Furstenberg's wrap dress (1974) and the launch of Victoria's Secret (1976), and by the mid-1980s unisex fashions had largely faded into the haze of nostalgia.

For the most part, "unisex" meant more masculine clothing for girls and women. Attempts to feminize men's appearance turned out to be particularly short-lived. The underlying argument in favor of rejecting gender binaries turns out to have been more binaries. First there was a forced decision between gender identities being a product of nature or nurture. For a while the nurture side was winning. Gender roles were perceived to be socially constructed, learned patterns of behavior and therefore subject to review and revision. Unisex fashions were one front in the culture wars of the late '60s and '70s, a war between people who believed that biology is destiny and those who believed that human agency could override DNA. As more people accepted the significant cultural nature of gender, a new binary emerged. Either culturally dictated gender roles were good and necessary, or they were outmoded and dangerous. Throughout this book I try to expose how categories and labeling, while useful in many ways, can also perpetuate stereotypical thinking. Stereotypes encourage simplistic ways of viewing a complex world. There is a reason why humans use stereotypes: they help us make quick decisions in confusing or chaotic situations. But quick decisions are not always the right ones. Many of our gender stereotypes are superficial, arbitrary, and subject to change. (This was the main point of my first book, *Pink and Blue*.[3]) Boys one hundred years ago wore pink and played with dolls. Legos used to be unisex. Field hockey is a man's game in India. Elevating stereotypes to the level of natural law is, well, silly. Most of our gender stereotypes depend on our believing that sex and gender are binary; to summarize the last fifty years of research on the subject, however, they are not. There are babies born every day who are not clearly boys or girls on the outside, and our insides—physical, mental, and emotional—comprise an infinite range of gender identity and expressions.

The unisex movement—which includes female firefighters, football star Roosevelt Grier's needlepoint, and *Free to Be . . . You and Me*—was a reaction to the restrictions of rigid concepts of sex and gender roles. Unisex clothing was a manifestation of the multitude of possible alternatives to gender binaries in everyday life. To reduce the unisex era to long hair vs. short hair, skirts vs. pants, and pink vs. blue is to perpetuate that binary mind-set and ignore the real creative cultural pressure for new directions that emerged during this period. Reducing the pursuit of equal rights to the clothes worn to a protest trivializes the most important social movement of our lifetime.

Lest anyone worry that this is going to be a memoir, my research draws on dress history, public policy, and the science of gender, not just my own frail memory. To describe the various styles and trends associated with unisex fashion, I consulted mass-market catalogs, newspaper and magazine articles, and trade publications. Each of these sources offers a slightly different perspective on the trends. Catalogs and the popular fashion press tend to be neutral or positive about new fashions; industry sources (*Earnshaw's, Women's Wear Daily, Daily News Record*) can be more sanguine, especially as a trend begins to fade. Critical views can come from newspapers and magazines but are especially plentiful in cartoons and other forms of humor. The legal and policy reactions to unisex styles include court cases, government regulations, and dress codes, such as those relating to hair length for men and pants for women. The judicial opinions handed down in these cases were particularly helpful in tracing the shifts in what is considered "generally acceptable" forms of dress. Scientific inquiry into gender and sexuality during this period expanded rapidly as a response to feminism, the sexual revolution, and the gay rights movement. The scientific literature, both academic and popular, provides vital insights into the competing schools of thought on what constituted "normal" sexuality and gender expression and how the scientific evidence was (or was not) translated into popular opinion and practice.

Sex and Unisex offers an interdisciplinary analysis of the gender issues raised during the 1960s and '70s in the United States. Each chapter focuses on one element of the unisex movement, illuminating the conflicts within it and how unresolved issues are still playing out today. At the same time, every chapter addresses some of the same organizing questions: What variations of gendered and unisex design are evident, and what do they reveal about underlying conflicts about sex and sexuality? How were conceptions of masculinity and femininity highlighted or subverted by unisex styles? Along the way I consider the reactions of those people who adopted unisex fashion and those who resisted them. My main argument is that this era, its conflicts and its legacy, reveals the flaws in our notions of sex, gender, and sexuality, right down to the familiar dichotomy of "nature or nurture." These flaws underlie the unfinished business at the intersection of the sexual revolution and the civil rights movement as revealed in today's culture wars.

The role of science and social science research in framing the public debate on gender is especially significant. It is no coincidence that studies of sex and gender expanded dramatically during the 1960s and 1970s as the women's liberation movement gathered momentum. Many of these were either reported in the newly launched *Psychology Today* (1967) or *Ms.* (1971), both of which played important roles in translating often-obscure scientific studies into popular articles. The credibility and persuasive power of scientific evidence is based on its reputation as objective, but critics have pointed out that the science of gender often falls short of perceived objectivity. The questions, protocols, and interpretation of gender science have often been shaped by the researchers' cultural context, if not by their personal concerns or political persuasions. At the publication level the decision of what reaches the public, and at what stage, affects not only public awareness of the findings but also whether it is accepted as scientific "truth." The story of unisex fashion, and the larger unisex movement, needs to be placed in the context of gender science as it developed as a field and as it informed the public. Each chapter in this book foregrounds a particular aspect of unisex fashion and connects it with both the public conversation surrounding it and the scientific knowledge that was shaping public opinion.

In chapter 1, "Movers, Shakers, and Boomers," I look at the generational push toward gender-free fashion as an expression of the coming of age of the postwar baby boom generation. Admittedly most teenagers in the 1960s did not have a "war on culture" in mind when they emulated their musical idols or adopted the fresh designs of Rudi Gernreich and London's Carnaby Street. Gernreich, the Austrian-born American designer and gay rights activist, introduced both the topless bathing suit and many of the most iconic unisex fashions. Even more than fashion designers, musicians were the undisputed style leaders of the early 1960s, with the televised appearances of groups such as the Beatles and the Supremes inspiring millions of young consumers. Besides changing American music, popular performers spread new expressions of sexuality, particularly for men. The conflict between styles that were intended to display and celebrate the human body and a movement to erase differences that result in inequality is a major theme in fashion from the mid-1960s on and remains unresolved as the baby boomers enter old age.

The next chapter, "Feminism and Femininity," traces the changing notion of femininity in the face of second-wave feminism, beginning with the 1963 publication of *The Feminine Mystique*. While I focus on the most visible sartorial change for girls and women during the period, which was the acceptance of pants outside of leisure settings, I also consider the impact of styles of teen-oriented fashions—part of the cultural movement *Vogue* editor Diana Vreeland christened the "Youthquake"—on women's bodies. Women's bodies themselves became more visible (literally, as hemlines rose) and were reshaped through exercise and new styles of undergarments (or none at all). The sexual revolution gave women credit for having sexual appetites, and the Pill gave them the means to satisfy those appetites without fear of pregnancy, but it also gave us a new "feminine mystique": the sexually liberated, available sex object, epitomized by Helen Gurley Brown's "*Cosmo* Girl." The paradox of this era is that the pressure on women to be attractive—young, slender, and sexy—intensified and gradually spread to all ages. I discuss the clothing worn by singer Cass Elliot of the Mamas and the Papas as an example of the resistance that was possible due to the sheer variety of available styles at the time.

Chapter 3, "The Peacock Revolution," focuses on the expansion of choices for men, ranging from Romantic revival (velvet jackets and flowing shirts) to a pastiche of styles borrowed from Africa and Asia. Journalist George Frazier popularized the phrase "peacock revolution" to describe the styles coming from London's young Carnaby Street designers, which promised to restore the lost glory of flamboyant menswear. Expanded color palettes, softer fabrics, and a profusion of decorative details represented a very direct challenge to the conformity and drabness of menswear at mid-century. For critics of new men's fashions, flowered shirts and velvet capes raised the specter of decadence and homosexuality, a fear reinforced by the emergence of the gay liberation movement. Just as women's unisex styles had to balance being sexy and liberated, men's styles tended to navigate the territory between expressiveness and effeminacy. That tension still exists, kept alive by unfolding controversies about LGBTQ (lesbian, gay, bisexual, transgender, queer) rights.

Barbershops felt the immediate effect of unisex trends: haircuts went from a weekly ritual to an occasional, do-it-yourself task. When men finally returned to regular styling, they tended to patronize "unisex salons," not barbershops. An entire new industry was born in the mid-1970s, as the once modest market for male grooming and grooming products expanded. Today not only are unisex hair salons still thriving, but upscale barbershops are competing with them for a portion of the huge market for male grooming, including manicures, antiaging treatments, and body hair removal, or "manscaping." The long hair saga provides insight into the continuing, often covert, movement to permit men as much personal expression as women.

In chapter 4, "Nature and/or Nurture?" I turn to children's clothing and the most fundamental questions of the unisex era: What is the origin of gendered behaviors, and can they be changed? As the women's movement challenged traditional female roles and popular media seemed to offer new expressions of masculinity and femininity, public attention turned to early childhood and the potential to alter the future by changing the way children learn about gender. Scientific evidence pointed to gender roles being learned and malleable in the very young. Children born between the late 1960s and the early 1980s were likely to have experienced nonsexist child raising to some extent, whether at home, school, or through media like books and television.

This particular aspect of the unisex movement offers the richest source of evidence of popular beliefs about sex, gender, and sexuality, which were often strongly influenced by parental ambivalence and anxiety. This chapter places changes in children's clothing styles in the context of competing scientific explanations of gender and sexuality, how well they were understood by the general public, and how children responded to the unisex movement. Nor have the questions raised forty years ago been satisfactorily answered; the public is still divided over issues of gender and sexuality. Whether the topic under discussion is same-sex marriage or gender-variant children, beliefs about nature and nurture—based on science or scripture—are fundamental to the arguments.

In chapter 5, "Litigating the Revolution," I examine the legal side of the unisex movement, focusing mainly on the battle over long hair on boys and men and the impact of the Civil Rights Act of 1964. The British Invasion in popular music deserves much of the credit for the early trend toward longer hair for men. But the Black Power movement further complicated questions of gender-appropriate grooming by intersecting them with expressions of racial identity. Men with long hair faced considerable criticism and resistance, with many confrontations ending in court, as had been the case with women wearing pants. African American women opting for Afros and braids also experienced criticism and discrimination as the dialogue about gender expanded to include "natural" versus "artificial" beauty. Battles over hair length began in high schools and gradually expanded into the workplace and the military. Young men daring to wear their hair long were accused of everything from anarchy to homosexuality, which suggests just how disruptive it seemed to their parents, teachers, and bosses. Within a few years many of those parents, teachers, and bosses also sported sideburns and hair creeping past their collars; by 1972 the judge in one long hair case noted, "The shift in fashion has been more warmly embraced by the young, but even some of the members of this court, our male law clerks and counsel who appear before us have not been impervious to it."[4]

Title VII (Equal Employment Opportunity) had an enormous impact on workplace clothing for women and for both men and women in formerly single-sex professions such as police officer and flight attendant. That story is told here through a description of the efforts to develop appropriate uniforms and through analysis of the initial changes in uniform styles. Title IX (Equal Opportunity in Education) was responsible for an expansion of girls' and women's sports programs at the high school and collegiate level. As women's sports gained funding and recognition, the clothing worn for those sports were redesigned.

Neither of these issues is yet settled in terms of policy or popular culture. Although women now account for more than half of the workforce, they continue to be paid less than their male counterparts for similar positions. Female sports stars are as likely to be recognized for their appearance as for their ability. The importance of beauty and sexual display, even in the workplace, seems even greater than it was before the unisex movement. This chapter juxtaposes sociological research on women's equality with the rise and fall of unisex clothing for work and sports.

The final chapter, "Culture Wars, Then and Now," summarizes and synthesizes the themes from previous chapters, bringing the discussion around to the current cultural landscape. Some of the innovations of the unisex era—pants for women, for example—represent permanent changes in cultural patterns but not a revolution in gender roles. Other trends from the 1970s—unstructured alternatives to men's business suits, for example—turned out to be short-lived fads. The sexual revolution and the gains of the civil rights era are still controversial, and the clothing changes that originally accompanied them are an important way to reveal the outlines of today's conflicts. Today's fashions and beauty culture continue to be sources of tension for women, between their need to be taken seriously (as workers, athletes, and human beings) and the traditional role of clothing as a form of self-expression and a means of enhancing one's sexual attractiveness.

In addition, new issues have emerged from the unresolved questions of the 1970s. Who in 1975 could have predicted that the 2012 presidential election campaign would feature arguments about the centerpiece of the sexual revolution, the contraceptive pill? That princess merchandise for preschoolers would be a billion-dollar industry? That *X: A Fabulous Child's Story* would be enjoying a revival among a new generation of young parents longing for ungendered clothing and toys for their babies? That the new frontiers in civil rights would be same-sex marriage, transgender rights, and the protection of gender-creative children? By examining the cauldron of the sexual revolution through everyday fashions, I hope to restart the dialogue we abandoned a generation ago and move us closer to resolving both old and new controversies.

The fashion industry has spent billions of dollars convincing us that fashion is frivolous. Yes, fashion is fun, but clothing is also bound up with the most serious business we do as humans: expressing ourselves as we understand ourselves. In the 1960s and '70s millions of Americans were struggling with existential questions: Who am I? What does it mean to be fully who I am? What rules are worth following and which should be discarded? Barriers of race, class, religion, and gender were being challenged by some and protected by others.

The story of these experiences is found in every trace of culture from that time period. It could be experienced through so many lenses—politics, music, humor, drug culture, alternative economies—but I have chosen to examine it through clothing and appearance, because dress has been my lens since I was very young. Having lived through that time as a teenager and young woman who followed fashion and eventually majored in it in college, I am amazed to admit that I did not fully comprehend the size and ferocity of the larger cultural conflict going on around me at the time. I cannot remove myself from the story, so I must place myself within it. Some of my academic peers, especially those outside American Studies, may find this self-reflexivity uncomfortable, but as I see it, I had a choice. I could omit my experiences and give the impression that my historical analysis, written decades after the fact, coincides with my original personal experience. But it doesn't. The 1970s Jo was too busy living to do a "close read" of her own times. So instead I've included my experiences as proof that we experience cultural change from such a personal stance that it can feel like we are and are not part of that change at the same time.

Readers of the era under discussion will find some familiar stories here, but they may also find themselves thinking "that's not the way I experienced it." I hope they will share their versions too. Readers who were elsewhere or not yet born know this era only through family stories and media stereotypes. They realize that what they've seen is probably not the whole picture, but it's all they have. Hopefully this book will help them get a more accurate idea of the relationship between gender and fashions of the times. And even more hopefully there will be more books, articles, and discussions to follow. The world we live in today is cluttered with the unfinished business of the sexual revolution, and too many of the questions in the 1960s and 1970s have never been answered.

Inevitably this is an incomplete account. Gender identity can never be separated from race, class, age, or other personal dimensions. One of the biggest challenges I have faced with this project has been discerning how to contain it without either oversimplification or confusion. Considering the many different effects generated by the social and cultural forces of the early 1960s, the more factors I introduced, the more I risked a tangled, confused argument. My decision to focus on the gender identity issues as they were manifested in the broad age/sex categories of the fashion marketplace (children, teens, women, men) resulted in a more diffuse treatment of race than I originally intended. Rather than add racial identity to the mix throughout, or craft a separate chapter to highlight the racial dimension of fashions, I have incorporated some of this material into each chapter. There were moments in the '60s and '70s when gender and racial stereotypes clearly collided in mainstream fashion—for example, the use of African American models to display "exotic" or flamboyant styles. A few of the early legal cases involving workplace dress codes raised issues of both gender and racial discrimination. Thankfully there are important recent works on the intersection of race and gender in fashion,[5] and this book will not be the last word; the door is wide open for future researchers.

Culture changes. In fact we are so used to the notion that it changes that we find it hard to imagine living in a society where the culture of our parents, grandparents, and great-grandparents is the same culture that surrounds us today. We have never experienced cultural stability, except as a childhood illusion. During our entire lifetimes culture has been changing around us, and we have changed culture. In our day-to-day lives we have argued about culture because we see that it can change, we believe that people can change it, and we are both excited and afraid. Women in our society exist in a reality where culture change, in the form of fashion, is an almost constant part of our lives, but industrial man has managed to finesse this by freezing masculinity with the adoption of the business suit. Through the suit and tie, men experience a common thread between themselves and earlier generations of men in a way that women cannot.

Perhaps the most perplexing puzzle when it comes to fashion is the relationship between masculinity and femininity. How does this underlying relationship influence what happens when one role or both change drastically? This is what happened in the 1960s and '70s, when it seemed that both masculinity and femininity were being redefined and yet there was no blueprint, no plan, and no endgame—only questions.

Movers, Shakers, and Boomers

In 1970 the Bayonne High School class of 1960 gathered for their reunion. Journalist Steven Roberts told their story as a participant observer, interviewing his old classmates and comparing notes with them, in a feature article in the Sunday *New York Times*. One common theme emerged: the class of 1960 had "just missed out" on the great changes of the upcoming decade. As one alumnus commented, "The last five years have really been the turning point." What had changed? Practically everything.

Between 1965 and 1970 the "police action" in Vietnam had escalated to a war, the civil rights movement had blossomed into Black Power and Nixon's "Southern Strategy," *Reefer Madness*(1936) became a cult laughing stock on the college film circuit, and *Playboy* discovered pubic hair. The women at the reunion discussed their marriages and children through the new lens of second-wave feminism. "We had been shaped," Roberts concluded, "in the dying years of a world that no longer exists." The basic assumptions instilled in them in the 1950s—"respect authority ... sex is dirty"—had been swept away.[1]

Or had they? While many younger Americans were embracing the sexual revolution, the civil rights movement, and the celebration of personal freedom, many others were not. Today's silver-haired conservatives did not spring from thin air during the Reagan administration. The story of Mitt Romney and a few friends forcibly cutting a classmate's long hair may have shocked voters during the 2012 presidential campaign, but there were dozens of similar incidents reported across the county in the 1960s, and probably many more that were unreported.[2] Contrary to popular media images, not everyone in the 1960s and 1970s was white, middle-class, and straight. Nor did we all become hippies and protesters in college. One of my most vivid memories of the Syracuse University campus was the sunny afternoon in May 1970 when I attended a vigil for the students who had just died at Kent State. One end of the Quad was a mass of students singing antiwar songs; at the other end some of our classmates were sunbathing and throwing Frisbees. Between us, students headed to their classes along the walkways that crisscrossed the lawn. Two of the students who died at Kent State had been passers-by like them, not protesters.

No generation is a monolith, no matter how society's institutions treat them. Baby boomers, as defined by Madison Avenue, did not exist in real life but were as much a construct as any other demographic or marketing segment. Contrary to popular stereotypes, there were—and are—black, Latino, queer, straight, celibate, disabled, and working-class baby boomers, with a diversity of opinions about politics and morality.

Nor was the older generation uniformly opposed to the transformations taking place in American culture. The doctor who raised so many of us—Benjamin Spock, then in his sixties—was a familiar figure at major antiwar rallies, and many other liberal heroes and heroines were contemporaries of our parents and grandparents. It may be tempting to frame the divide that emerged as a "generation gap"—a term popularized during the early 1960s—but it is more useful to see it as the opening wedge in the culture wars that have engulfed the United States for the past fifty years.

Like huge tectonic plates colliding to reshape continents, three simultaneous forces began to interact during this time period. The first was the postwar baby boom, which in 1960 began pumping millions of teenagers a year into the consumer marketplace. The second was the sexual revolution, which had its roots in the sexology studies of Masters and Johnson, Hugh Hefner's dream of sexual freedom, and the uncoupling of sex and procreation. Finally, the civil rights movement focused national attention on individual rights, beginning with African Americans but soon expanding to include youth and women of all races and, to a lesser extent, gays and lesbians. The civil rights movement and the sexual revolution were well under way when baby boomers were still watching *Howdy Doody* (1947–1960) and would have been major influences on American culture with or without them. The adolescence and young adult years of the baby boom accelerated the conflagration, and our diverse experiences during those formative years are reflected in the conflicts that have dogged my generation ever since.

Why look at the tensions and controversies of this era through clothing trends? It's common to think of fashion as superficial, bearing little relationship to the serious issues of its time. This is wrong on two points. First, clearly there have been times when fashion changes have expressed deeply held convictions in times of change. The best example is the abandonment of knee breeches (associated with the aristocracy) in favor of trousers in revolutionary France, a shift that foreshadowed the triumph of commercial culture over hereditary power in the nineteenth century. (A more cynical explanation, but equally valid in some cases, is that the sudden taste for proletarian pants reflected an acute desire for survival by the French aristocracy.)

The other reason to look past the apparent triviality of fashion is that it is an important way that individuals connect themselves to others in modern consumer culture. We dress to express ourselves—age, gender, race, religion, as well as personality—and to place ourselves in context: place, time, occupation, kinship, and communities. Theater critic Eric Bentley, observing the clashes over clothing and hair, wrote in 1970, "If hair-dos and clothing are hardly, in themselves, worth a fight to the death, in the nineteen sixties they did become symbols of more than just a lifestyle; they became symbols of another life, and this the essential life of human beings, the life of their deep affections and their cherished thoughts."[3]

This juxtaposition of "lifestyle" and "life" brings to mind the rhetoric of modern opponents to gay rights. To label the way someone lives a "lifestyle" is to reduce their existence to a spread in this month's issue of *Esquire* or *Vogue*—a whim, subject to change with season or mood. The fashion controversies of the 1960s and 1970s—for example, whether women should wear pants to work, or if boys' long hair or girls' miniskirts disrupted education—were not about lifestyle. They were, in the words of the era, about "doing your own thing." To be your own person and express yourself fully was and always will be a serious and complicated process, and the efforts of people struggling to make lives for themselves through the upheavals of that era are still influencing our culture. That doesn't mean the baby boomers' struggles were more important; it's their (our!) sheer numbers that have made that generation so influential. In fact I take care in this book to consider both the experiences of people who were not teens or young adults as well as those who were baby boomers but were outside of "mainstream" boomer culture by choice or exclusion.

I grew up knowing that my brother and I were part of a "baby boom" that happened when World War II ended and couples settled down to start long-delayed families. We weren't "baby boomers" until 1970, when the label first appeared in a *Washington Post* article, according to the *Oxford English Dictionary*. As "leading edge" boomers (born in 1947 and 1949), we had a front-row seat for the cultural changes of the 1950s—television, the growth of suburbs, the Cold War. Those seats always seemed pretty crowded; in the early 1960s we attended a school so overrun with kids that we were on half session: seventh and eighth graders attended in the afternoon, and ninth graders and up attended from 7:00 AM to noon. Frankly, being part of a baby boom seemed more of an embarrassment and an inconvenience than anything else—that is, until Madison Avenue discovered the youth market. The first national brand to target baby boomers was Pepsi, with its 1963 ads that shouted, "Come Alive! You're in the Pepsi Generation!"[4] *Vogue* editor Diana Vreeland coined the term "Youthquake" in 1965 to describe the sweeping influence of young people in seemingly every facet of life: music, fashion, and politics. Suddenly we were leaders!

Although baby boomers made up nearly 50 percent of the U.S. population in 1965, we weren't alone on the cultural scene. Our older siblings and cousins, born between 1925 and the end of the war, dubbed the "Silent Generation," were just coming into their own in the mid-1960s, with their own lives and desires. They were often forced to choose sides between the seasoned survivors of the "Greatest Generation" and the defiant baby boomers rather than blaze their own trail. The Silent Generation has not produced a president of the United States, the nation having gone in 1992 from our last World War II–era leader (George H. W. Bush) to our first boomer, Bill Clinton, and staying with that cohort long enough to block them permanently. But the Silent Generation did provide the Youthquake with its sound track: the Beatles, Jimi Hendrix, Joan Baez, Brian Wilson of the Beach Boys, Johnny Cash, Aretha Franklin, Barry Manilow, and Bob Dylan were all born between 1925 and 1946. So were fashion designers Mary Quant, Ralph Lauren, Yves Saint Laurent, and Betsey Johnson, as well as iconic hair stylist Vidal Sassoon. (The other major names of the era—Courrèges, Cardin, and Gernreich—were born just before 1925.)

Born between the early 1960s and 1981 (demographers differ on the date for the end of the postwar baby boom), Generation X was emerging, though blessedly unlabeled until 1991, when Douglas Coupland's novel *Generation X: Tales for an Accelerated Culture* christened them as such.[5] These were the beneficiaries—or victims, depending on your point of view—of the social and cultural transformations of the 1960s. They never knew Jim Crow laws or "Help Wanted" ads divided by sex or race, and they were legal adults when they turned eighteen, while first-wave boomers had to wait until they were twenty-one to take advantage of adult privileges. For the most part they missed the free love and high times of the boomers' youth, thanks to PCP, crack cocaine, the War on Drugs, the resurgence of STDs, and the discovery of HIV/AIDS. Still, they play an important role in this story, because they were the guinea pigs for parents and educators attempting to prepare the next generation for the Age of Aquarius, the Apocalypse, or whatever else they thought was on the horizon. Of course there were also our elders: men and women in their prime or in their twilight years, who had lived through so much and now found themselves irrelevant to marketers and challenged, baffled, or infuriated by their children and grandchildren.

In every age group there were atheists and believers, political views that spanned the spectrum from Marxists to John Birchers, prudes and libertines. The usefulness of generational categories stems from their adoption by manufacturers, retailers, media, and advertisers as a means of targeting customers. Since we are examining consumer culture, these niches tell us something about how groups of Americans were perceived by the commercial world. It is truly rare for any of us to have never felt pointedly targeted or ignored by advertisers.

If you were born after 1981, don't worry. The party that started in the 1960s is still going strong, and you're invited—like it or not. As I reveal in the rest of the book, the styles of the '60s and '70s were just the visible signs of the questions on everyone's mind—questions we are still struggling to answer. Many of them deal with the most essential aspects of our beings: sex and gender.

Baby boomers were sometimes accused of behaving as if we had invented sex; in fact we would have been the dimmest generation in human history if we hadn't responded to the national fascination with sex that coincided with our own adolescence. And we would not have been normal teenagers if we hadn't responded to that environment with hyper-hormonal enthusiasm. Like most revolutions, this one had been decades in the making. Unbeknownst to us, our grandparents had already witnessed a first sexual revolution in the 1920s among writers, artists, and other bohemians inspired by Freudian psychological theory, which introduced the concept of a human unconscious driven by sexual desires and fantasies. The music, clothes, and literature of the Roaring Twenties celebrated a hedonistic, sensual youth culture that arose from the horror and destruction of World War I, only to be submerged again in the Great Depression. The academic study of sex continued in biology and psychology departments, building up a body of work that began to attract wider public attention with the 1948 publication of Alfred Kinsey's *Sexual Behavior of the Human Male,* followed in 1953 by *Sexual Behavior of the Human Female.* Hugh Hefner, as a graduate student in journalism at Northwestern University, wrote his master's thesis on Kinsey's work before launching *Playboy.* The pornography cases over *Lady Chatterley's Lover, Tropic of Cancer,* and *Fanny Hill* in 1959 opened up a market for racy novels that became more and more explicit. By the mid-1960s curious teenagers could find just about any kind of information they might desire about sex, though probably not in any public library. Personally, I learned a great deal just browsing the books and magazines in the homes where I babysat.

Explicit straight extramarital sex in books and movies was just the beginning. Homosexuality, once hidden and persecuted, became, if not completely open and still far from accepted, a titillating subject of conversation and art. More common was bisexuality, which several cultural observers identified as the latest cool thing in the early 1970s. Love triangles have been a time-honored plot device, but in the early 1960s group marriage and other forms of polyamory caught the imagination of the many fans of Robert Heinlein's *Stranger in a Strange Land* (1961). A steady stream of popular works on multiple relationships followed, including Robert Rimmer's novels, particularly *The Harrad Experiment* (1967); the film *Bob and Carol and Ted and Alice* (1969); and Nena and George O'Neill's book *Open Marriage* (1972), which sold 1.5 million copies. Of course much of this sexual freedom was facilitated by the availability of the Pill (approved in 1960), which made possible the separation of intercourse and reproduction and also the uncoupling of "love and marriage" (which, we had learned from Frank Sinatra in 1955, "go together like a horse and carriage"). Not surprisingly, baby boomers are more likely to admit to smoking dope than to any form of sexual experimentation beyond "shacking up" before marriage.

This upheaval in intimate relationships is usually characterized as the "sexual revolution," but I suspect that had it happened a decade later we would be calling it the "gender revolution" instead. The concept of "gender identity"—the acquired cultural traits that proceed from biological sex—was quite new, having been just introduced to the scientific literature in 1955 by sexologist John Money (more about his troubling career later in the chapter "Nature and Nurture"). Betty Friedan does not use the word "gender" once in *The Feminine Mystique* (published in 1963); at that time "sex role" was the more common term, signifying the close relationship between biology and our lives as social beings. The distinction between sex and gender has never been easy to grasp or even generally accepted. No matter how scholars have tried to explain the distinction between nature and nurture, popular media and consumer culture reflect the general uncertainty as to which traits, tastes, and behaviors were cultural and which were innate. After all, we've known for hundreds of years that the earth circles the sun, yet we still speak about the sun setting, because that's how it feels. In the case of sex and gender, the jury is still out on how separate they really are. While the sexologists, evolutionary psychologists, anthropologists, and neurobiologists sort it out, the rest of us will continue to mingle and confuse them.

Before John Money introduced the notion of a cultural dimension called "gender," the variations in human sexual activity and expression could be labeled as natural or unnatural, normal or abnormal, legal or illegal. What was natural, normal, and legal was good; the unnatural, abnormal, and illegal required treatment, correction, or punishment. Adding cultural influence to the mix was brilliant and clearly true. Anthropologists and historians could provide ample evidence of the mutability of cultural patterns over time and geography. But it also raised some very thorny questions. If an individual's gender expression did not match their biological sex, was that necessarily the result of biological or psychological abnormality, a character flaw, or incorrigible criminality? Could culture be the problem in such a "mismatch"? Were cultural norms automatically right? After all, they were subject to change and variation. Without using the word "gender," Betty Friedan argued that suburban lives were an alien and toxic culture and that the scientific arguments used to justify consigning women to lives of nurturing and consuming were false. Treating biological sex as a defining, existential characteristic denied individuality and human agency. To achieve her highest potential a woman must be as free as a man to pursue her interests and use her talents, and it was culture—not biology—that was standing in her way.

The Pill is often credited with launching the sexual revolution, and reliable, hormonal birth control was certainly a biological solution to what appears to be a biological problem. But a closer look reveals the problem with this perception. First, as my mother, a registered nurse, was fond of telling me, not only had my generation not invented sex, but neither had they discovered birth control. Remember that one of the reasons the postwar baby boom was so dramatic was the "birth dearth" that preceded it. People did not stop having sex when the economy crashed in 1929; they stopped having children or had fewer of them. They used condoms and diaphragms (which worked pretty well), withdrawal and rhythm (with less success), and when those methods failed they sought abortions.

One of my professors in college told the story of her mother, who had five children during the Great Depression—and four abortions, one between each live birth. My own mother, who had been the third oldest in a family of eight children, had a tubal ligation in her late twenties after producing my brother and me.

The convenience and certainty afforded by oral contraceptives would not have been possible without cultural change driven by a desire among young women and men for different lives from those of their parents. The alternative visions included a life with fewer children, or children later in life, but, more important, it included a sexual life without marriage, monogamy, or even commitment. When social commentators raised the alarm about the sexual revolution, it wasn't the birthrate that concerned them; it was women's sexual freedom, the severing of the connections between sex and love, the decline of premarital chastity. From the perspective of young, sexually active single women, oral contraceptives were a powerful weapon against the old double standard and a means of escaping the pattern of early marriage and motherhood that had become the standard during the 1950s. This was not about sex and reproduction, it was about gender: about life, not lifestyle, about the cultural expectations of women.

The gender revolution was not just about femininity; it was also about masculinity and about homosexuality. There was no male equivalent to *The Feminine Mystique* on the best-seller list, but men were subject to as many restrictions as women, just different restrictions—ones that resulted in, and reinforced, power and privilege for some. Those advantages came at a cost, as studies were beginning to show in the late 1950s. Men's lives were shorter, they were at much greater risk for heart disease and stroke, and they began to regret their absence from their children's lives in the mom-dominated suburbs. A men's movement and scholarly interest in masculinity emerged, led by psychologists Joseph Pleck and Jack Sawyer, who organized a "Male Liberation Festival" at Harvard University in 1971. Their groundbreaking anthology, *Men and Masculinity* (1974), inspired even more academic interest in male sex roles, though the subject has never enjoyed the visibility or influence of women's studies.[6]

The gender revolution touched homosexual men and women as well and in even more complex ways. In 1960 homosexuality was still considered a mental illness by the American Psychological Association, and to be a sexually active homosexual man or woman was to be an outlaw, thanks to sodomy and public indecency laws. The erotic possibilities of bisexuality appealed to many young people, straight or otherwise, who made it the "in lifestyle" in the early 1970s. For gays and lesbians this popularity meant that bisexuality could work as a culturally acceptable location between the closet and complete coming out.

In the scientific community the idea that sex and gender could ever be completely separate was controversial, especially as women began to demand full legal equality with men. In 1972 *Time* published an article about the work of John Money and his contention that gender identity could be shaped independently from biological sex. (He based his argument on his work with intersex children who were surgically assigned as females and treated with hormones and behavioral therapy to produce happy, well-adjusted girls—or not, as the case turned out.) An assembled panel of experts, including Money, discussed the possibility and desirability of a "unisex society." They considered the supposed differences between men and women—verbal ability, creativity, temperament, and so on—and came to the conclusion that culture played a greater role in all of them than did biological difference. For most men and women, claimed psychologist Jerome Kagan, "the biological differences are totally irrelevant." Psychiatrist Donald Lunde agreed: "There is no evidence that men are any more or less qualified by biological sex differences alone to perform the tasks generally reserved for them in today's societies."[7]

When asked if a truly egalitarian "unisex" society would ever exist, however, the experts were unanimous in saying it was not only unlikely but also undesirable. For the experts in the first camp, modification of gender norms was impossible because they were ultimately connected to physical reality. Anatomy was still destiny (or, as Therese Benedek put it, "biology precedes personality"). According to psychologist Joseph Adelson, efforts to alter cultural norms were misguided and doomed to fail, "as though the will, in pursuit of total human possibility, can amplify itself to overcome the given."[8]

Others considered cultural change possible but stopped short of an endorsement. "Perhaps the known biological differences can be totally overcome, and society can approach a state in which a person's sex is of no consequence for any significant activity except child-bearing," suggested Jerome Kagan. "But we must ask if such a society will be satisfying to its members." Psychoanalyst Martin Symonds agreed: "The basic reason why unisex must fail is that in the sexual act itself, the man has to be assertive, if tenderly, and the woman has to be receptive. What gives trouble is when men see assertiveness as aggression and women see receptiveness as submission." Besides, a family where Mom and Dad were too similar would be "a frictionless environment in which nobody would be able to grow up," because children need roles to identify with and rebel against.[9] Symonds was not alone in this opinion; he was echoing critics of women's liberation dating back nearly a century, who had warned of a dire future of manly women and effeminate men. Two years earlier an opinion piece by Barbara Wyden in the *St. Petersburg [Florida] Times* had suggested that unisex parents (shorthaired working mom in pants; longhaired, bead-wearing dad doing housework) was a sign that the family was in trouble.[10]

As Betty Friedan had pointed out, many of these scientists were failing to take into account the powerful influence of their own culture. They were like the proverbial fish unable to comprehend the water in which they swam; I would take it a step further and suggest it was not actually the water: science can help very smart fish understand how they move through water and why they breathe in it but suffocate in air. What the scientists had not taken into consideration was the fishbowl, the container that, like culture, determines the size and shape of their environment.

Reformers, advocates, and activists working to expand civil rights were essentially trying to change the dimensions of the fishbowl. The Declaration of Independence and U.S. Constitution offer definitions of human rights that initially promised more than they delivered to many people living within our borders. The civil rights movements in our history have been efforts to include people who had been excluded from the promise of "life, liberty, and the pursuit of happiness" offered in 1776 and the guarantee of "equal protection under the law" added in 1868. This may seem heady, serious stuff for a book on fashion, but it was the civil rights movements that made clothing and hair into national, contentious issues. Much of the controversy centered on issues of gender expression and gender equality, which raised different questions for women and men and for adults and children.

Many of the initial questions were seemingly trivial: Why can't girls wear slacks to school? Why must men always wear ties, which seem to serve no practical purpose? Why do so many dresses button or zip up the back? Why can't a boy wear his hair long just like the Beatles? Why do I have to wear white gloves and a hat just to go shopping downtown? Why is it cute to be a tomboy but not a sissy? If these sound like children's questions, maybe it's because at first they were. I remember puzzling over these and many other rules when I was growing up. The answers were even more confusing—and annoying! "That's just the way it is." "Because I said so." The cultural authority of grown-ups, which we had accepted as small children, lost its credibility as we reached our teen years. In the 1960s the baby boom generation started to question more and push back harder, along with some allies in older generations. They were aided and abetted by a consumer culture that was more interested in their buying power than in cultural and political change.

Along with the push for progress came resistance. For some the changes were dangerous and threatening, for others perhaps they just came too fast. Evolutionary biologists have a useful concept called "punctuated equilibrium," which can be applied to cultural change as well. Instead of Darwin's model of smooth, steady evolution, punctuated equilibrium means there are long periods of stasis between events of sudden change when the new ecological system settles in. These eras of little change may be a period of adjustment or a time when populations are migrating to a more hospitable environment. A biologist friend explained it this way: the internal or external events (mutations, crises) that result in significant change can be stressful. Like a rubber band that is stretched too far, a species can either snap (extinction) or retreat to something like its original size and shape, just slightly altered. She made this suggestion when I was struggling to explain the apparently sudden change in the U.S. cultural climate after 1972, which includes the gradual decline in enthusiasm for the Equal Rights Amendment as well as a revival of "classic" elements and styles, from Diane Von Furstenberg's dresses to the power suit and Preppymania. Perhaps, she said, the changes of the 1960s had been "too much, too soon" for enough people that we had relaxed into a period of stasis.[11] That will be one of the ideas worth testing as we survey the evolution of fashion between 1960 and 1980.

The most obvious fashion-related flashpoints in the gender revolution are pants for women; long hair and colorful, flamboyant dress for men; and unisex for just about everybody. But there is both more and less than meets the eye in each of these trends. Women and girls had been wearing pants in some form for some time prior to the 1960s. Rompers and overalls for little girls were unexceptional, as were slacks, capris, and even shorts and jeans for women, at the right time and place. These were casual or leisure styles; in a culture where dressing up still mattered, even the nicest slacks were unacceptable for work or school. Backyard cookouts, yes; shopping or church, no. When my family moved to a small New England town in 1961, my Midwestern mother was scandalized by the housewives in slacks she saw at the grocery store. (Hollywood stars like Katharine Hepburn and Marlene Dietrich were exempt from these rules, because they were not like the rest of us.) The objection to women in trousers was based on gender but not on the rules of the Victorian era (pants are masculine; skirts are feminine). It was part of the particular construction of being "ladylike," the image that allowed women special status and protection, layered onto rules about informal as opposed to formal behaviors. One school dress code specifically banned "play clothes," for girls listing slacks, jeans, shorts, and pedal pushers as examples. When the formality of the early 1960s began to relax, trousers were often permitted if they were part of a pantsuit and if they had a side or back zipper and the jacket or top covered the wearer's rear end. The decision to permit pants if they were part of a suit is related to the shifting boundary between formal and informal dress, but the other limitations are about the erotic associations of pants, especially tight-fitting trousers that draw attention to the hips and buttocks, or even—with a center front fly—the crotch.

The exuberant splendor of menswear, especially between 1967 and 1973, and the battles over long hair, mustaches, and beards reveal the very different gender rules as they applied to men. The public response to each of these trends also gives us an indication of the differences between the cultural expectations of men and women. Femininity and masculinity are not simple opposites; they are more like two sports with a few commonalities but with totally different sets of rules. Consider, for example, figure skating and ice hockey. Athletes in both must be able to skate, but they wear different costumes, use specialized equipment, and are judged by vastly different standards. Is figure skating the "opposite" of ice hockey?

The rules of femininity value different attributes and behaviors than do the rules of masculinity, and they are not always opposites. Even though both men and women were governed by the formal/informal standards of dress and grooming, the demands of gender resulted in noticeably different effects. A man in formal dress was dressed identically to every other man in the room and completely covered from neck to toe. A formal gown for a woman was revealing (more or less, depending on her age and marital status) and, as popular humor reminds us, hopefully, unique. For another woman to have the same dress was cause for mortification. Women and men could both wear shorts and bathing suits, but only women needed to shave their legs and underarms when they did so.

The rules for young women dictated careful management of an image that oscillated between ladylike and seductive. There was a proper time and place for each, and part of a girl's education—whether at home, in home economics class, or cotillion—was learning the boundaries and nuances of feminine performance. The rules had a different meaning for women of color and working-class women, for whom a genteel appearance and quality clothing signified access to respect and privilege. For men there was very little space or place for sexual display, or even individual expression; instead, boys and men were trained to operate with a very limited visual range. Again, these restrictions played out differently for men of color. African American and Latino men's dress includes a tradition of flamboyance despite or, as Monica Miller has argued, as a response to oppression or subservient status.[12] Appropriation of minority or subcultural masculine style by straight white men was an important feature of the 1960s and 1970s, as if dressing like the super masculine movie hero John Shaft would inoculate them from accusations of effeminacy.

When young men and women began to break out of their respective limits, the disparity in the public response was remarkable. Girls exchanged "ladylike" rules and trappings for sexier, more revealing clothing to much fanfare and little protest. Miniskirts rose inch by inch, and school dress codes followed them, resignedly. Only a handful of legal cases involving dress codes dealt with too-short skirts or girls wearing pants, compared with the dozens of boys who went to court to argue for their right to wear their hair as long as they wished. (This issue is discussed in much greater detail in chapter 5, "Litigating the Revolution.")

The most obvious manifestation of the gender revolution is unisex. The term "unisex," referring to styles intentionally designed to blur or cross gender lines, dates to the mid-1960s. The trend peaked during the 1970s and affected men, women, boys, and girls, all in different ways. On one level, for many people it was a fad, an amusing flash in the pan. For others it was a movement generated by serious, existential questions about the very nature of sex and gender, what constituted appropriate social roles for men and women, and how to raise children. Unisex includes many different ways of challenging gender rules. Some styles are best described as "androgynous," or combining elements of masculine and feminine styling (a longhaired girl in a miniskirt, button-down shirt, and tie). The opposite approach to androgynous design is a neutral style, devoid of masculine or feminine elements (a turtleneck sweater, jogging suits). The third approach to unisex dressing is best termed "cross-dressing," although I mean that term in a broader sense than is popularly meant. The rules of masculinity rarely permit cross-dressing, and even in that defiant time doing so was limited to details, not entire outfits. Women, on the other hand, could not only wear "man-tailored" clothing and "boyfriend sweaters" but could also wear actual men's clothing, as was the case with young women who bought their jeans in the boys' department.

When teenagers and adults wore unisex clothing, the resulting confusion might be the desired effect, a poke in the establishment's eye. Complaining "you can't tell the boys from the girls these days" was a sure way to mark yourself as an old fogey. But to younger children, gender mix-ups could be irritating or embarrassing. Baby boomers and Generation Xers tend to have very different memories of the unisex era, which is significant because it is the younger generation that has helped drive fashion change from the late 1970s on.

If you were to ask someone in the fashion industry, unisex was a fad that came and went in one year: 1968. For that brief moment the fashion press hailed gender blending as the wave of the future, and department stores created special sections for unisex fashions. Most of these boutiques had closed by 1969. However, in the more mainstream realm of Sears, Roebuck catalogs and major sewing patterns, "his 'n' hers" clothing—mostly casual shirts, sweaters, and outerwear—persisted through the late 1970s. The difference between avant-garde unisex and the later version is the distinction between boundary-defying designs, often modeled by androgynous-looking models, and a less threatening variation, worn by attractive heterosexual couples.

The work and thought of designer Rudi Gernreich, the visionary master of unisex fashion and its most famous proponent, shows how complex the trend actually was. Born in Austria, Gernreich and his mother had fled to the United States when he was a teen in order to escape Nazi persecution of the Jews. Besides being a leading American designer, he was also an early gay rights activist, providing financial support to the Mattachine Society, through cofounder Harry Hay, who was his lover in the early 1950s.[13] Most of his work with homosexual rights was unknown to the wider public until after his death in 1985. As a very public figure, who had once been arrested and prosecuted as part of police entrapment, Gernreich understood that his political and personal life could threaten his livelihood. Nevertheless, it is clear that sexuality and gender identity played important roles in his fashion vision. He thought naked bodies—female and male alike—were beautiful, an attitude variously attributed to his reaction against prudish Nazi edicts against nudity, his training as a dancer, and a night job washing bodies in a hospital morgue. Designs such as the topless bathing suit and the soft, transparent "no-bra bra" were intended to emancipate women's bodies from the artifice of boning, uplift, and elastic. But he wanted to give equal attention to men, asking in 1969, "Why should the male not also be a sexual object?"[14] He also designed futuristic styles such as the costumes for the TV series *Space: 1999*: jumpsuits, turtlenecks, and tunics.

These seemingly opposite creations represented two important strands in the gender revolution: a focus on "natural" bodies (not the girdled, air-brushed versions of the 1950s) and a futuristic vision of an egalitarian world. Ironically, the latter minimized sex differences, with fabrics and silhouettes that erased curves and even facial features, while Gernreich's other designs left nothing to the imagination, exposing breasts and even pubic hair. These fashions perfectly encapsulate the central conflict in fashions from this era, between displaying and celebrating the human body and minimizing or even erasing differences that result in gender inequality. Thus we have contradictions such as his 1974 thong bathing suit, "a unisex garment which nonetheless enhanced the difference between the sexes."[15]

Liberation is a fine thing, but it does not come with instructions. Baby boomers who came of age in the 1960s wanted freedom to "do their own thing," which meant many different things to different people. For racial and sexual minorities, the goals were probably clearer than for those who were straight white folks. We already had the right to vote, the right to public displays of affection and marriage, and the all-important right to pursue happiness, unhassled and unmolested—as long as we followed the rules. But many of the rules chafed; they didn't make sense to us as they clearly did to most of our parents and grandparents.

It is striking to me how many of the sympathetic commentators on the youth movement seemed to think we knew what we were doing. Prominent liberal intellectual Alfred Kazin practically proposed American young people for sainthood, calling us "the visible conscience of society," leading the nation toward an egalitarian and unmaterialistic future.[16] According to socialite/designer Gloria Vanderbilt, young women had "more choice of what they want to do and be."[17] But having more choice didn't automatically make the choices more clear; we have been fretting and arguing and judging over those choices ever since. Young men, freed from our culture's "sick preoccupation with virility," could instead "dress in terms of how they feel about themselves,"[18] but that assumed they understood those feelings and were prepared for negative as well as positive reactions. The fashions of the 1960s and 1970s articulated many questions about sex and gender but in the end provided no final answers.

One reason for this lack of resolution was that the experts from all the various "-ologies"—sexology, psychology, theology, and the rest—were still experimenting, still theorizing, and still arguing. In his history of sex research, Vern Bullough identifies two major strands in the field during the 1970s.[19] The first is the interactionist model of gender identification, which credited genetic, physiological, and social forces with the creation and maintenance of our feminine or masculine selves. Interactionism suggested that these influences have different impacts at different stages of human development. Within interactionism there was a tug-of-war among the various disciplines to determine which academic specialty was best equipped to unlock the formula. There were also still disagreements over which was more important, nature or nurture. John Money, of course, argued that behavioral therapy and hormones could override physiology; Milton Diamond engaged in a long-running public feud with Money over his claims, eventually successfully exposing the flaws in his research.

The second area of controversy was even more fundamental. In order to study a behavior, psychologists must develop tests and instruments to measure it. The existing measures were based on a bipolar model of gender, with femininity and masculinity as opposites. "Normal" men and women would have scores at the appropriate end of the spectrum. People who scored too high on the opposite scale or who ended up in the middle were believed to have problems ranging from gender identity disorder to homosexuality. Alternative models began to appear in the 1970s, most importantly by psychologists Anne Constantinople and Sandra Bem, who rejected the linear model of femininity and masculinity as polar opposites.[20] Bem developed the BSRI (Bem Sex Role Inventory), which measured masculinity and femininity on independent axes. An individual's score would place that person in one of four quadrants: low masculine/high feminine ("feminine"), high masculine/low feminine ("masculine"), low masculine/low feminine ("undifferentiated"), and high masculine/high feminine ("androgynous"). Bem argued not only that this instrument was a more reliable measure of femininity and masculinity but also that research using the BSRI supported her theory that androgynous individuals were psychologically healthier than the other categories.

Against this backdrop the unending disagreements and divisions over everything having anything to do with sex and gender seem inevitable. Even where there is agreement in the scholarly community—the declassification of homosexuality as a mental disorder by the American Psychological Association in 1973, for example—common knowledge and public opinion have lagged far behind. This is the setting for our next four chapters: the foggy, uneven landscape of gendered and unisex fashion at the dawn of the culture wars.

Feminism and Femininity

I turned thirteen in 1962. Before I graduated from middle school, three books hit the best-seller lists, each offering a completely different, competing view of what sort of woman I should try to be. Let the authors speak for themselves:

> When a man thinks of a married woman, no matter how lovely she is, he must inevitably picture her greeting her husband at the door with a martini or warmer welcome, fixing little children's lunches or scrubbing them down because they've fallen into a mudhole. She is somebody else's wife and somebody else's mother.
>
> When a man thinks of a single woman, he pictures her alone in her apartment, smooth legs sheathed in pink silk Capri pants, lying tantalizingly among dozens of satin cushions, trying to read but not very successfully, for he is in that room—filling her thoughts, her dreams, her life.
>
> —HELEN GURLEY BROWN, SEX AND THE SINGLE GIRL, 1962

> The problem lay buried, unspoken, for many years in the minds of American women. It was a strange stirring, a sense of dissatisfaction, a yearning that women suffered in the middle of the twentieth century in the United States. Each suburban wife struggled with it alone. As she made the beds, shopped for groceries, matched slipcover material, ate peanut butter sandwiches with her children, she ferried Cub Scouts and Brownies, lay beside her husband at night—she was afraid to even ask herself the silent question—"is this all?"
>
> —BETTY FRIEDAN, THE FEMININE MYSTIQUE, 1963

Never before in history has there been a generation of women so dis-
illusioned, disappointed, and unhappy in marriage as in our times.
Many feel that married life does not offer what they had hoped and
dreamed it would. Some feel neglected, unappreciated, and often un-
loved. When they search for answers, they feel lost in a sea of darkness.
Some are resigned to this condition, but others still hope and search
for answers.

There are, of course, many women who have achieved a high level of
happiness, but in many cases it is not the happiness of which they once
dreamed, and it falls short of their goals. They feel a need for a richer,
fuller life. They, too, need light and understanding.

—HELEN B. ANDELIN, *FASCINATING WOMANHOOD*, 1963

I hasten to say that although I didn't read any of these books at the
time, the ideas each author advocated swirled around me throughout my
high school and college years. (And they are all still in print fifty years
later, which is certainly telling.) Which women should I be? Helen Gurley Brown's independent, sexy, young, single girl? Betty Friedan's liberated woman with a career and perhaps an equally liberated husband? Or
Helen Andelin's domestic goddess, realizing her power by cultivating her
femininity? When faced with a multiple-choice test, I turned it into an es-
say exam. Like many women of my generation, I tried a bit of each.

American women's fashions in the 1960s and '70s—and today—were
the battlefield for these competing visions of the feminine. In this chapter
I examine two main themes that emerged during this period in women's
clothing. The first is the desire for an independent existence that is equal
in political and social status to men; the second is the very real drive to
be sexual beings. Yet these were not separate strands at all. As we'll see,
unisex or androgynous dressing, while intended to level the playing field
between men and women, was often perceived as sexually attractive as
well, and sexually attractive clothing can be powerful. It is the very tension between these two impulses that helped drive fashion change during
this period and that made it so very complicated.

Each of the three works that open this chapter had a different impact
with a different audience. *The Feminine Mystique* is credited with launch-

ing second-wave feminism and routinely appears on lists of significant books for required reading. *Sex and the Single Girl,* in contrast, is listed on Amazon.com as a "cult classic," and amateur reviewers on the site disagree whether it is a humorous period piece or the best advice book ever written. It not only helped Brown rebrand *Cosmopolitan* from house-wifely to collegiate when she took over as editor of the magazine in 1965, but it also inspired new popular culture heroines, from a film version of the book, starring Natalie Wood, to the fashionista girlfriends of *Sex and the City.* All three books have sold millions of copies. *The Feminine Mystique* could boast three million copies sold by 2000 (in just less than forty years)—no small feat for a serious nonfiction title—but *Sex and the Single Girl* claimed two million sold in three weeks. Compared to both of these, *Fascinating Womanhood* was more of an underground success. Self-published in 1963, it sold four hundred thousand copies before Random House bought it and republished it in 1965. It really caught on as Andelin developed courses and teacher training that fed the conservative antifeminist movement in the 1970s. Total sales today have reached over two million.

Of these three books, *The Feminine Mystique* offers the least amount of fashion commentary or advice. Friedan was critical of the consumerist role of suburban housewives and, by extension, the preoccupation with fashionable clothing promoted by women's magazines. She did, however, convey a sense of fashion being a frivolous feminine pursuit as opposed to the more serious pursuits of political power and legal careers.

In contrast, both *Fascinating Womanhood* and *Sex and the Single Girl* provide fairly specific advice on clothing choices, although Helen Gurley Brown goes into much greater detail; she devotes an entire chapter to clothing as opposed to just a few pages in Andelin's book. Brown's imagined reader was a young woman with lots of ambition but not a whole lot of money, so her advice focused on getting the most attractive looks for the least amount of money. She also argued that young women should please themselves with their clothing, not men, since if they appear confident and well put together, men will find them attractive regardless of the style. To round out the image found in *Sex and the Single Girl,* it helps to understand that the chapter preceding the one on clothes includes quite a bit of diet and exercise advice, and the chapter following dispenses make-up and hairstyling information.

In *Fascinating Woman,* on the other hand, a woman's appearance is considered the reader's first step toward regaining lost femininity. To look feminine, women must avoid any materials or styles that men wear unless they can be feminized through color, trim, or accessories. The main strategy is to emphasize the differences between women and men. Both authors agree that overly sexy clothing, or at least obviously sexy clothing, is undesirable. For Helen Gurley Brown, too-revealing clothing is low-class and attracts the wrong sort of man; for Helen Andelin, sexy clothing violates one of the most important rules of true femininity: a woman should be modest.

Imagine that the millions of readers of these three books constitute three categories of female consumers. Then consider the larger reality that these categories—feminists, "*Cosmo* girls," and domestic goddess-es—were neither exhaustive nor mutually exclusive. There were women who were "none of the above." Consider, for example, the young lesbian who wants to succeed in her clerical job with a big firm and also dreams of love and romance with a woman. Then there were the countless women like me, whose heads spun with the options and possibilities and wanted a bit of each (or, in the cliché of the 1980s, "to have it all").

Women had started wearing pants before the 1960s. First-wave femi-nists had challenged men's exclusive right to trousers in the nineteenth century, winning small but significant victories: overalls and rompers for children's play clothes and bloomers and knickers for women's active sportswear. By the early 1960s trousers in many forms—jeans, capris, and shorts—were acceptable leisure styles for American women, particularly the young. Between 1965 and 1975 this acceptance pushed past existing boundaries into the workplace, the schoolroom, and even formal occa-sions, to the point that trousers were no longer considered masculine, but, rather, neutral garments. Although this change represented a fun-damental shift in public attitudes and perceptions, it ultimately did not result in neutral clothing styles. By the late 1970s women's trousers were acquiring feminine details and fit more closely to the hips and thighs, accentuating the sex of the wearer rather than creating a neutral effect.

Once pants were no longer seen as inherently masculine, they simply became another vehicle for displaying the female body.

In medieval Europe trousers were underwear; men wore these tight-fitting leg coverings under their robes, and women did not wear them at all. Between the fourteenth and sixteenth centuries, shorter and shorter robes and doublets revealed the legs, and eventually the buttocks, up to the waist, and men's lower garments became important fashion items in their own right. Loose or skin-tight, knee-length or longer, trousers distinguished men from women and men from boys, who wore dresses from infancy until old enough to be "breeched" at six or seven years. Early advocates of equal rights for women took note of the relative freedom of men's and women's clothing and argued for dress reform to erase the restrictions of women's fashionable dress. Corsets, layers of petticoats, and wide, sweeping skirts were all indicted as markers of women's dependent and subservient status. Activists including Elizabeth Cady Stanton and Amelia Bloomer advocated adoption of simplified dress consisting of a knee-length dress over a pair of wide trousers based on those worn by women in the Middle East. They called it the "American Costume," to emphasize their goal of emancipating women from the dictates of foreign designers, but it was popularly known as the Bloomer dress. It didn't last long: it was introduced in 1851 and abandoned by Amelia Bloomer herself in 1859 when lightweight cage crinolines replaced heavy layers of petticoats as skirt supports. But the seeds had been sown; there is ample evidence that women continued to defy convention and put on trousers, whether for practical or political reasons. Early photography provides a wealth of images of women in pants as workers, soldiers, performers, and just for a bit of cross-dressing fun.[1] In the struggle for women's rights, wearing trousers was considered a subversive, even disruptive act, and cartoonists often depicted a post-suffrage future of mannish, trousered wives and hen-pecked husbands.

By the 1950s a woman in pants was no longer a cause for alarm or an object of ridicule, as long as she observed the new rules. Slacks, shorts, capris, pedal pushers, and other trouser variants were for leisure, not for school, office, or church. *Women's Wear Daily* publisher John Fairchild declared in his 1965 book, *The Fashionable Savages,* that pants for women were fine "at home, [for] winter sports and the country, not in city streets," a sentiment echoed by most designers and retailers.[2] In a setting where either slacks or a dress could be worn, it was more "ladylike" to wear a skirt, and skirts were clearly preferred for grown women. A bowling manual for women in 1964 suggested "culottes, skirts and blouses, sports dresses and *even slacks* are suitable for lane-wear," but only one adult woman in the entire book is shown in slacks. Only the girls are wearing slacks or shorts.[3] Menswear tailoring was rare, images of Katharine Hepburn notwithstanding; most pants for women and girls were cut and styled differently from men's. They were slimmer, with tapered legs and side or back zippers and few or no pockets. Panty girdles worn beneath slacks ensured the control and smooth line expected under all women's clothing, even for active sports such as tennis.

But by 1965 the door had already been opened by some Paris designers, especially André Courrèges, whose August 1, 1964, show featured rock music and "pants, pants, pants,"[4] while the venerable but still iconoclastic Coco Chanel offered flowing pants for home entertaining. Within a few years most designers were showing pants in some form, and pantsuits were rapidly gaining in acceptability. Some schools and workplaces were more resistant than others; nurses in Los Angeles won the right to wear tunics and pants instead of dresses in 1973, and other hospitals followed suit fairly quickly, since pants were clearly more practical than skirts. Banks and fine restaurants held out against pantsuits until the late 1970s. Jeans, as a subcategory of pants especially associated with leisure, were a special case for both men and women, so I discuss them separately when I get to unisex styles.

If unisex and the trend away from formality helped launch the fashion for pants, the surprise accelerant was controversy over skirt lengths. Ever since the introduction of the first miniskirts—which just grazed the knee, a length that hardly seems shocking today—women had faced some serious challenges. Some were practical: according to etiquette, bare legs were déclassé. Skirts called for stockings or, in the case of casual styles or school clothes, tights or knee socks. Tall girls quickly learned that the shorter the skirt, the more it was likely to reveal the gap between stocking top and garters. Tights and pantyhose solved that problem, although at first they were at least twice the cost of regular hosiery. (Never mind the fact that if you were above average height, tights and pantyhose were never long enough.) Tired of the uncertainty generated by pants and miniskirt controversies, the French fashion industry conspired to introduce mid-calf-length (midi) skirts in January 1970, in an attempt to force "wardrobe-killing change," as Christian Dior had done with his 1947 New Look, which had rendered square shoulders and A-line skirts obsolete in a single season, replacing them with voluminous styles with a Victorian-revival sensibility. Women reacted angrily, interpreting the move as a reactionary attempt to shut down youth culture or to boss women around. For manufacturers and retailers the uncertainty over skirt lengths posed nothing but confusion; they responded by stocking more pants.[5] Amid all of this controversy, many women began to see pantsuits as more tasteful, flattering, and modest than either minis or midis. Restrictions on pants evaporated in schools and workplaces across the county; in suburban Detroit the dress code for teachers was changed to permit pantsuits.[6]

There was some resistance from more conservative women, but even in those quarters slacks were more acceptable if they were feminine. Helen Andelin thought pants had their place ("sports, outings and mountain climbing") but when worn in other settings they should be distinguished from men's clothing in some way—color, trim, or accessories. Women who chose mannish clothing for activities such as yard work, she warned, would find themselves treated like "one of the boys," which would upset the natural male-female relationship.

Perhaps the oddest source of anti-pants opinion was physician Robert Bradley, author of the popular book *Husband-Coached Childbirth:*

> I strongly feel that the current rash of vaginal infections is related to women dressing in men's-style clothing. I'm an old square who thinks women look graceful and feminine in long skirts with lace and frills to accentuate their femininity. Pioneer women wore long skirts with no underclothes—at least for working—and had far fewer bladder infections than modern women who wear slacks, especially tight, rigid denims, and panty hose. In addition, the exercises of squatting and tailor sitting can be performed so much more easily in a large, loose skirt than in tight-fitting slacks.[7]

Later studies found trousers innocent on all charges; instead the major culprits were nylon panties and pantyhose.[8]

Youthquake fashion was about more than style. It established a new standard of beauty: young, slender, and unabashedly sexy. Fashion models had been slender since the 1920s, but they had exuded a cool, mature elegance that matched the sophisticated environment of most haute couture salons. In the mid-1960s young designers such as André Courrèges and Mary Quant challenged this staid image, presenting their fashions on very young models—teenagers or women who looked like teenagers—who hopped or danced down the runway to loud rock music. As women quickly discovered, these new looks went beyond superficial style changes. There were also invisible shifts in sizing and basic pattern design that made a minidress not only look better on a young, slim body but fit better as well. If you were a fashion-conscious woman between 1964 and 1966, you might have wondered if you were gaining weight, but it wasn't you that changed.

Women's clothing sizes are not now, and never have been, standardized in the United States, though not for lack of trying. There was an effort in the 1940s and '50s to develop a statistics-based sizing system that would be adopted by all manufacturers, but, as any woman who buys her own clothes knows, a size 10 from one manufacturer is not a size 10 from another (not to mention companies like Chico's that have invented their own sizing systems). Catalog retailers and sewing pattern manufacturers were the most transparent in their sizing systems, in order to avoid costly returns and exchanges. The sizing charts from the Sears catalogs in 1964 and 1966 reveal some interesting changes in size categories and measurements. Women's fashions were organized in three main sections: Junior (odd numbers), Misses (even numbers, usually up to 18 or 20), Women's (even sizes above the Misses range), and Half Sizes (even numbers with a $1/2$ added—for example, $141/2$). These were distinct proportions as well as measurements. Size chart listings for a Junior 13 and a Misses 14 in the Sears spring 1966 catalog would have the following measurements:

	Junior 13	Misses 14
Bust	$35^{1/2}$–$36^{1/2}$	36–37
Waist	26–27	27–28
Hips	37–38	$37^{1/2}$–$38^{1/2}$

A woman of average height measuring 36-27-38 might be able to fit into either size; the main difference in fit was bust fullness and location. High, small bustline? Juniors. Full bust, lower on the torso? Misses. There were also differences in style: Junior sizes were for young women in high school, or possibly just starting college or work. Misses designs were a bit more mature—not old-ladyish, but less casual and more covered up. In the 1960s and '70s, with a large, young population driving consumption, the Junior department became *the* fashion department for most retailers. A woman who wanted the latest trends looked there first; Misses fashions had longer hemlines and more conservative styling. Given that dynamic, the changes in sizing are all the more revealing about the transformation of women's fashion at the time.

An observant regular Sears customer in the lower end of the Junior or Misses size ranges might think she had gone up a size since her last purchase, but that was all. The 1966 waist measurements for both size ranges were slightly smaller in proportion to bust and hip, and the Junior styles included shorter skirts; lower, "hip-hugging" waistlines; and more trousers and pantsuits. Because the Junior sizes topped out at about a 38–39-inch bust, women who were larger had to shop in the Misses department, forgoing the hottest trends. This represented a significant shift in the center of gravity in the fashion world, where the teenage market had once been a small, specialized segment.

This shift was not limited to mass-market producers. In 1965 *Vogue* reported that the basic master patterns (called "slopers") for the trendiest designers had also changed.[9] Not only was "the look" slimly androgynous, but so was the body for which it was designed. The new ideal body had a small, high, wide-set bosom and slender, almost preadolescent hips. Accordingly, the revised patterns featured smaller, higher-cut armholes and higher bustlines. Sleeves were slimmer; pants and skirts were tighter at the hip. None of these changes would have shown in the size charts, but would be noticed in the dressing-room mirror. Short skirts; sleeveless dresses; and tight, hip-hugger pants demanded toned arms, knees, and legs. The author of the *Vogue* article offered helpful exercise advice to help readers achieve the required effect.[10] Bicep curls and leg lifts wouldn't help the girl with an hourglass figure, of course, or indeed anyone who wasn't stick-thin. Designer Ruben Torres, predicting jumpsuits for the twenty-first century, declared that they were "for lean, sleek bodies." What about women who didn't measure up? the interviewer asked. Torres's answer was, "Plastic surgery and, for those too old, some veiling, draped at the vital part."[11] It strikes me that if gender ambiguity was the object, unisex fashions were most effective on androgynous bodies. For adults, androgynous bodies come in essentially two varieties: skinny and fat. Skinny men and women could carry off the tiniest unisex styles— hip-hugger pants, for example—because our culture is comfortable with exposed slender bodies. Fat bodies—male and female—were excluded or hidden.

When Junior sizes had been intended for high school girls, their sexiness had been downplayed. The desired effect was fresh and maidenly: the chaste ingénue, not Lolita. But as the size range became more about style than age, the clothing became more revealing and the advertising poses more provocative, even in the pages of the Sears catalog. Women in their late teens and early twenties in the late 1960s were on the front lines of the sexual revolution, with some fairly consequential decisions to make about their lives and bodies. For starters there was the paradox of being encouraged to embrace your sexuality while not being a sex object. The Pill made sex without the fear of pregnancy a reality, but it did not erase the double standard. Intercourse before marriage, or even promiscuity, was judged more harshly for women than men, and wearing clothing that expressed one's identity as a sexual being could be risky.

Another quandary was the contradiction between second-wave feminist ideology that beauty culture was an artificial distraction that limited women from achieving their full potential and the alternative view, found in both *Cosmopolitan* and *Fascinating Womanhood,* that fashion and cosmetics were valuable tools for a woman to get what she wanted. Was it better to "go natural" or embrace commercial enhancements? Didn't that depend on your natural body and the extent to which it fit the ideal? What about women over thirty? Young mothers in their early twenties? Society women "of a certain age" who were used to dressing well and following trends? Marylin Bender of the *New York Times* detected this bias toward youth quite early, in 1964: "old maxims to the effect that life begins at 40 and elegance at 30 don't hold true in fashion any more. The latest news from the Paris couture showings confirms the fact that it is no longer possible to age gracefully and still be in high style."[12] The new mod styles, with their skimpy cuts and juvenile attitude, were just for the young, and older women followed them at their peril. The miniskirt was especially problematic, as it moved from just above the knee to a few inches below the crotch. Women who a few years earlier would have considered trousers "unladylike" found tailored pantsuits a reasonable alternative to dresses in unfashionable lengths or trendy dresses that made them look foolish.

At the other end of the age spectrum were young teens or preteens. Standard sizing usually placed them in the 7–14 girls' size ranges, but girls who were developing breasts in fifth or sixth grade often found themselves awkwardly stuck between girls' and women's fashions. Girls' dresses were too short and the wrong shape; Junior and Misses styles might fit but often looked too mature. Sears' clothing for "junior high girls" in the 1960s and '70s gives us a glimpse into the early stages of age compression, or "kids getting older younger" (KGOY). This concept—younger and younger children adopting styles and products initially designed for an older age group—has been controversial for years. We might think of this today as thong underwear and colored lip gloss marketed to five-year-olds, but in the late 1960s and early 1970s it was a bit subtler. The Junior section of the Sears spring 1967 catalog featured popular model *Colleen Corby* (born in 1947) in an outfit that in style and sizing was aimed at young women about her own age, in the high school to college age range. Modeling separates in bright, bold stripes, Corby appeared in what had already become a typical "Junior" pose: a wide stride, as if the photographer caught her mid-frug. Both the A-line skirt and sleeveless dress are about three inches above her knee, in contrast to Misses styles of that season, which just skimmed the knee. Corby's shoulder-length hair is in a long, off-center braid when she models the pants outfit. Every detail would match well with campus styles from 1967 to 1968. In 1970 Sears introduced a young teens line called "The Lemon Frog Shop," sizes 6J to 18J, described as for girls from eleven to fourteen years of age. Colleen Corby, by then in her early twenties, is a featured model. The Lemon Frog styles include a midriff-baring top, hip-hugger pants, and mid-thigh-length micro-miniskirts worn with knee socks. Corby and the other models have their hair in pigtails or looped braids. Whether these styles looked little-girlish or sexy depended on both the wearer and the viewer. Even more problematic is the reality that from this point on, clothing for preteen girls could be both little-girlish and sexy.

"Natural beauty" was not achieved easily, even for women in their late teens and early twenties. Stiff, pointed bras and constricting girdles were out, but a smooth line under clothes was even more desirable when the clothes were made of slinky knit fabrics. Not everyone wanted to go braless—or could. Enter pantyhose, bodysuits, and soft-cup bras. Rudi Gernreich's soft, unstructured "no-bra bra" was specifically intended for women who wanted to "fake the braless look."[13] Young girls in minidresses replaced both girdles and regular hose with pantyhose, including patterned styles that drew attention to the expanse of leg.

Slacks were revealing in new ways, especially if they were fashionably tight. *Vogue's* fashion adviser noted the need for a panty girdle, or even pantyhose with a panty girdle over them, for "smooth thigh transition." To be a woman, especially to be a lady, was to be restrained. Not just restrained physically by foundation garments and shoes but also restrained socially, economically, and culturally. However, although discarding girdles and bras gave women physical comfort, in some ways it gave them less freedom. After all, now the control was exerted through exercise and dieting.

One way to interpret this trend toward greater body consciousness is that it helped create a culture that redefined "fat," by changing how clothes fit, and also marginalized fat women by rendering much fashionable clothing unwearable. But a closer look at the choices available also reveal how some trends could be used to dramatic effect by fat women, following the example of singer Cass Elliot of the Mamas and the Papas, a woman who, although she loved fashion, didn't match designers' vision of the new body yet managed to negotiate an image that was right on trend—and fabulous.

The Mamas and the Papas' first big hit, "California Dreamin'," was released in December 1965 and dominated the charts for the first three months of 1966. They represented not just a new sound, folk rock, but also a new look for groups. Instead of carefully coordinated costumes, they each wore what they liked. The look of the group seemed to symbolize a new, free way of living, each person absolutely idiosyncratic. From the beginning the star of the group was Cass Elliot, who was big in every way—big personality, big voice, and a big body. At just over five feet tall, the former Ellen Cohen from Baltimore was reported to weigh more than 200 pounds.

People who wrote about her found it impossible to ignore her size, which they mentioned directly, or metaphorically, as when *Newsweek* described her as "that volcano of sound." As *Time*'s reviewer pointed out, former model Michelle Phillips's willowy frame was a dramatic contrast to "Big Bertha" Cass. Of course no one ever gave the weight of the two "Papas."

Stories of her life reveal a woman who especially loved glamorous, feminine styles. In high school Cass refused to dress according to the rules and was well known for her eccentric dress: Bermuda shorts paired with high heels and white gloves. A pre–Mamas and Papas boyfriend recalls that she always dressed impeccably and in a very feminine style, favoring big hats, pretty scarves, and flouncy dresses. When "Mama" Michelle Phillips opened the door to her New York flat and first laid eyes on Cass Elliot, she was also just starting to feel the effects of her very first hit of LSD. Seeing Cass in a pink angora sweater, great big false eyelashes, and hair in a bouncy flip, Phillips recalled, "I remember thinking, 'This is quite a drug.'"[14]

Despite her public self-confidence, Cass was privately uncomfortable with her weight, which varied from 180 (after a particularly intense bout of dieting and diet pills) to more than 300 pounds over the course of her career. Still, she dressed herself enthusiastically and found plenty of styles she adored in the flowing lines and visual effusion of the mod and hippie eras. Relying on personal dressmakers, she created a blend of current styles—miniskirts, caftans, custom-made boots—and old Hollywood sparkle and glamour. She and Michelle had many of their stage looks created at the same Hollywood boutique, Profile du Monde, which specialized in made-to-order clothing from sari silks.[15] In her solo career as well, Cass embraced Hollywood glamour. The performances began with Cass, in a beaded gown, being lifted onto the stage by an elevator. According to reviewers of her final appearances, in 1974 in London, she looked "glittering, stunning and magnificent," "like a pink sunrise."[16]

If she had lived, she would have joined the pantheon of super-size, glamorous female singers: Kate Smith, Aretha Franklin, and others. But instead she died at thirty-two, first attributed to choking on a ham sandwich, but then discovered to have been a heart attack, which the headline writers swiftly translated into "obesity." But in her heyday with the Mamas and Papas, she received the lion's share of the fan mail and was often surrounded after their concerts by young girls asking for her advice. In an era where "do your own thing" was a mantra for the young, Cass Elliott's personal style showed that it could mean for the "rest of us" above a size six. Like her contemporary Barbra Streisand, she was not conventionally pretty. But as *Esquire* noted in 1969, "What Streisand did for Jewish girls in Brooklyn, Cass Elliot was doing for fat girls everywhere. The diet food people must have hated her the way nose surgeons are said to hate Streisand. While the Mamas and Papas were defining a lifestyle for their fans to emulate, Cass was redefining the concept of beauty among the young."[17]

Cass Elliot epitomized the female archetype of "earth mother," a label often applied to her ("Cass looked like the mother of all mankind," "Earth Mother in a muumuu"[18]) that combines size and procreative power. Her solo debut album, "Don't Call Me Mama Anymore," was an attempt to shed both the "Mama Cass" moniker and the maternal image, but she was fighting an uphill battle when it came to the fashion industry. There is a long-standing relationship between weight and "motherliness" in women's clothing; plus-size powerhouse Lane Bryant began with maternity clothes before expanding into "mature styles," which also happened to run larger than the Misses range. Determined not to be left out of the Youthquake, Lane Bryant put on a fashion show in 1968 featuring above-the-knee skirts for "stout women." The *New York Times* described the models as "fuller," "chubby," and "plump" but also as "motherly" and "grandmotherly."[19] A young, full-figured woman, frustrated by the matronly looks in the ready-to-wear marketplace, could look to celebrities like Mama Cass Elliot for inspiration.

It is obvious to me as a lifelong jeans wearer that dungarees formed the popular foundation for unisex clothing. I am not referring to designer unisex, futuristic jumpsuits; his-and-hers pants suits; or matching crocheted granny-square ponchos. Relatively few people actually adopted most of these, despite what the fashion press was reporting or retailers were pushing. Jeans opened the door for all of these and were the common denominator in many outfits. Just about everyone wore jeans, regardless of age, sex, class, or race. There are several reasons for this.

Jeans were a childhood favorite. For many American kids, blue jeans were the play clothes of choice. Perfect for backyard games of cowboys and Indians, jeans were also often soft from years of wear if you were fortunate enough to have older siblings who broke them in. Sears catalogs throughout the 1950s and early 1960s displayed classic denim jeans in children's sizes 2 to 6 or 7 without gender distinction. Baby boomers may have dressed like little ladies and gentlemen at school and on Sundays, but our freest times were in jeans.

Jeans were sexy. No sooner had we outgrown backyard games than we discovered the allure of jeans on young bodies. James Dean and Marlon Brando. Girls in jeans, looking tomboyishly cute. You bought them to just fit, shrank them to fit closer, and then let them adjust themselves to your body over months or years of wear. The marriage of jeans and rock music sealed the deal. Grown-ups hated them both, which made it even better. Jeans were a blank, neutral canvas. If the ad men had their gray flannel suits and ladies had their little black dresses, we kids had our jeans. New, dark indigo jeans were practically formal and could be paired with a sport coat, leotard top, or dashiki. Once they softened up and started to rip, they could be held together with patches, appliqué, or embroidery, or lead new lives as shorts, skirts, or even shoulder bags.

At first everyone was wearing basic dungarees, and that meant women were usually wearing men's jeans. But that was soon to change. The first Gap store, selling just Levi's jeans and records, opened in 1969 in San Francisco. The key to the store's success, besides a savvy exploitation of the generation gap (thus the name) was that they carried every size that Levi's made, guaranteeing a perfect fit for men and women. One of the biggest brands of the 1970s, the Ditto brand of jeans was created when owner Richard Jaffe realized that young women were buying young men's jeans because they liked the fit and construction. So he created a line of jeans that were tagged with both men's and women's sizes. Then Ditto produced men's pants (in construction) made for women to wear (curvy, with booty-emphasizing seams). By 1974 women and girls were buying 98 percent of Ditto's production. The company's ads were usually a close-up of a woman's rear end with a man's hand on or near it, emphasizing the cut of the jeans and the way it curved around the woman's butt. In less than a decade, jeans had gone from masculine, to neutral, to gendered and sexy, which is pretty much the story of unisex fashion for women in a nutshell.

How was unisex fashion connected to the various strands of femininity, feminism, and sexual liberation that wove through women's lives in the late 1960s and early 1970s? It is tempting to say that it was figment of high fashion designers' imaginations, but designers do not work in a vacuum. They respond to what is happening around them, in the arts, in the street, in diners, and in four-star restaurants. What was in the air was change, with no clear future direction. Women, particularly white, middle-class women, had been moving toward greater equality and self-determination since the turn of the century. The seductive detour through the suburbs had been satisfying for some, but Betty Friedan had correctly detected growing dissatisfaction with its limits. Astute marketers sensed that some women were looking for new sources of self-actualization and fulfillment. Of course this disillusionment with the postwar American Dream did not extend to those who hadn't yet achieved it, so the old messages needed to be revised, not totally discarded. America's fascination with sex was pushing the boundaries in film and literature, and between *Cosmopolitan* and the Pill, the sexual double standard was being challenged. For women in particular the sexual revolution centered on the decline of premarital chastity and with it the delusion of "technical virginity," which defined everything short of actual intercourse as "not sex." The birth control pill made "free love" possible, the new music made it attractive, and the fashions made it visible.

The postwar babies were approaching prime fashion consumer age, creating opportunity and confusion for manufacturers and retailers.

Both the sexual revolution and second-wave feminism were generationally based; the children were renouncing the world of their parents. In a market where half of the population was under the age of twenty-five, the sanest course seemed to follow the young. But that assumed they knew where they wanted to go.

The most futuristic versions of unisex demonstrate the limits of unisex dressing for women—for example, the costume designs for *Star Trek* (1966–1969), *2001: A Space Odyssey* (1968), and *Space: 1999* (1975–1977). The body-hugging clothing assumed to await us in the future revealed the figure, making the wearer's sex obvious. Women still wore body-shaping underwear, makeup, and jewelry; men did not (except for male aliens, apparently). Futuristic unisex was more practical, perhaps, but made physical differences even more apparent.

What about the other styles was considered unisex? Menswear influences, or downright appropriation of masculine signifiers such as neckties, had been a feature of women's fashions for centuries. Although these trends multiplied during the late 1960s and 1970s, the final effect was not that women's clothing became more masculine, it was that most of the elements they borrowed became either feminized (like jeans did) or were no longer considered masculine.

What the gender trends in women's clothing reveal is the opening of a conversation about femininity—its definition, its desirability, its naturalness, and its expression—amid an even more serious discussion of women's place in society. The profusion of options and rejection of old rules of propriety meant that women had more freedom to choose among an even greater abundance of options. About twenty years ago one of my doctoral students, a young woman from Korea, embarked on an independent study of American fashions of the 1970s. Having been a teenager in another country at the time, she had no memory of the period and relied entirely on *Vogue* magazine for her paper. While she did an excellent job of primary research, I realized that I had worn hardly any of the trends she identified. Consulting my personal photo albums, I realized why: I had made just about everything I wore, except jeans and T-shirts. Not only were my clothes home-sewn, but the patterns I used were also heavily modified, as I took the "do your own thing" dictum to heart. My fash-

ion bible was not *Vogue* or *Mademoiselle,* but *Cheap Chic.*[20] This 1975 guide
to alternative fashion by Caterine Milinaire and Carol Troy was the *Our
Bodies, Our Selves* of fashion for many women, offering inexpensive ideas
for creating an individual style. In the 1970s my mother would ask me
what the right hemline was "this year," and there wasn't one: it depended.
Everything depended—on the weather, the occasion, and one's mood.

The *New York Times* noticed this proliferation of choice in 1968, reporting so many different trends that the only common theme they could
find was escapism. Some women's clothing was dressy, glamorous, and
exotic, but casual looks were invading places and occasions where they
once had been prohibited. Hems ranged from micro-mini (a few inches
below the crotch) to floor-sweeping "granny" length. The economy was
booming, and consumers were buying—everything, it seemed. The new
eclecticism was even showing up in rock 'n' roll bands. The Beatles had
abandoned their look-alike mod suits for an idiosyncratic mix of vintage, uniform, and Eastern styles. This stylish abundance—and confusion—lasted through the late 1970s. The August 1973 issue of *Mademoiselle* shows young women from various colleges wearing everything from
houndstooth check pants, to jeans, to above-the-knee skirts, to maxi-
skirts, to midi-length skirts.

This suggests a temporary shift away from something I call "personality dressing," referring to the common women's magazine trope that asks,
"What kind of woman are you?" and then offers style and grooming advice based on the responses. For example, in 1965 *Seventeen* featured "Personality Types and the Clothes That Go with Them," using the categories
"dainty vs. sturdy," "dramatic vs. demure," and "dignified vs. vivacious"
for three pairs of outfits.[21] A fragrance ad from the same year offers just
three choices: "romantic," "modern," and "feminine."[22] Clara Pierre, noticing the same trend, used the term "event dressing" for the new, more
situational rules, but I think the term "moment dressing" is more descrip-
tive.[23] Which outfit came out of the closet depended not only on the occasion but also on the woman's mood at the moment. Moment dressing was
a sign that the essentialist view that women came in a few, easily catego-
rized varieties was passé, at least for a while. Like the W-O-M-A-N in the
Enjoli perfume commercial who could "bring home the bacon, cook it up

in a pan, and never let you forget you're a man," the woman of the 1970s could do anything, or at least dress for anything.

All fashions end; that's why they are called "fashions," not paradigm shifts. It was inevitable that trends so generationally driven would change as the leading edge of the baby boom reached their late twenties and thirties. Careers replaced summer jobs, and suburban houses replaced dorm rooms. The economy tightened, and there was less money to spend on whimsical clothing, bringing classics back to center stage.

Although women had made significant gains in civil rights—equal opportunity in employment, Title IX opening up school athletics, the ability to establish credit and financial autonomy—second-wave feminists still felt they had unfinished business, but there were signs of public fatigue and, more seriously, backlash. In the nine years between the publication of *The Feminine Mystique* and the passing of the Equal Rights Amendment, while some women were raising their consciousness and reading *Ms.,* significant countermovements had also gained strength. Blue-collar women, lesbians, and women of color were excluded by the feminist leadership's emphasis on finding a place for women within the existing societal structure. These fissures within the women's movement existed early on, at the ironically named Congress to Unite Women in 1969 and 1970. Appearances had something to do with it, just as they had during the first women's movement in the nineteenth century. Amelia Bloomer, Elizabeth Cady Stanton, and others had abandoned dress reform and the revolutionary outfits associated with it in the 1850s, because they were convinced the clothing was distracting from the "real issues" of women's rights. Betty Friedan and others in the National Organization for Women leadership were afraid that activist lesbians, especially the more visible, "mannish-looking" ones, would attract too much hostility and negative press, thus hindering the movement.

Stereotypes are stubborn things. Just as the suffragists had been lampooned as pants-wearing Amazons for decades after the Bloomer costume disappeared, the popular image of the bra-burning, man-hating, hairy-legged feminist became lodged in the popular consciousness. Never mind that the bras in question (outside the Miss America pageant in 1968) were tossed in a trash can (along with mops and fake eyelashes), not burned. The July 1973 issue of *Esquire,* proclaiming on the cover "This Issue Is about Women," is a snapshot of the male response to feminism. While including young journalist Sara Davidson's straightforward history of the modern women's movement and a thoughtful set of interviews with men who were sympathetic to the cause, the issue also included such choice pieces as a chart of the women's liberation leadership titled "Women Who Are Cute When They Are Mad" and a satirical piece asking "What If... Gloria Steinem Were Miss America?"[24] The answers:

> People would say she won because she dated Bert Parks.
>
> She would not have won Miss Congeniality.
>
> Her talent would be a modern dance interpretation of the Bell Jar.
>
> She would accept a $5000 wardrobe consisting of three dozen turtlenecks, a gross of T-shirts and 250 pairs of jeans.
>
> She would wear purple aviator contact lenses.
>
> She would still be a royal pain in the ass.[25]

Not all women were enthusiastic feminists, either. Some were devotees of Helen Andelin's vision of power femininity, a movement that gained a political face with the emergence of the new conservative leader Phyllis Schlafly. Schlafly organized a STOP ERA movement that was instrumental in blocking or rescinding ratification of the amendment before the deadline in 1982. (STOP stood for Stop Taking Our Privileges, a reference to Schlafly's contention that the ERA would end women's protected status and result in women being drafted and everyone being forced to use unisex bathrooms.) Probably one of the most articulate expressions of intellectual opposition to women's liberation was George Gilder's *Sexual Suicide* (1973). Like many other critics, he argued that the prevailing culture exalted women and gave them a privileged place in society. But he also noted one of the basic problems with the liberation movement—and perhaps the social reform effort. He responds to a question posed by Nora Ephron in an article for *Esquire:* "What will happen to sex after liberation? Frankly, I don't know. It's a great mystery to all of us." "Ms. Ephron is honest and right. The liberationists have no idea where their program would take us. The movement is counseling us to walk off a cliff, in the evident wish that our society can be kept afloat on feminist hot air."[26]

In fact none of us knew what would happen if women and girls had equal rights, or if the sexual double standard were eliminated, or if women had complete reproductive choice. We wouldn't know for sure until long after these things happened; we still don't know. But in the meantime the pace of change slowed as millions of individuals turned inward and made their private choices.

Women's fashions begin to reflect these changes in the early seventies as dresses made a comeback. When twenty-two-year-old Diane Von Furstenberg arrived in the United States in 1968, she found a chaotic, disappointing mix of "hippie clothes, designer clothes and drip-dry polyester."[27] There was nothing, she believed, for young mothers or working women, and she felt there was an untapped market for "simple sexy little dresses" that were comfortable, easy to care for, and figure-flattering. The result was her iconic knitted jersey wrap dress, which she modeled herself in a full-page ad in *Women's Wear Daily*. The unstructured dress, with its modest length and sexy slit skirt and V-neck, was a gigantic success and was seen everywhere, whether in the original version or any of the many knock-offs, and is credited with wooing women away from pantsuits.

Influential as the wrap dress was, it was also well timed, not just great design. Women's fashions were acquiring a vintage sensuality, propelled by nostalgia for the 1930s in popular culture and design. One barometer of this trend is Frederick's of Hollywood, known in the 1960s mainly as a mail-order purveyor of hard-to-find lingerie items. Frederick's claimed to have invented the push-up bra and offered not only a sexier selection of bras than Sears or Montgomery Ward, but also pasties, crotchless panties, padded girdles, and, in the late 1960s, sex toys and how-to manuals. The firm went public in 1972 and opened 150 stores in the next eight years, becoming a fixture in suburban malls. Competition was not long in coming; in 1976 Bloomingdale's department store hired French photographer Guy Bourdin to create "Sighs and Whispers," a lingerie catalog that created such a sensation that original copies sell today for hundreds of dollars. Women in skimpy, even scandalous undies populate the dramatically lit tableaux. They are not just lounging passively, but jumping and dancing. They even "flash" the reader, revealing see-through bras under filmy negligees. In 1977 Victoria's Secret upped the ante with more sophisticated unmentionables, reminiscent of pre–sexual revolution boudoirs, but with a postrevolutionary frankness.

The final element in the shift in women's fashion was the publication of *Dress for Success for Women* (1977),[28] John T. Molloy's sequel to his 1975 best-selling book for men.[29] In his introduction he described the biggest problem facing women in the professional workplace: the lack of appropriate office styles for women with aspirations beyond the secretarial pool. The available choices were usually too casual and either too mannish or too sexy. Like the original men's version of *Dress for Success*, Molloy's advice was based on his own extensive research, most of it for businesses that hired him to provide guidance to their own employees. Since I've already admitted that I did not read any of the three most influential books for women published in the early 1960s, I'll confess that for my research for this book I used my original paperback copy of *Dress for Success for Women*, purchased in 1978 when I was in graduate school. By the next year, every female grad student in my department owned a "success suit" as described by Molloy in the chapter by the same name: a blazer-style jacket and a skirt hemmed just below the knee, worn with low-heeled, plain pumps. My suit was deep maroon wool, one of his "approved" colors. Mass merchandisers lagged a bit in adopting the style; Sears and Montgomery Ward showed their first Molloy-style outfits in fall 1979. But they usually offered separate pieces, not suits, and always included matching trousers, an option Molloy did not endorse. "The pantsuit is a failure outfit," he warned, except in female-dominated workplaces.[30]

By the late 1970s skirts and dresses were back for work and formal occasions, pants were uncontroversial (but had been feminized with colors and trims), and lingerie sales were up. But were these steps backward or forward? If you believed that dresses and sexy underwear were the tools of patriarchy, you saw retreat in these events. If you believed that clothing, including power suits worn with a lace-trimmed slip, was your ticket to the executive suite, you saw progress. If you believed that gender differences were a moral imperative, you would be very pleased that women were "dressing like women again." The one permanent change was that the monolithic image of women had been shattered, or at least had a few cracks in it.

Fashion historian James Laver, observing the clothing of Great Britain in the early 1960s, mused, "When a woman becomes emancipated, you would think she would go in for an orgy of femininity. Instead she flattens her figure and cuts off her hair. She did it after World War I and again after World War II."[31] He found this behavior contradictory, but I don't believe it is. Women's rights movements have been, at least in part, a rebellion against the cultural construction of femininity, what Betty Friedan called "the feminine mystique," probably because these supposedly innate characteristics of women—kindness, emotionality—have too often been used to define our place and then confine us within it. Trying to break away from that confinement means engaging with the cultural products that connect the female and the feminine, sex and gender. For clothing that can mean reassessing either the fashions we wear or the industry that creates and promotes them—or both.

Bras and beauty products were thrown in the trash at the 1968 Miss America pageant as a protest against the artificial construction of femininity, yet both lingerie and cosmetics are bigger business today than they were forty years ago. Cosmetic surgery, just in its infancy in the 1960s, has grown as the baby boomers have aged. Was fashion a form of oppression created and perpetuated by patriarchy or a pastime enjoyed by many women as a means of self-actualization? There have always been many views on fashion among feminist activists and thinkers. There is no single feminist perspective on fashion; there is a multitude. One of the oldest conflicts within the feminist movement has been the one between people who wanted to eschew fashionable clothing and those who believed it was an important form of personal expression.

How deep were the changes in women's dress from this era, and how many of those changes persist today? Attempts to develop unisex clothing in the 1970s had about as much success as the Bloomer costume did in the 1850s. Doors were opened and new choices appeared, but it is difficult to argue that the cultural construction of femininity in 1980 was radically different from what it had been in 1960. Even though women had adopted pants, most preferred to wear trousers that fit their curves and were worn with blouses and sweaters that were designed for women, not men. Two changes appear to have been permanent: greater sexualization of clothing and the demise of many of the old rules of etiquette that had governed dress. These two trends were not unrelated. "Sexy" clothing had long been permitted or denied according to age, marital status, profession, and occasion as one element in a complex set of rules within broader gender codes. What was worn in the bedroom, ballroom, or bawdy house varied according to subtle standards learned through popular media. In 1963, movie streetwalkers such as those in *Irma la Douce,* were immediately recognizable because they wore exaggerated makeup in the daytime, boots when it wasn't raining, and very short skirts. Ladies wore white gloves and hats and donned pants for only the most casual activities. By the late 1970s women had abandoned white gloves and hats and wore pants everywhere. Sandals, once considered strictly beachwear, appeared in offices across the country. Some of these rules had separated casual from formal, public from private, and girl from woman. They also helped to communicate one's availability for flirtation or more. Without the rules were all females sexy? Did that become part of the basic job description for all girls and women? That may be one unintended legacy of the sexual revolution.

The Peacock Revolution

3

Journalist George Frazier is credited with popularizing the phrase "peacock revolution" to describe the styles coming from London's young Carnaby Street designers, which promised to restore the lost glory of flamboyant menswear.[1] Frazier was describing the explosion of choices that were suddenly available to men, ranging from Romantic revival (velvet jackets and flowing shirts) to a pastiche of styles borrowed from Africa and Asia. Expanded color palettes, softer fabrics, and a profusion of decorative details represented a direct challenge to the conformity and drabness of menswear at mid-century. For critics of the new men's fashions, flowered shirts and velvet capes raised the specter of decadence and homosexuality, a fear that was reinforced by the emergence of the gay liberation movement. Just as women's unisex styles had to balance being sexy and liberated, men's styles tended to navigate the territory between expressiveness and effeminacy. But like many revolutions, the peacock revolution ended in repudiation and regression. Although fashion prognosticators in 1970 were predicting the demise of neckties and gray flannel suits, within ten years the pendulum had swung back with a vengeance. John T. Molloy's *Dress for Success,* in 1975, had codified a return to conservative dressing for business. Within a few years the more flamboyant styles of the late 1960s and '70s had been relegated to the back of the closet, if not the thrift shop.

Part of the reason for this stylistic whiplash is that the impact of the peacock revolution was exaggerated at the time and seems only to have grown in the popular imagination. The reality is that many men, even young men, did not succumb to the trend, and few of those who did adopt the new styles continued to experiment with new expressions of masculinity for long. To understand what was going on beneath the surface of men's fashions, we need to enter relatively unexplored territory: the masculine mystique.

Multiple competing models of masculinity and femininity characterize modern culture. Girls and boys are presented with an array of options as to what kind of men and women they will be, and they are also aware, through photography, movies, television, and the millions of images on the Internet, that these models have changed. Anytime a boy reads, watches movies or television shows, sings along with rock lyrics, or engages in a dozen other popular culture activities, he is aware of his options (and of the models he must avoid). Men's fashions enclothe these different choices, or, more exactly, allow men to clothe themselves in just the right masculinity for the moment or the company. After all, they're just the costumes that men use when they are playing different roles: suburban dad barbecuing on the weekend, young man on a date, businessman at a meeting, hip-hop fan at a concert.

Isn't this just what women do? Superficially yes, but men's and women's fashions differ significantly, from design and distribution to the psychological impact they have on wearers and viewers. In a consumer society the advertisements in magazines and television and the other cultural products that surround us are what communicate the ideal patterns and the desired effect. If, as Betty Friedan argued, women's magazines shaped our cultural expectations of women, then men's magazines—*Playboy, Esquire, Gentleman's Quarterly,* and, beginning in 1965, *Penthouse*—wielded similar influence in men's consciousness. Like the women's magazines, men's lifestyle magazines dispensed visions of modern gendered consumerism tailored to their respective demographic. Instead of the housewife in her kitchen, the *Playboy* archetype was the swinging bachelor in his penthouse, packaged for a readership that was young and educated (more than half of *Playboy* subscribers were college graduates or still at university). Members of *Esquire's* target audience were somewhat older and more established in their careers. *Penthouse* sought readers who were more affluent than *Playboy's* and even more engaged in the hedonistic lifestyle of the late 1960s. *Gentleman's Quarterly* (or *GQ*), a spinoff from *Esquire,* originally aimed at the menswear industry insider, by the 1960s and 1970s was appealing to the clothes-conscious male consumer in a range of professions.

The vivid, revolutionary nature of young men's clothing in this period is evidence that the time was ripe for a rejection of the masculine mystique along the same lines of second-wave feminism. At the very least it's worthy of an analysis similar to Freidan's: an examination of the underlying fantasies, desires, and aspirations embedded in their articles and advertisements. A few scholars have paid attention to masculinity as a cultural artifact—very few, compared to the huge numbers who have examined women and the media. In this chapter I take a look at the myth and reality of the peacock revolution and its unisex aspects and set them against a backdrop of what we know about men and masculinity. Too widespread to be a fad but falling short of the predicted paradigm shift, the experimentation and conspicuous outrage of this period offered men, particularly white men, an escape into alternate lives. There were some permanent changes, though not the "revolution" predicted in the 1960s. By the 1980s, grooming products and cosmetics for men were a large and permanent addition to the American scene, and "casual Friday" had expanded to "business casual," weeklong and year around. Options for casual clothing, whether active sportswear or leisure styles, were much greater than before the 1960s. The peacock revolution was no more a failure than women's dress reform in the era of the Bloomer costume, and in subtle ways it was much more of a success.

It's always been a puzzle to me why more dress historians don't study men's clothing. Even when they are outwardly drab, men's suits are a marvel of construction, requiring vastly different skills than are required for women's clothing. Neckties have to be the most tenacious vestigial appendage outside the human body; now, there's a story! It seems to me that the relationship between men's sexuality and homophobia is at least as interesting as the cycling male gaze between women's legs and breasts. (Admittedly, women's clothing lends itself to more visually exciting museum exhibits, but must cultural history always be about pretty things?) Men's fashions have their own stories to tell, and the 1960s and '70s are rich with them. What was changing during this era was not masculinity in isolation, but masculinity as it related to the feminine, which was also in a state of rapid change.

More than femininity, masculinity in America had acquired a uniform—the business suit. Introduced in the middle of the nineteenth century, the boxy "lounge" or "sack" suit had originally been intended for casual wear at a time when the well-dressed man had a wardrobe of jackets, each appropriate for a specific time of day and occasion. (As any fan of *Downton Abbey* knows, the phrase "dressing for dinner" in period dramas refers not just to ladies; gentlemen, too, were expected to exchange "daytime" frock coats or cutaways for dinner jackets and white ties.) A well-fitting morning coat or cutaway was the work of a tailor, whereas the less structured sack coat could be presentable off the rack with perhaps just a few alterations. By the mid-twentieth century this style of suit had dominated the American office for three generations. There were trends in details such as lapel width and fit (tight or loose), but these tended to be subtle and slow-moving, compared with women's fashions. A good, basic, neutral-colored sack suit could last a man for many years, because it could be trusted not to go out of style.

The image of "the man in the gray flannel suit" is one of the most enduring icons of masculinity: the organization man, struggling to maintain his identity while conforming to professional standards. But it was not the only brand of masculinity available. Like women, men could choose among a range of myths and media images to emulate, from working-class hero to dapper aristocrat. Nor were they wedded to a single image: the man in the gray flannel suit could be a frontiersman in rugged jeans on weekends or indulge his love of color in a Hawaiian shirt. Men's departments before the peacock revolution were not completely devoid of color or frivolity; however, the colorful, fun clothes were consigned to a very restricted set of occasions. Vintage photographs of men on city streets, in offices, and even at sporting events in the 1950s are striking in their uniformity. Hats, suits, and overcoats are so similar in appearance as to make the gathering look like a military muster. The changes that took place in the 1960s and '70s added variety to "office clothing," limited the most formal elements to fewer settings, and opened the door to more individual expression.

Just as Freudian psychology contributed to popular attitudes about women and femininity, it also shaped beliefs about "normal" expressions of masculinity. The main problem with the psychoanalytic approach to gender was the failure of Freud and his followers to realize not only that was there culture at work in attitudes and behavior but also that there was culture at work in the environments in which attitudes and behaviors were learned and even in their own research. What psychologists in the 1950s attributed to the subconscious human mind was not as universal as they thought, but shaped by unique circumstances of society and culture. That included their own professional worldview, their assumptions, and even their research design and conclusions, which were far from being objective science.

One of Freud's most powerful legacies is the idea that masculinity is fragile and subject to "corruption." This is behind modern efforts to protect boys by shielding them from imagined threats ranging from exposure to feminine-stereotypical activities to mere knowledge of the existence of homosexuals. We also have Freud to thank for the idea that children are born as sexual beings, although most of us no longer believe those feelings are attached to our mother or father. Part of the problem is that when the science of psychology is translated into pop psychology, it is out of the scientists' hands, subject to the whim of cultural expectations. There's no way for the experts to steer it as it works its way through our culture and back into our attitudes and behavior. There's no peer review, no public discourse. The concepts, images, and discarded truths take on a life of their own and are passed on from one person to another as common knowledge or urban legend. Yesterday's "discoveries" live on, infecting new minds and seemingly immune to correction or retraction.

So despite post-Freudian psychology and second-wave feminism, the notion persists that femininity is not only the opposite of masculinity but also its inferior and its enemy. The fear of the feminine goes back to ancient Greece, which combated this threat by developing a culture in which boys were mentored by older men (including homosexual intercourse, which was considered masculine for the older man). What has changed in three thousand years is mainly what comprises appropriate "feminine" activities and expression (education, work outside the home, domesticity, sexual freedom—and, of course, modes of dress), but because masculinity is defined in terms of what is considered to be unique to men, nearly every expansion of the feminine has initially been considered a threat to masculinity. The exception is the nineteenth-century invention of the "separate sphere" for middle-class women. One reason this ideology has been so enduring is that it protected male occupations and territories from female encroachment.

What happens in the 1960s when teenage boys and young men begin to adopt seemingly feminine traits? The reactions of the menswear industry and various subsets of American society are one way to discern the masculine mystique. Another is to examine the fashion trends through the lens of the some of the most popular arbiters of men's consumer culture: men's lifestyle magazines such as *Playboy* and *Esquire*.

Modern men's dress is a paradox: dull but interesting. For at least the past 150 years it has been conservative and resistant to change. This contrasts with the ornate and expressive dress worn by men at other times and in other cultures. Considering the dominant role of men in most aspects of American life, this situation should strike most of us as strange. Many scholars have tried to explain it, beginning with cultural Darwinists of the nineteenth century, who saw loose-fitting male dress as evidence of Western man's position at the top of the evolutionary ladder. Comparing a man in business dress to the more flamboyantly dressed man of earlier times and unindustrialized societies seemed to prove that the business suit represented the triumph of intellect over emotion or civilization over primitivism. For those who believed that men were more highly evolved form of humans than women, this also explained why women's clothing was more ornamental than men's: either women were less evolved than men (which left open the possibility that someday they, too, might eventually adopt more rational dress), or they had been selected to be ornamental as a means of fulfilling their own biological destiny to attract a mate and produce offspring.

This evolutionary view of clothing makes some superficial sense. The males and females of most species have an array of markers that help them find each other and choose among potential mates. Human primary sex characteristics (our genitals) are visible at birth, but our secondary sex characteristics (pubic and facial hair, breasts, vocal changes) appear at puberty. Nearly from the beginning of human history, we have used various means to emphasize and amplify sexual, age, and status differences, including body paint and clothing and a wide variety of modifications and accessories, both temporary and permanent. These artificial secondary sex characteristics not only express biological sex but also communicate the attributes and behaviors associated with masculinity and femininity.

Of course there were huge flaws in these early evolutionary theories of dress. The first is that nineteenth-century humans were not a different species from Etruscans or Tang dynasty Chinese. Another is that neither males nor females of the same species are more highly evolved than the other. Lastly, describing societal or cultural change as "evolution" is metaphorical. It should come with a disclaimer like those found on the printed labels of herbal remedies: "This conclusion has not been validated by empirical study and is not intended to be used to justify the present or predict the future." Primary and secondary sex characteristics in their natural states are biological realities; everything we do to enhance, hide, emphasize, or otherwise modify them is cultural. That goes double for most of our everyday attempts to explain differences between men's clothing and women's.

British essayist Harold Nicholson expressed the dilemma of men's clothing as "the problem of how to be individual without being funny."[2] Interestingly, and probably not coincidentally, this concept of vulnerability to ridicule also appears in the psychological research on modern male sex roles. In one of the earliest studies of clothing and human behavior, "fear of ridicule" was given as a motive in clothing selection more often than any other motive by men. For women, however, it fell below reasons such as "to appear attractive," "to impress others," and "to express myself."[3] Later studies suggested that men were more conforming than women and more likely to bow to peer pressure about dress.[4] The blossoming of masculinity studies after 1970 provides us with more insight into men's behavior. James Babl found that highly sex-typed men (that is, men who scored in the high masculine/low feminine quadrant on the Bem Sex Role Inventory) responded to an audiotape on the decline of masculinity by behaving in a more masculine manner and scoring even higher on masculinity scales. (Androgynous men did not.)[5] Educational researchers Jean Grambs and Walter Waetjen found that school-age boys were especially vulnerable to the accusation of effeminacy or homosexuality, adding, "*The most powerful word in the English language is 'sissy.'* Within a group males dare to be nonconforming only when there is no sex-linked factor in the behavior or attitude. If there is any element suggesting that something is masculine or feminine, males will adhere to the 'male position.'"[6]

The dominant style in business wear in the early 1960s was an off-the-rack version of British menswear: white dress shirt, a suit in a dark neutral color (usually black, gray, or navy blue) and a rep tie—ribbed silk, with diagonal stripes. Casual clothing might include sport shirts (plaid, striped, or even Hawaiian), knitted polo shirts, or sweaters, and could be more colorful. The main deviations in color and cut came from society's margins: jazz musicians and beatniks with their turtleneck shirts, generously cut suits, and loud ties, or fashion-forward sophisticates who favored the new "Continental Look"—slim jackets with side vents (or no vents at all) paired with tight trousers with beltless waistbands, like Sansabelts.

But the first signs of change were already visible in England, where young working-class men were emerging from the wartime rubble looking like Edwardian dandies. These "Teddy Boys" adopted a blend of Continental and American elements—tight Italian-style trousers worn with a flowing zoot-suitish drape jacket and "duck's arse" hairstyles, with echoes of their grandparents' day—the Edwardian era had been just forty years earlier—such as long, double-breasted jackets with velvet collars. Demand for these styles, and modifications of them, influenced staid Saville Row, which responded with their own touches of Edwardian elegance. The Teddy Boys were succeeded by the Mods and Rockers, rival subcultures with their own distinctive uniforms. The Rockers were the British counterparts of the American "greaser"—working-class toughs in jeans and leather jackets, whose lives centered on motorcycles and rock 'n' roll. The more fashion-conscious Mods, who favored American blues and Continental-style clothing and scooters, were the leading edge of what would become the peacock revolution.[7]

The changes already simmering in Great Britain barely stirred the surface of American menswear in the early 1960s. *Esquire* was reporting on the Mods as an interesting novelty but for the most part offered its readers a choice of Saville Row (traditional English) or Continental (recommended only for the slimmer man, ideally in the creative department, not accounts). *Playboy,* with its younger readership, touted the Ivy League style—a slightly looser, younger version of Saville Row—as the preferred mode of dress. This was evidently the influence of the magazine's fashion director Robert L. Green, since Hugh Hefner himself had been known to prefer jazz-influenced drape suits when he launched the magazine.[8] Sears echoed these suggestions, with English and Continental styles for adult men and Ivy League for teens and young men. The range of colors was limited, although more leeway was allowed for leisure wear, with golf shirts, cabana sets, and sport shirts available in a range of hues and patterns.

But beneath the surface there was a desire for change. Fashion historian James Laver, best known for his theory of "shifting erogenous zones," predicted in 1964 that men would soon start dressing more for physical attraction and become more erotic.[9] His reasoning echoed other evolutionary/cyclical theories of fashion change, including the idea that one of the drivers of innovation was sexual display, but that the focus of the display must shift from time to time as the imagination becomes bored. His reasoning was that men had suppressed their desire for display so long that they were way overdue for a change. Elaine Kendall, writing in the *New York Times,* reasoned along the same lines and came to the same conclusion: "Women's fashions through the ages have reflected social conditions. Have men's fashions done so, too? Well, the case is harder to prove, but the evidence is there—if the observer is in the right place at the right time."[10] Men's outward appearance may have been conformist and conservative, but underneath rebellion was simmering. Marylin Bender noted a few years later that this may have been connected to women "rethinking their place in society . . . the respective roles of men and women . . . [are] . . . revised."[11]

Credit for launching the revolution in menswear was claimed by many designers and probably belongs to many more. Individual designers certainly played a role—a number of them the same innovators who transformed women's fashions, including Courrèges and Cardin. But neckwear designer Michael Fish is perhaps the most overlooked actor of the

1960s. It was his brightly colored neckties (dubbed "kipper ties" as a play on his last name) that made the revolution palatable to men who wanted to appear "with it" but still had to maintain a mainstream businesslike appearance. While other designers were reinventing the jacket or discarding it altogether, Fish was offering a few square inches of liberation, noting, "Fashion, you see, is in the mind. You have to think differently before you can dress differently. By changing their clothes, people risk changing their whole lives and they are frightened."[12]

Kipper ties made their first appearance at the venerable British outfitter Turnbull and Asser in 1965, where Fish was employed as a designer. In some ways they represented a revival of a style from the not-too-distant past: the so-called "Bold Look" neckwear of the postwar era, which had featured colorful geometric and scenic designs displayed on a generous five-inch-wide canvas. The Bold Look had been replaced by conformist restraint to the extent that by the early 1960s some men's ties were reduced to 1–2-inch strips of solid blue, gray, or black adorned with a single tiny embroidered motif. Michael Fish reintroduced polka dots, bright colors, and prints and made the ties wider, growing from 3 inches to 5 inches by the late 1960s. Through his own store, called Mr. Fish, he sold ties, shirts, suits, and dresses (women's and men's) to the trendiest Brits and tourists from all over the world from 1966 to 1973. Name a style icon from this era and Michael Fish dressed him, from Sean Connery as James Bond to Mick Jagger and David Bowie.

Across the Atlantic a young tie salesman named Ralph Lauren, having tried unsuccessfully to introduce wide neckties to his company, set off on his own in 1966. He hit the jackpot with an order from Neiman-Marcus for one hundred dozen ties and was able to open his own store in New York in 1967, establishing the Polo brand with its nostalgic English vibe but a young, American tilt. The drawn-out progress of the new tie styles in the national marketplace suggests something less than a revolution. Although 3-inch-wide ties made their debut in *Esquire* in fall 1967 and in *Playboy* one year later, the more mainstream Sears catalog held off on the trend until spring 1970. Similarly, while *Esquire* reported a trend for patterned shirts worn with a patterned tie (a striped shirt with a floral tie, for example) in 1968, they did not appear together in Sears until spring 1970, and even then just combined two different stripes in shirt and tie. Of course, catalogs don't tell the whole story; men could mix shirts and ties to accomplish a range of looks, from fairly conservative to maniacally mod.

The high-water point for the British mod influence on American fashion was 1965–1966, before the "summer of love" introduced West Coast hippie styles to the mix. Even *Playboy*'s Robert L. Green featured "modified mod" in the September 1966 issue,[13] with a photo of "two urban guys" dancing at a go-go, wearing American adaptations of English mod attire. One man sports a herringbone tweed double-breasted jacket with epaulets, a cotton floral shirt with solid-color long-point button-down collar and a polka-dot tie. The other has a three-piece suit with a double-breasted short vest cut straight across and a paisley tie. To the modern eye the look is conservative—after all, they are both wearing suits—but in 1966 the suits they wore were an exciting departure from the style of just a few years earlier. Epaulets? A floral shirt with a tweed suit? A wide paisley tie in green and blue? If Michael Fish was right, there was just enough fashion difference to suggest a difference in thinking.

One of the most striking features of the peacock revolution is the success of women's fashion designers in entering and transforming the menswear industry. Some of the most iconic brands in menswear—including Pierre Cardin and Bill Blass—made their debut during this era and rode to success by tapping men's desire for fresh design. French designer Cardin was the more revolutionary of the two, having already earned a reputation as a bit of a rebel within the Chambre Syndicale de la Haute Couture (the venerable French trade union of high-fashion designers) by showing a ready-to-wear collection in 1959. (For his transgression, he was promptly expelled from the Chambre Syndicale but reinstated soon after.) His women's fashions and entrepreneurial innovations were equally avant-garde, as described in chapter 2, and he had been producing some menswear since 1957. When his styles first became available in the United States in 1966, they had an immediate impact, and many imitators. Introducing his Paris couture collection in July 1966, he announced, "You are going to see some slightly strange boys and girls," accurately predicting how disruptive his designs would be.[14] His solution to the tie problem was to eliminate them altogether; he declared neckties "bourgeois" in

1967 and offered scarves and turtlenecks instead. Cardin offered other forms of unconstructed and innovative suits, including vest suits, tunic suits, and shirt suits (matching trousers and shirt worn with no jacket, a precursor to the 1970s leisure suit). He is also credited with the revival of wider jacket lapels. In 1968 *Playboy* highlighted the new cut associated with Cardin's designs: higher armholes, narrower sleeves, and longer, shaped jackets. Like women's clothing, menswear was not only changing the look of men's bodies but also requiring that men reshape their bodies to a younger, slimmer version in order to wear fashionable clothing.

The Nehru jacket was just one of a number of tie-free options that Cardin popularized. Worn by celebrities ranging from Lord Snowdon (with a silk turtleneck) to Sammy Davis Jr., the Nehru jacket with its stand-up collar and soft construction did not originate with Cardin. It was based on a style created in the 1940s and associated with Indian prime minister Jawaharlal Nehru (1889–1964); the Beatles wore matching jackets in this style for their 1965 Shea Stadium concert, two years before Cardin's interpretation in gray flannel. But it was Cardin's version that launched the real craze, which peaked in the fall of 1968. Although it was to become a symbol of middle-age wannabe swingers, the Nehru jacket represented a powerful desire at the time to hang on to the idea of a jacket but open it up to the possibility of greater self-expression and comfort. Accessorized with beaded necklaces or medallions dangling on chains or fabricated in traditional suiting materials, the Nehru jacket appealed—just briefly—to a wide swath of American men. Its heyday was short, however; after a slow ascent (in various forms but without the "Nehru" label) beginning in 1965, it was hailed by both *Esquire* and *Playboy* as the big news of fall 1968. Reception by mass merchandisers was mixed. Sears never bothered with it for adult men; their spring 1969 catalog featured Nehru jackets for boys 2–6x and 7–14 only. In contrast, J. C. Penney took a gamble and embraced the style, offering for boys and men from size 6 through adult not just Nehru jackets but a coat and shirt in the same style as well. As it turned out, Sears was right. Many Nehru styles were purchased, but few were worn much if at all. The Fashion Archives and Museum of Shippensburg University in Pennsylvania has a brilliant red-and-gold print Nehru shirt. In his letter the donor of the garment admitted, "I bought

Nehru shirt, 1968.

this Nehru shirt in 1968 at Hutzlers Department Store in Baltimore and I have never worn it. I was going with a woman at the time who had worked at Hutzlers and was certain that the Nehru look was for me. It wasn't."[15]

By fall 1969 the Nehru fad was over, and the American menswear industry moved in a slightly different direction: a cautious blend of traditional and modern, epitomized by the designs of Bill Blass.

Like Cardin, Indiana-born Bill Blass had already made his name as a women's wear designer, but the similarity ends there. While Cardin had found a niche with the jet-set avant-garde, Blass's work for Maurice Rentner Ltd. was later characterized as "trim social-circuit luncheon uniform—a crisp suit worn with a good set of faux pearls."[16] His blend of classic tailoring and updated features made him popular with younger socialites, however, and his work appeared regularly in *Vogue*, modeled by the emerging "new" models such as Jean Shrimpton and Penelope Tree. In 1967 he began to design menswear for Rentner, and by 1968 he had earned a Coty Award for menswear—the first such award given by the organization. Nora Ephron interviewed Blass and his customers to find out his secret and revealed a rather conservative designer who understood just how far middle-class, middle-aged American men were willing to go to stay abreast of their sons and younger brothers. He recognized that the Nehru jacket was about rejecting neckties but believed that most men were more interested in wider, more colorful ties than a complete overthrow of the suit. Gray made him "sad," so he made lots of suits in shades of brown, which he felt was more flattering to most men. Turtlenecks were all right in their place ("the country") but not for formal wear. His large-scale plaids were a bit of a shock to conservative men but a welcome shot in the arm to the most adventuresome.[17] As *Playboy* noted in 1969, Blass and Ralph Lauren offered just the right blend of traditional English styling and a dash of hipness, without venturing too far into the land of Mod, or worse yet, hippieness. Leaping "fashionably forward by way of the past," the menswear of Lauren and Blass was reminiscent of English landed-gentry life between the wars, all Norfolk jackets and heathery tweeds.[18]

What was clear to some observers was that the shift in men's appearance was neither trivial nor superficial. Just as some women were chal-

Caftan pattern, 1976. McCall's M5354.
Image courtesy of the McCall Pattern Company, 2014.

lenging societal and cultural conventions that limited their educational
and career aspirations, some men were finding the masculine mystique
inhibiting. No less a cultural critic than Marshall McLuhan noted that
men and women were beginning to share experiences and communicate
as equals, which included granting men the freedom to express themselves through dress.[19]

Nor was fashion just a means of self-expression. After all, the peacock's
display has a purpose beyond vanity or self-expression: to attract admir-
ing peahens. The new clothing was supposed to be sexy, in stark contrast
to the business suit, which projected an image of a reliable breadwinner.
In fact even the definition of "sexy" was in flux. *Women's Wear Daily* noted
that the girls were all crazy for "fragile, unmasculine" men—slender,
longhaired boys in their romantic velvets and ruffles.[20] Rudi Gernreich
offered futuristic menswear that was abbreviated, tight-fitting, or both,

asking, "Why should the male not also be a sexual object?"[21] Rather than simple polar opposites, masculine and feminine clothing began to intermingle along a continuum. Cardin, Gernreich, and Fish offered skirts, dresses, and caftans for men; eventually caftans were acceptable enough for men that mainstream companies offered patterns for home sewers.

Besides the Nehru jacket and pantsuits, which were worn by both men and women, the most newsworthy innovation of the late 1960s was luxury fur coats for men. These were not a revival of jazz-era raccoon coats; these were expensive full-length seal, beaver, or mink coats worn by wealthy and prominent men, including Interior Secretary Walter J. Hickel and star quarterback Joe Namath.[22] Namath was not the first professional athlete to embrace the new masculine glamour; that was Joe Pepitone, first baseman for the New York Yankees, who grew his hair long and favored skinny, mod-style suits. Pepitone is credited with breaking the hair barrier in baseball, being the first player to bring a blow dryer into the clubhouse.[23]

At the extreme fringes of male style of the late 1960s lay the hippies, who embraced a do-it-yourself, anything-goes aesthetic that mixed thrift-store finds, military styles, and exotic cultural appropriation. As the inheritors of the freedom injected into menswear by the British Mods, members of the 1960s counterculture represented an effort to break with mainstream culture altogether—to drop out of the system and forge an entirely new path. Although associated with the United States, there were similar movements in other countries. British peer Mark Palmer, who dropped out of the upper class to travel in a caravan with various pop stars and dress in Druid robes, offers a succinct explanation of the appeal of the hippie culture: "It is not escapism leaving a bad scene to start a new one."[24]

How widespread was this revolution? Certainly it varied by region, class, and race. *Playboy*'s fashion director Robert L. Green inserted none-too-subtle criticisms of both mod and hippie "excesses" in his seasonal updates. Selected styles were acceptable; the September 1965 issue of *Playboy* featured both a mod-influenced Chesterfield overcoat and a short red jacket with a stand-up collar, along with pages of very traditional Ivy League tweed jackets and loose trousers.[25] By the next year it was clear that mod influences were encroaching on Ivy-style dominance, with the appearance of large-scale plaid trousers, worn with Ivy League–inspired natural shoulder, three-button jackets. Slimmer trousers were growing in popularity, Green acknowledged, but he warned that *Playboy* readers should "leave the skintight styles to high school dropouts."[26]

Playboy's sartorial conservatism is not surprising; menswear manufacturers and retailers were major advertisers. Just as editorial and advertising content in women's magazines reinforced the feminine mystique, the financial realities of publishing demanded congruence between advice and commerce in *Playboy* and *Esquire*. In the same issue where Robert Green threaded the needle carefully between good mod and bad mod, major advertiser h.i.s. (which usually occupied six full pages toward the front of each issue), ran an ad depicting a very Ivy League–looking young man carrying a hand-lettered sign advocating rebellion "against non-conformity," and a few pages later an ad for Jayson shirt company enthused, "Mod shirts are here," showcasing their new collection by Harvey of Carnaby Street.[27]

By 1967 the "Back to Campus" issue could no longer ignore youth fashion or dismiss it as the purview of "high school dropouts." Jazz critic and civil libertarian Nat Hentoff contributed an article detailing the harassment of young men based on their "long hair, sandals, [and] other markers of rebellion" and indicting the older generation for "trying to enforce and preserve their own values, which are among the reasons the young are rebelling."[28] Nor was Hentoff a lone voice; he also cites two other recent articles on the generational divide. Marya Mannes of the *New York Times* had observed that America had become "a society grown set in its ways: resistant to changes, hostile to difference." And according to a *New Yorker* writer, "smooth men represent modern interchangeable machine-ready" masculinity, and "individuality is threatening to gum up the works of the machine."

With so many of its readers matching the college student or recent graduate demographic, *Playboy* needed to tread carefully in its criticism of the younger side of the generation gap. The magazine's September issues for the next few years document the march of the male rebellion across the nation's campuses. In 1967 one group photo includes a bearded student in the shadowy background wearing tight jeans, a turtleneck sweater, and sandals.[29] By the following year Green was reporting an "explosive assortment of revolutionary attire," including Nehrus, tunics, shaped suits, wide ties, and medallions. Even in the traditionally conservative South, more colors and patterns were worn. Unsurprisingly, the West Coast schools were the most "far out," with floral bell-bottoms, ponchos, and meditation shirts (loose, light-weight Indian cotton tunics). Turtlenecks were ubiquitous, as were wider lapels and ties expanding to five inches.[30]

In the 1969 "Back to Campus" issue the cultural fault lines among the young are clearly revealed. According to Southern Methodist University junior Tim Kelleher, two factions had emerged: ultraconservative (Ivy) and fashion liberals, the latter being "quick to try something new if it turns them on."[31] New trends included facial hair of all kinds, bell-bottoms (worn by 20–30 percent of males and increasing), opera capes from the Salvation Army, six- and eight-button double-breasted jackets, huge loud plaids, and billowy sleeved tapered shirts in voile and crepe. The peacock "revolution" was turning into a civil war.

Of course trend-setting magazines are not the only windows into mainstream adoption of fashion. For comparison, let's examine how mass merchants like Sears, Roebuck and Company incorporated various innovations and when. The mod look made a tentative and late appearance in the menswear section of the company's catalogs. This aligns with *Esquire's* and *Playboy's* reluctant embrace of British influence after a few years of resistance and a clear preference for Ivy League styles. Just as mod styles for women appeared in *Vogue* and *Seventeen* long before they were promoted by men's magazines, Sears introduced Carnaby-inspired collections for Junior Misses years before its King's Road line for young men debuted in winter 1968. "King's Road" was code for mod-influenced British styling, since King's Road in west London was the center of innovative male fashion in the mid-1960s. J. C. Penney's equivalent, also appearing in 1968, was "The Inn Shop."

Unisex in the world of catalogs translated into "his 'n' hers" styles, not gender-bending menswear. Beginning in spring 1967, Sears highlighted matching shirts, sweaters, and casual outerwear for men and women in a section of the men's department, as did J. C. Penney and Montgomery

His and hers crocheted ponchos, *Ladies Circle Knitting and Crochet Guide*, Fall 1975.

Ward. Penney's fall 1968 catalog featured sixteen pages of identical designs for men and women—shirts, sweaters, and casual jackets—shown on models whose poses and expressions suggested they were couples. These "his 'n' hers" sections continued through the late 1970s. Similarly, the more daring men's styles in knitting and crocheting pattern books were modeled by men with women (girlfriends? wives?) leaning against their manly chests or holding their hands. Another version of the couples motif was family styles, which appeared toward the front of the catalog or even on the cover. Though sized according to sex and age, the fabrics, colors and decorative details were identical. The underlying message seemed to be strictly heteronormative: it's okay to wear this flowered shirt, crocheted vest, or poncho, because the model is a bona fide straight guy.

Other important trends appeared in the fashion press and the catalogs with a slight lag. Turtlenecks were reported to be the next big thing in *Esquire* and *Playboy* in 1967 and appear all over Sears by the fall-winter 1968 catalog. The main distinction was that although fashion editors were reporting the acceptability of turtlenecks for evening and in posh clubs and restaurants (even in Playboy Clubs), the Sears versions showed casual clothing and sport jackets at first, not suits. The vest suit (matching vest and trousers worn without a jacket, as opposed to the venerable three-piece suit) was reported as a trend in *Esquire* in 1967 but not carried by Sears until 1971. My fashion-forward husband wore a rust-colored suede cloth vest suit, purchased at a menswear shop in Syracuse, New York, to our wedding in 1970.

Bold madras plaids and paisleys had popped up in London in 1964 but moved more slowly into the American mainstream. *Esquire* and *Playboy* were featuring both of these patterns approvingly by 1966, and madras jackets, ties, trousers, and shorts were abundant in the retail catalogs. Paisley (beyond small prints on neckties) took a bit longer to break into the mass market but then arrived with a bang; in addition to shirts and ties, Sears offered a large-scale dark blue paisley suit in 1969. The introduction of innovative fibers and fabrics, especially polyester double knits, was quickly embraced in the menswear universe. They were featured in *Esquire* and Sears practically simultaneously in the fall of 1969. Between

1968 and 1973 it seemed that the once conservative American male was ready to blossom in glorious color and style.

The seeds for the end of the peacock revolution were sown in 1967 with the release of *Bonnie and Clyde,* director Arthur Penn's groundbreaking film about the Depression-era outlaws, starring Warren Beatty and Faye Dunaway.[32] The movie not only ushered in a new era of on-screen sex and violence but also struck a chord with fashion designers looking for fresh inspiration. Theodora Van Runkle won an Oscar for the costumes—Dunaway in slender, mid-calf skirts and Beatty in chalk-stripe, double-breasted suits—and some menswear designers took note of the film's romantic aesthetic. Baby boomers had heard plenty about the Great Depression from their parents, and it seemed an unlikely source of nostalgia, but emerging American designers Ralph Lauren and Bill Blass both rode to their early successes on '30s-inspired clothing.

From the vantage point of the early 1970s, the future of men's fashions seemed both clear and confusing. On the one hand, the drab, conformist model of menswear had apparently been shoved to the back of the closet. Even bankers and politicians wore sideburns and had hair curling over their shirt collars, and *someone* must have bought all those plaid trousers and leisure suits. Once Pandora's box had been opened and men had become accustomed to expressing themselves through clothing, could they turn back? On the other hand, the road ahead was far from clear. The new expectation was not only for more color and pattern or innovative designs but also for more expressive forms of masculinity. Men, like women, were supposed to dress according to their fashion "personality," to follow trends and care about hairstyling, not just a haircut.

Predictions abounded. *Penthouse* fashion editor Rodney Bennett-England included several pages of fashion predictions from various designers in his 1968 book, *Dress Optional.* The designs range from fairly tame—pants with no creases or cuffs, collarless unstructured jackets—to molded plastic clothing and space-age jumpsuits that resemble *Star Trek* uniforms. Of course there were no neckties at all, just turtlenecks and scarves.[33] Rudi Gernreich's predictions, commissioned for *Life* for its January 1, 1970, issue, offered unisex in the form of near-nudity—just

Men's hairstyling guide. Brylcreem ad, *Gentlemen's Quarterly,* September 1974.

miniskirts and wigs—for youthful men and women and neck-to-toe caftans for the old and unattractive.[34] In 1972 the *Journal of Home Economics* posed the provocative question, "What will happen to the gray flannel suit?" The answer, the author argued, was obsolescence, as men's fashion would become more globalized and the industrial-revolution-fashion lost its relevance.[35] The reality, of course, was just the opposite. Within a decade, men were investing in "power suits" and the Ivy League style was rebranded as preppy and sweeping the country. Let's untangle the '70s to see what changed, how much, and for whom.

Amid the visual cacophony of the late 1960s and early 1970s, trends were sometimes difficult to detect, but a return to quieter elegance was certainly in the air, and it hit full swing with the release of *The Godfather* (1972) and *The Sting* (1973). That same year saw a flurry of publicity around the filming of *The Great Gatsby* (1974) in Newport, Rhode Island, over the summer; *Esquire* waxed eloquent about the "Newport Look," a sort of hybridized version of the Gatsby style that mashed up the 1920s and '30s and incorporated linen suits, country tweeds, and vintage-y sweaters. The death of onetime king the Duke of Windsor, who was also a well-known fashion icon, in 1972 also generated quite a bit of nostalgia in the fashion press for the elegance of bygone days. The eccentricity of the mod and hippie era was gradually replaced with trends that often broke as many rules, just not all in a single outfit. The leisure suit offered an alternative to jacket and tie for the new, more casual lifestyles of the 1970s.

After several years of long, unkempt, and unstyled hair, men turned to hairstylists, who gave them a neater, well-groomed appearance. The prices were higher than in a barbershop, and he might find himself in a chair next to a women having her hair cut in the same manner, or even with a woman styling his hair. But unisex salons were a booming business, and even today they are one of the locations where the "unisex" label persists. Hair-care products made a comeback, promising men that their expensively styled hair would be both long and neat.

The transition from barbershops to unisex salons was not easy, particularly for barbers. Barbershops felt the immediate effect of this trend; haircuts went from a weekly ritual to an occasional, do-it-yourself task. Barbers were flummoxed. They felt the economic effects almost immediately, not only from teenagers but also from boys as young as four and five, all of whom were demanding Beatles styles. Some of this stemmed from hero worship, but there was also an element of rebelling against a ritual—the weekly or biweekly trip to the barbershop. The barbers' initial reaction, to complain and ridicule the hirsute young, was not likely to win them customers.

When men finally returned to regular styling, they tended to patronize "unisex salons," not barbershops. An entire new industry was born in the mid-1970s as the once-modest market for male grooming services and products expanded. This was not easily accomplished; many state regulations had separate licensing rules for barbers (whose clients were mostly men) and hairdressers (who cut and styled women's hair). Barbers naturally resisted efforts to revise the regulations; hairdressers, who had been seeing more and more men in their salons, welcomed the change.

The old regulations required shops to have separate entrances or separate hours for men and women. Early unisex salons had ignored these rules, and so had the law. Barbers were incensed. They were losing business at an alarming rate, and the number of licensed barbers and apprentices was declining. In New York State between 1964 and 1971 there had been a decrease of 2,183 barbers at a time when the male population was increasing. In comparison, the number of cosmetologists (who were licensed to work on women's hair) had gone up by 21,810. The new licensing requirements, approved in July 1972, were still rather restrictive; a barber could cut women's hair, but a hairdresser would need a barber's license as well as a cosmetology license in order to work on men. Unisex salons were also required to have a separate area for customers who wanted privacy.

Angela Taylor of the *New York Times* described an early "his 'n' hers" salon in Greenwich Village that opened in 1968. The cosmetologist owners were skirting the New York law, since neither of them had a barber's license and they failed to provide separate entrances or spaces for male and female customers. There is no indication that having their establishment featured in the city's major newspaper created any legal repercussions.[36]

It wasn't just style that was affecting demand for barbers' services. Many barbers, especially the older ones, had strong ideological reactions to longhaired men. In a small town in Nebraska an elderly barber refused to allow young men with long hair to come into his shop and then began complaining about how bad business was. An article from 1970 described the experience of one customer who noticed the barber roughly pushing his head as he was trimming his hair and protested, "Hey, what's going on?" "You fags with your long hair, you're the kind of guys that are ruining the country," the barber reported angrily. The customer got up and walked out.[37]

Besides his-and-her salons, new men-only establishments began appearing across the country. In many cases these were run by barbers who had been able to make the transition from clippers and shears to razor cuts and blow dryers and were beginning to offer additional services such as manicures and facials. Many of the men's styling parlors had some kind of private or semiprivate cubicle available for customers who did not want to be on display.

With the renewed popularity of classic tailoring, menswear in the mid-1970s divided along several lines. One strand continued along the colorful alternative trends; another followed the practical, outdoorsy styles of L. L. Bean and Eddie Bauer, the bicoastal leaders in flannel shirts and khakis. Conservative business clothing made a resurgence, buoyed by economic need; inflation and higher unemployment made conformity to office standards more popular and "investment dressing" more attractive than rapidly changing trends. *Gentleman's Quarterly* illustrated this variety in its winter 1974–1975 issue with a spread featuring twenty men divided into four groups based on their "look": *classical, experimental, eclectic,* or *free.*[38] Those in the classic, "no flash, no fuss" group are all in suits and ties, with an assortment of trendy details (wide lapels, mustaches, a vintage-looking double-breasted jacket). "Experimental" men also wear suits (four of the five) or sport coats but wade a little deeper into the style waters with less-traditional fabrics and accessories. No suits for the "eclectics"; their outfits are a mix of separates in more casual materials. The avant-garde "free" group—the only men shown smiling broadly—sport even more colorful and casual-looking styles and intentionally break the soberness of suits by pairing them with scarves and graphic T-shirts. Art director Nick Peters gets a full-page spread for his unstructured black cotton Italian suit worn with a white silk scarf—and no shirt.

There is one noticeable commonality in these photographs: the vivid flamboyance of previous years has virtually disappeared. There are no awning stripes, no giant plaids. If the shirts and ties have overall designs, they are small and appear in low contrast, because they really don't show up in the photographs. Two of the four group photos are in color, and the palette is fairly neutral, except for a yellow sweater and a dull red shirt. Only the "eclectic" plaid shirt and the moon face in a graphic T-shirt disturb an otherwise calm tableau. The color choice may be strategic, as the black-and-white photos make those two even more "classic" and timeless.

The menswear press had been predicting the end of the peacock revolution for several seasons, even for traditionally lively resort clothing, which had been moving toward subtler colors and a return to neutral classics such as white linen suits. "Gentlemen should look like gentlemen, not bougainvilleas," *Esquire* counseled its readers in March 1974.[39] Popular youth culture was once again at cross-purposes with this segment of the fashion industry. In September 1973 *Rolling Stone* ran a story about an underground trend called "disco"; eventually the popularity of the music—and its body-conscious, colorful fashions—exploded after the release of *Saturday Night Fever* in 1977.[40] Even mainstream retailers such as Montgomery Ward and Sears included a few pages of polyester open-necked shirts and tight knit pants, even as their business suit selection calmed down in the late 1970s.

Another powerful influence on business clothing in the mid-1970s was John T. Molloy's *Dress for Success,* which was based on extensive research into American corporate culture. Molloy's underlying message was that men who dressed according to the unwritten dress codes of business would be more successful than those who attempted too much expression or experimentation, especially at a junior level. *Dress for Success* hit a nerve in the shaky economy, and millions of copies were sold. Today Molloy's observations offer an interesting insight into the realities of how much freedom men enjoyed if they worked in a business environment. He noted regional variations in the rules that are reminiscent of the landscape described in *Playboy's* college fashion issues: avoid pink or lavender shirts in the South and suits and ties in California. He found generational differences in how men judged appearances as well: men over

Men's disco-inspired fashions, Montgomery Ward catalog, Fall/Winter 1974.

48 were likely to make "moral judgments," men 34–48 were more aware of class implications of dress, while the youngest men (28–34) were the most open, as they seemed to have no significant prejudices against any patterns or colors. Nor did Molloy shy from controversy; he included advice aimed directly at men of color and at homosexuals. He did grant exceptions to the otherwise conservative rules for men in three categories: athletes, musicians, and black men all had permission to be flamboyant. The role of race in determining the parameters of masculine expression is complicated; Monica Miller attributes the greater leeway to a tradition of dandyism dating back to the liveries of slaves used for display in England and America.[41] One of my more uncomfortable discoveries in conducting this research was noticing that just as African American models appeared in the pages of Sears, Ward's, and other mainstream catalogs, they were usually used to display the most colorful or exotic styles. Leopard-print underwear? Probably on the black model.

Male vanity and display were especially acceptable for athletes, and advertisers sought out these familiar faces to promote products that might otherwise seem effete. Jockey featured Baltimore Orioles star Jim Palmer in a series of underwear ads beginning in the late 1970s that are now legendary. Joe Namath wore fur coats on the sidelines during games, inspiring many imitators until the NFL ruled that only official uniform gear could be worn on the field. Off the field, of course, full-length coats in mink, fox, beaver, and other luxurious furs became status symbols for players and fans alike. Both *Esquire* and *Playboy* routinely featured athlete models in editorial fashion spreads.

Is men's clothing sexy? The sexual messages of much of men's clothing of the 1960s and '70s are hard to miss. Jeans, worn tight and low around the hips, are sexy. Many reasons are given for the popularity of jeans after the war, but whether the models are cowboys, motorcycle toughs, or teenage rockers, the common denominator is clear: jeans aren't just denim pants; they're sexy pants. Open-front shirts (with or without chains) are sexy. And then there's the entire question of underwear. Once strictly utilitarian, men's underwear during the 1960s and '70s became more varied in cut, color, and pattern and, even if not visible, part of the public consciousness. *Penthouse* editor Rodney Bennett-England drew not only on his own fashion experience but also on many letters that readers contributed to the magazine about what women did and did not consider sexy in a man. His opinion was that the late 1960s were clearly years devoted to reviving sexuality in male dress. He also notes that the fewer differences there are between men's and women's clothing, the more important it is for men to pay attention to those elements of his clothing that are masculine.[42]

The problem is that male sexuality, prominently displayed, carries with it ambiguity of sexual orientation. After all, a sexy male should be attractive, but according to the dominant culture he should be attractive only to women and oblivious to his own gorgeousness. A character like James Bond, whose impeccable clothing, whether formal wear or swimsuits, was clearly intended to be sexy but needed to be assertively—even aggressively—heterosexual in order to carry it off.

Of course James Bond was fictional, as were all the hard-boiled detectives and rugged cowboys that littered the popular landscape at mid-century. Psychologists were interested in examining the real American man, especially the suburban species, to determine why so many men seemed to have trouble adapting to their prescribed role. According to common psychological wisdom in the 1950s, just as the natural state for adult women included marriage and motherhood, being a breadwinner was the natural, desired state for men. A man who remained single into his thirties was suspect. If he was clearly straight—that is, if he dated many women but avoided commitment—he was immature. If he appeared to have no social life and, heaven forbid, showed too much interest in the arts or was too carefully dressed, he was suspected of being homosexual. Some of the once mainstream beliefs about homosexuality from this era are astonishing now, and most have been abandoned, at least by professionals if not by the general public. With no clear understanding of how homosexuality was "caused," psychiatrists and psychologists seemed free to speculate to their hearts' content, based on Sigmund Freud's culturally limited view of the subject. For example, one of the most common reasons once given for homosexuality was immaturity, a kind of arrested development. The sexually promiscuous playboy was also failing to grow up; he was just stuck at a different stage. A man's failure to mature into a breadwinner, or his insistence on avoiding the role, was a symptom of misdirected sexuality. In the same way that "normal" woman should desire motherhood, a "normal" male should desire to be the head of a household. Note that the desire was not necessarily to be a dad; it was the breadwinner role that was important. This masculine mystique was just as much a trap for men in the 1950s and early 1960s as the feminine mystique described by Betty Friedan was for women. There were attempts at alternative lives: the Beats lived lifestyles that were intentionally non-suburban, non-procreative, and non-conformist. But popular criticism of the Beats and their transformation into the caricatures known as "beatniks" in the humor pages and television skits were either effeminate arty types or overgrown adolescents, reflecting the notion that a man who objected to the breadwinner role was either an infantile sissy or a hormone-driven teenager in a man's body.

Small wonder, then, that the first restless movements of the peacock revolution and the youthful rebellion in the 1960s raised the specter of homosexuality among its critics. The irony was that at that time true homosexual men tended to be purposely invisible, except when it was safe to be noticed. As Russell Lynes observed in 1967, it was highly unlikely that the longhaired young men appearing on America's streets were all homosexual, because for the most part homosexuals did not advertise so conspicuously.[43] To do otherwise was to risk one's career or even being arrested.

With all the emphasis on apparent sexuality, what did gay men think of the peacock revolution? As I completed this book, the Museum at the Fashion Institute of Technology in New York City had launched a major exhibit, *A Queer History of Fashion*, exploring topics that have often been the subject of whispered conversations and crude humor but are long overdue for serious treatment.[44] Fashion is about sex and sexuality as much as it is about gender, and human sexuality is varied and complex. That many of the leading designers associated either with unisex clothing or with the peacock revolution were gay should not come as news. Rudi Gernreich was openly gay, as were Pierre Cardin, Saville Row icon Hardy Amies, and Yves Saint Laurent. When I read interviews with them about the changes in menswear or the new sexuality in fashion, it is hard to envision them as disinterested observers. What they could not be was completely open participants in the public conversation.

Shaun Cole provides a detailed look at the urban worlds of gay men in the early twentieth century, worlds that were hidden from the eyes of the mainstream public and carefully coded to be visible only to each other. Stereotypes could work in one's favor; if effeminacy was assumed to be a sign of homosexuality, cultivating a stereotypically masculine image could provide effective armor.[45] Certainly it worked for Hollywood stars such as Rock Hudson and Raymond Burr, among others. Passing as a straight playboy was probably even easier once Hugh Hefner provided such a popular template. A powerful and publicly flaunted (straight) sex drive could inoculate a man from the suspicions that often greeted sophisticated taste in music, art, and theater. In gay bars and nightclubs the impact of the adoption of flamboyant, gender-bending styles by straight men resulted in a hyperbolic "macho" image, iconically represented by the members of the disco group Village People. The original ad recruiting performers for the group specifically called for "macho types" with mustaches. Their appearance reflected a "virilization" trend in gay presentation that has been noted by several historians of the period—boots, beards, denim, and leather replacing earlier Continental or mod styles.

The boundary between the straight and gay world was being crossed and even erased in both appearance and behavior. Sexual practices such as anal sex, fellatio, and cunnilingus, which once were strongly associated with homosexuality, became less taboo for heterosexual couples. Nor was it necessary to pair off to engage in sex: from *Hair* and *Oh! Calcutta!* to *Bob and Carol and Ted and Alice,* popular plays and movies explored the idea of polyamory and group sex.[46] Once a straight couple added a third (or more) person to the mix, homosexual activity was practically a given. Men and women who could "swing both ways," in practice and in appearance, found themselves very popular. This openness, in turn, made it easier for people who saw themselves as sexually liberated to adopt unisex, androgynous, or ambiguous fashions. Clara Pierre described this moment in 1976: "But with that uncertainty past, and the fear of sexual ambivalence reduced by our knowing that we are all 'a little bit both,' clothes no longer have to perform the duty of differentiation and can relax into just being clothes."[47]

In her view the sexual revolution produced a culture that was more comfortable and open about sex, which led to greater comfort with homosexuality and androgyny. With the clarity of hindsight we understand that the world Pierre described was limited and eventually doomed, in the short run. Not everyone was comfortable with the idea of sexually aggressive women, unmarried couples cohabiting, or nudity in the movies, much less open marriage, discussions of homosexuality, or swingers clubs. The frightening appearance of AIDS in the early 1980s put a damper on the sexual revolution and slowed the progress of gay men's liberation. People are still arguing whether bisexuality is an orientation—the way some individuals experience sexual attraction—or an opportunistic preference, a position between the closet and complete openness. Unisex and androgynous clothing, far from being proof of more relaxed attitudes toward gender and sexuality, now appear to have been just the opening salvos in our own cultural Hundred Years' War.

So what did change in men's clothing? The late 1970s return to safer, classic styles did not mean a complete rollback of every innovation. Just as women's hemlines became a matter of taste, with lengths varying based on the occasion and the wearer's own preference, men's clothing had permanently negotiated some flexibility. The suit was less important, replaced in many workplaces and previously formal situations by separate trousers and sport jackets. Beards, mustaches, and long hair (or shaved heads, for that matter) are unremarkable variations. Men's casual and active sportswear may lack the blinding colors and patterns of the 1970s but still offer many options, sometimes more color options than in women's clothing. A recent Lands' End catalog lists men's pima cotton polo shirts in twenty-five colors (including pink) and women's in only fourteen. The demand for men's cosmetics, grooming products, and even cosmetic surgery has been well documented for decades. Like their baby boom sisters, the young men of the 1960s helped establish a cult of youth and a desire for eternal fitness that has pursued them into retirement age. When these men were in their youth, the menswear industry satisfied their demand for body-conscious styles that emphasized their slim hips and tapered torsos—styles that could not be sustained as they reached middle age.

Sociologist Joseph Pleck observed in 1981 that stereotypical gender roles are not only impossible to live up to, but they also impose psychological strain when they are not achieved.[48] Like women, men were affected by the feminist movement and the sexual revolution, and like women, they were left to shape new roles without a clear sense of direction. The peacock revolution was an attempt to shake up the culture, to ask "Why not?" and to challenge the prevailing masculine myths. It succeeded in upsetting the applecart, and men are still searching for the answers.

Nature and/or Nurture?

Where do masculinity and femininity come from? After all, it is fairly obvious that newborn humans have neither set of qualities. Yet by the time they are two or three years old children not only know the rules, but they also have become its primary enforcers, as any observer of a preschool playgroup can confirm. With the women's movement challenging traditional female roles and popular culture offering a range of new expressions of modern masculinity and femininity, it seems inevitable that children would get swept up in the excitement and confusion. If nothing else, the link between adult and children's clothing would mean that kids and grownups would wear similar styles. This clearly happened during the 1960s and '70s, but there was something else at work too. Emerging scientific evidence pointed to gender roles being learned and malleable in the very young. This affected children regardless of where their parents stood on women's rights or sexual morality. Given the drive to transform women's roles and promote gender equality, it's likely that if you were born between the late 1960s and the early 1980s, you experienced non-gendered child raising to some extent. If you didn't wear your sibling's hand-me-down Garanimals outfits, the kindergarten teacher might be reading *William's Doll* to you at story time. Or you might be singing along to your *Free to Be . . . You and Me* record on your Fisher-Price record player, after watching *Sesame Street,* which featured Susan Robinson as a working woman who liked to fix cars in her spare time.[1]

Looking at children's fashions we can see just how complicated the ideas and arguments were during this period. There were so many different popular beliefs about sex, gender, and sexuality, mixed with parental ambivalence, disagreement, and anxiety about the right way to raise children. In this chapter I describe changes in children's clothing styles and place them in the context of the competing scientific explanations of gender and sexuality. I also address how well those were understood and accepted by the general public. As children of the unisex era grew up, their reaction to ungendered clothing became apparent in the ways they dressed their own children. Not that we are that much closer forty years later to knowing where gender comes from. We're still arguing over gender, gender roles, sexuality, and sexual orientation. Whether the hot topic is marriage equality, the Lilly Ledbetter Act, or gender-variant children, beliefs about nature and nurture in determining our personal characteristics are fundamental to the arguments. Some of those beliefs are based on religion, others on science, but many of them are likely echoes of forgotten lessons learned in early childhood.

A note about the messiness of studying the history of childhood is in order. While studying gender expression in adult fashions can be complicated, the task is even more daunting when we turn to children's clothing. Babies don't pick their own clothing, which reflects adult tastes and preferences. After all, how many week-old Yankees fans are there, really? It's not surprising, then, that of the 762 individual specialists listed in the Costume Society of America directory, only 19 report expertise in children's clothing. In American consumer culture, children begin to have some say in what they wear when they are toddlers, between the ages of one and three years. Sociologist Daniel T. Cook has argued convincingly that American preschoolers have been consumers-in-training since the dawn of the twentieth century, which means that several generations of us have grown up to accept the spectacle of an adult arguing with a three-year-old over the relative merits of a tutu or a sundress for a trip to the mall.[2] Our great-great-grandmothers would have brooked no such behavior: children wore what Momma bought or made, period. In short, beyond infancy it is hard to know the extent to which the wearers or their parents are driving trends in juvenile clothing. Children's voices are missing from the popular history of the 1960s, and although it is possible to interview grownups about their childhood memories, the problem is that adults' memories tend to be selective and influenced by later experience, hindsight, and nostalgia.

The most abundant source of information about children's fashion is mail order catalogs from various time periods. Until the mid-1980s the retail giants in children's wear were Sears, Roebuck and Company, Montgomery Ward, and J. C. Penney, who together accounted for a quarter of the infant and toddler market.[3] The structure of the children's clothing market beyond these big three department stores was similarly limited. Unlike women's apparel, with its many designers, manufacturers, and retail outlets in all sizes, a significant proportion of children's clothing was produced by a handful of companies. A few large manufacturers such as Baby Togs, Carters, and Health-Tex dominated the market, reaching consumers through local department stores or national chains. Pattern companies like Butterick and McCall's were still important players as well, at a time when most women learned the rudiments of sewing in school. Home sewing enabled women to modify current fashions to their own tastes and abilities, giving them more choice than is available today. When I examined the trends in infants' and children's clothing for this period, I drew mainly on the plentiful images available in catalogs and pattern books, along with the observations of industry reporters such as *Earnshaw's*. If your childhood was middle-class and mainstream, much of this will ring true.

Children's clothing choices are not simply a matter of taste—a favorite color or cartoon character, a dislike for scratchy fabrics—they are also a way that children try on, rehearse, and express their burgeoning identities. Even two-year-olds have a rudimentary understanding of the prevailing gender rules. In fact it is striking to consider how complicated the "rules" are—far beyond pink for girls, blue for boys—and what an accomplishment it is that young humans master them over the course of early childhood.

In *Pink and Blue: Telling the Boys from the Girls,* I offer a more detailed description of these complex rules and how they have evolved since the late 1800s, which I will summarize here.[4] The main point is that not only have the rules for boys and girls changed, but so has the definition of "neutral" clothing. Our traditional conception of gender may be a simple either/or binary, but the actual costumes and props with which we enact those roles are not. In addition to gendered clothing—designed according to shifting standards—there have always been other options, be they called "neutral," "unisex," or just "children's."

Before the twentieth century all babies wore long white dresses; slightly older boys and girls wore dresses and skirted outfits that were shorter and more colorful than baby dresses. Neither style indicated the child's sex, because that would have been considered horribly inappropriate. Pants were considered so quintessentially manly that women and girls could not even wear underdrawers until the middle of the nineteenth century. The timing of a child's graduation from baby to boy was a matter of taste and parental perception; the growth spurt that transformed the chubby toddler into a taller, leaner child was one sign that his masculine nature was about to manifest itself. Other parents might select their son's first pants in time for his first day at school, or they might watch for signs of "manly" behavior before putting his dresses away. Parents in the 1880s did not believe that boys needed masculinity lessons any more than they needed instruction in crawling, walking, or talking. The advice was just the opposite: pushing a baby into boyhood too early was dangerous, because he might become sexually precocious.

Freudian psychology and social Darwinism replaced this long-held view that identity was innate (or "nature"), with the opinion that while *sex* may be innate, *sexuality* was learned—nature strongly influenced by nurture. They also mingled what we today would call gender—masculinity and femininity—with aspects of sexual orientation. As sexuality historian Hanne Blank points out, this particular "nature plus nurture" hypothesis has turned out to be an imperfect explanation, and the scientific evidence once used to support it has been largely discredited.[5] There is, however, a stubborn cultural insistence on reducing complexity to binary choices (nature or nurture, male or female, masculine or feminine), which encourages even more stereotyped thinking. All men are not aggressive, all women are not passive; most gay men are not effeminate, and vice versa. Within the categories we have constructed there is huge variety, which binary, stereotyped thinking ignores.

One telling indication that these notions of gender had a cultural bias is the inconsistency with which gender-variant boys and girls have been treated. Science alone could not explain why "tomboyism" was an acceptable and even desirable stage in girls, but "sissyish" boys needed stern correction and psychological treatment. The homophobic subtext of the works of G. Stanley Hall and other child psychologists clearly indicates that unmasculine behavior in little boys was perceived as pathological while similar, unfeminine behavior in girls was "normal."

Once nurture had been introduced as a factor in sexual development, the bulk of twentieth-century studies of gender development were devoted to trying to figure out how nature and nurture interacted and which was more powerful. In the meantime, parenting advice was constantly changing, as any woman can verify who lived near her own mom or mother-in-law when her children were small. Each generation had its own experts who published books and articles denouncing their predecessors as old-fashioned and unscientific and dictating new approaches to infant and child care. Attitudes about gender and sexuality were part of this turmoil. In the first half of the twentieth century, many people apparently held a composite belief that gendered behaviors were present in an immature form at birth and developed as the child grew but that sharp gender distinctions could wait. In their view baby boys were male but not masculine, although they contained the germ of masculine behavior. Babyishness would become boyishness as the child matured, inevitably ending in manliness. Male babies and small boys, not being physically mature enough to dress like men, wore clothes that were appropriate to their tender years and subordinate status. In those days decorative touches such as smocking and embroidery were as acceptable on a baby boy as they were on a girl. A male toddler's long curls were charming and baby-like. To the extent that little boys' clothing was distinguished from that of girls, it was along much subtler lines than that of older children and adults. Babies—even male babies—were fragile, vulnerable, and soft; strongly masculine clothing was just not suitable. The widespread use of pastel colors for infant furnishings reflects this view, as does the incorporation of details like rounded collars and puffed sleeves.

The ungendered children's clothing of the nineteenth century was gradually discarded in favor of a complicated and regionally variable pattern of boy-girl symbolism. The iconic use of pink and blue, for example, spread unevenly throughout the United States between 1900 and the 1940s. As late as the end of the 1930s pink was a perfectly acceptable choice for baby boys in some parts of the South. Pastel pink and blue used together continued to be a traditional combination for baby gifts and birth announcements through the 1960s. Dresses for boys, on the other hand, went out of fashion fairly quickly. For toddler boys they were rare after 1920, although the use of white baby dresses for newborns continued into the 1930s and '40s. By 1960 boys never wore dresses outside of a christening ceremony, and even under those circumstances suits with trousers or short pants often replaced dresses. On the other hand, overalls, pants, and shorts for girls became so commonplace that by the 1950s knit shirts and jeans were as neutral for American children as white baby dresses had been for their grandparents.

For the children of the 1950s and early 1960s who have no historical memory, the gender rules for clothing of that time were "traditional." From their parents' point of view, the more gendered styles for babies and toddlers were an innovation, as were the more masculine styles for little boys, complete with neckties and long trousers. For parents who preferred them there were still plenty of neutral choices for babies and toddlers. Compared to the styles available in our own recent times, there was actually considerably more leeway available in the '50s and '60s. Pink and blue had become nearly universal symbols of femininity and masculinity but lacked the moral imperative of modern "pinkification." Like wearing green on St. Patrick's Day, dressing baby girls in pink and boys in blue was a lighthearted custom, not a requirement. Other pastels—yellow, green, and lavender—were convenient and popular choices for baby shower gifts and for thrifty parents planning a large family and lots of hand-me-down clothing (or people who simply thought their baby looked best in those colors). Baby boys' fashion had not yet acquired the "just like daddy" style and still might incorporate decorative elements that in another generation would be considered feminine. The spring 1962 Sears catalog offered embroidered, sleeveless "diaper shirts" in packages of three—all white or one each of pink, blue, and yellow—and dressy outfits for infant boys that were babyish, not at all manly (unless you count the tiny pocket and the mock fly stitching on the front of the underpants). Some girls' clothing was sufficiently feminine that no boy could wear it, but boys' styles tended to be so plain that they could be appropriate for girls as well.

Toddler clothing for dressy occasions was sharply gendered; party and holiday fashions featured pastel-colored Eton suits with short pants and bow ties for boys and frilly dresses worn over poufy underskirts for girls. But play clothes usually consisted of overalls and polo shirts for both boys and girls, with a few feminine styles included as "fashion items." The lowest-price items, often sold in packs of two or three, were nearly always neutral styles, and the more gendered items were likely to be the most expensive. This reveals an important element of gendered clothing for children at a time when clothing was still relatively costly: neutral clothing was more economical in the short run (when first purchased) as well as in the long run (as hand-me-downs). But cost was not the only consideration. Had parents in the early 1960s believed as strongly in gendered clothing as did parents in the early 2000s, there would have been fewer neutral choices back then.

School-age boys and girls had a range of styles and colors to choose from within acceptable bounds of masculinity and femininity, but those limits still allowed for a range of expression, at least for girls. A sewing book in 1954 suggested a wardrobe of six to eight school dresses, two party or Sunday dresses, and just two pairs of "sturdy slax" [sic] for play.[6] School dresses came in a variety of styles and colors to suit every taste from tailored to frilly. In every classroom girls' gender expression ranged from tomboys in skirts and sweaters to "girly-girls" in ruffles and bows who had their hair set in pin curls every night, not just on Saturday. Boys' fashions, once they were no longer in the toddler size range, tracked fairly closely to adult men's clothing, with whatever expansions or contractions of cut and color they experienced.

Throughout the period, acceptable gender expression depended not only on the wearer but also on the context, especially the setting and the activity. Neutral clothing existed long before the term "unisex" appeared, particularly for younger children and for active play clothes for all ages. Pants, shorts, and overalls were widely available in infant and toddler sizes and for the most part were ungendered long before the unisex trend began. In fact, because the younger they are, the more ambiguous their

Styles for schoolgirls, Montgomery Ward catalog, Fall/Winter 1961.

Children's jeans, Montgomery Ward catalog, Spring/Summer 1960.

appearance, babies and toddlers modeling play clothes in Sears catalogs of the 1950s and early '60s were more "unisex" than adults could ever hope to be. The older the child, the fewer androgynous casual styles were available. Pants and shorts for girls sizes 7–14 featured more feminine details than those for younger girls: floral prints, decorative flourishes, and side or back closures. Only classic, Western-style jeans were neutral (right down to the fly front for both girls and boys), although "girls' jeans" with side zippers were also available. Expensive, seldom-worn children's items such as coats and snowsuits were made hand-me-down friendly by avoiding feminine or masculine details, but the lowest-cost items were also likely to be neutral. Dressy clothes were not only more gendered for all ages but also more likely to mimic adult fashions. The girls modeling the trendiest clothes also posed like grown women, underscoring the connection between those styles and the adult fashions on which they were based. Throughout the 1950s and '60s, "dressy" clothing literally meant dresses for girls from infancy to adulthood. Party and holiday clothing was the most elaborate and also the most feminine and masculine. Between play clothes and dressy fashions lay school clothes, which meant dresses and skirts for girls, although they were offered in a range of styles from plain to fancy.

Gender patterns in children's clothing shifted between 1962 and 1979 in ways that parallel the changes in adult clothing. For most of the 1960s the postwar rules prevailed: younger children had more neutral options than school-age boys and girls. The dressier the occasion, the more gendered the clothing. The clothing for active play was decidedly "masculine" and located in the boys' section of the catalog. A page from the fall-winter 1964 Sears catalog is typical. A boy and a girl are shown in jeans and striped T-shirts; no "boy" or "girl" versions are offered either in sizing or in style.

Like Victorian fashions, mid-century styles continued to mark age distinctions from infancy to adulthood, though with fewer rigid rules. No longer restricted to short trousers, toddler boys now enjoyed a greater range of colors and patterns than older boys and men. Younger girls' fashions were shorter and more whimsically decorated than those for older girls and women. Party and holiday fashions for little girls featured

Children's play clothes, Montgomery Ward catalog, Fall/Winter 1960.

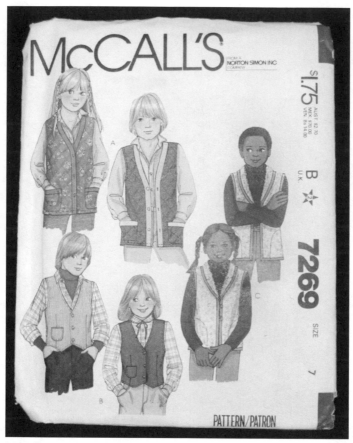

McCall's unisex vest pattern, 1980. McCall's M7269.
Image courtesy of the McCall Pattern Company, 2014.

frilly dresses worn over poufy underskirts, not child versions of women's trends. Misses styles could be more revealing and more sophisticated than the Junior fashions designed for high school and college-age consumers. Different flavors of femininity were available depending on age and dating or marital status. Little girl femininity was dainty, pastel, and whimsical. Bigger girl femininity was ladylike and paid attention to current trends and to becomingness (colors that flattered the girl's complexion, for example). Teenage clothing was trendier and figure-flattering, but not revealing. "Sexy" was for adult women.

The innovative styles popular with adults in the late 1960s were available for children, including pantsuits for girls, collarless or Nehru jackets for boys, and turtleneck sweaters and shirts for both. Many of the options for boys and girls were truly neutral, with no strong, preexisting gender significance. Most of the neutral styles were based on adult unisex trends, including hairstyles like the Afro and novelty items such as caftans, ponchos, and belted sweater vests. Styles such as turtleneck sweaters, T-shirts, sweatshirts and sweat pants, and jeans, which had been acceptable casual wear for both boys and girls for some time, became more popular and permissible for a wider variety of occasions. Some of these represented new classics, which have continued to be available ever since the 1970s. By the late 1970s feminized versions of once masculine or neutral styles were appearing such as turtleneck shirts with puffed sleeves or denim overalls with ruffled shoulder straps. Vests survived ungendered into the 1980s.

Unisex clothing and fashion for boys meant a kind of flexibility that had not been seen in several decades: more patterns in fabric, including floral prints and bright colors generally, and more embellishment, especially embroidery. These trends echoed similar freedom in men's clothing, described in the previous chapter. Boys' hairstyles became longer and longer and in many cases were quite similar to girls' hairstyles.

One interesting feature of unisex clothing for children was not only the phenomenon of designers of girls' fashions borrowing styles from the boys' department but also girls actually buying boys' clothes. Sears acknowledged this practice by including size conversion charts in the boys' pages of its catalog. *Earnshaw's* reported in 1978 that as much as 25 percent of "boys'" jeans and pants was actually sold to girls. The practice also apparently reversed, though not to the same extent; one manufacturer of girls' stretch pants and tops increased his business when he realized that mothers were buying the comfortable, easy-care garments for little boys and started including boys in his ads. To further complicate the story, the manufacturer added a "boys'" line, which girls also began to wear.[7] In the same year, some feminine elements started to make a comeback. Red, yellow, or green shortall (short overall) and overall sets in the spring 1978 Sears catalog featured ruffled straps and puffed-sleeve shirts.

The unisex trend reached every member of the family beginning in 1970 when the Sears catalog that spring featured six pages of "his and hers" styles for adults (in the men's section) and "family styles" modeled by school-age children. Toddler play clothes for boys and girls had always been grouped together, but the unisex influence was visible in fashion-forward styles mimicking adult trends: collarless jackets, longer haircuts, and bright colors for boys and pantsuits for girls. There were fewer dressy, traditional gender-specific styles for children under size 14 as casual styles dominated the scene.

"Family" fashions, in the form of coordinates for adults and children of both sexes, had been popular since the end of World War II, perhaps as a celebration of the nuclear family. These styles in early 1960s Sears catalogs reflected current trends in colorways, whether for heathered neutrals or citrusy brights, but they were limited to a page or two. For boys and men these "his and hers" styles offered a rare respite from the limited range of appropriately masculine hues. Overall one of the most striking characteristics of all clothing between 1968 and 1978 is the explosion of color and pattern that assaults the eye in every magazine and catalog. From apparel for the tiniest babies to men's suits, each page is a kaleidoscope of stripes, plaids, and prints in brilliant colors. For the first time in generations, older boys and men were enjoying colors and expressive patterns formerly considered effeminate, juvenile, or both. Pastels for babies and toddlers were "creeping into the background," replaced by red, white, and blue and green, orange, and yellow.[8] Orange, gold, and olive green dominated kitchens and closets alike in the early seventies, and bicentennial red, white, and blue was everywhere in 1976.

Pastel pink had become a nearly universal symbols of femininity by mid-century, but dressing baby girls in pink was still optional. For most girls pink was one choice among many, and pastels in general were clearly associated with warmer weather and dressier occasions as well as gender. Spring and summer fashions featured pastels and light colors while the fall-winter catalogs were full of darker, more saturated hues. The plaid cotton school dresses familiar to so many baby boom girls were seldom light in color because they had to stand up not only to recess but to penmanship lessons with real ink as well. From season to season the colors and fabrics in the children's sections of clothing catalogs generally followed adult trends and patterns. If burnt orange was a fashionable color, the entire family wore burnt orange.

The details of clothing trends can be overwhelming; underlying rules and patterns can be frustrating to discern amid the contract flow of colors, shapes, and patterns. They also make for boring reading. Rather than recap the trends already described in the previous chapters for women and men, most of which were transferred directly to children's clothing with little modification, what follows is a brief summary of changes in gendered and ungendered clothing for children from birth to puberty for the years 1962 to 1979.

Two of the "bedrock" rules from the previous decades did not change: the dressier the outfit, the more gendered it was, and it was perfectly acceptable for girls to wear boyish styles for play, or even clothing from the boys department. However, some of the key existing rules disappeared, including

- age separation (babies are not toddlers are not children are not teens are not adults)

- pants for girls are for casual wear only

- neutral styles for babies may include some otherwise feminine elements (floral prints, puffed sleeves, smocking, pink and blue in combination)

A new pattern emerged during this time that not only survived the 1970s but also persists today in an even more decided form. As the age separation rule faded, the distinction between "girly" feminine and "sexy" feminine dissolved and moved lower in the age range for girls. This began with preteen or young Junior styles aimed at girls in the 10–12 age range, but by the late 1970s they were evident in the 7–14 size range as well.

One last shift that occurred during this period was the boys' equivalent of the peacock revolution. Like teens and older men, boys enjoyed a wider spectrum of colors, patterns, and styles and wore their hair longer and longer. Like the more mature styles, this trend showed signs of disintegrating after the mid-1970s.

All of these changes together resulted in more options from which to choose. This was true for gendered clothing, which was reimagined and expanded: more pants for girls, in styles ranging from boyish to fussy, and more expressive, colorful, and even flamboyant styles for boys. But the number and proportion of styles designed for both boys and girls—the neutral or unisex styles—also increased. As a result there was more choice than had been available for children before or since. The question remained, what to choose?

Unisex clothing could be dismissed as just another trivial fashion trend, except that it coincided with heightened scientific, popular, and political attention to the differences between men and women, including the sources and consequences of those differences. Much of the excitement boiled down to a very old question: Are we products of nature or nurture? Unisex clothing posed this question not only visually, to the observer, but also in a very intimate way to the wearer. Who was right? Erasmus, when he penned *vestis virum facit* (often translated as "Clothes make the man"), or Shakespeare, who observed, "Clothing oft proclaims the man"? The women's movement introduced new urgency to the question of the origins of gender roles, along with a corollary: Is it possible to explore new social roles? Almost immediately there was a conservative reaction: just because new roles were possible didn't necessarily mean they were desirable.

For many scientists these questions were already being answered by work suggesting that nature and nurture interacted, although in unknown ways. The either/or binary choice persisted in the popular mind, however, especially when it came to children and gender. Many parents (and psychiatrists) clearly held the view that biological sex, as indicated by a baby's genitalia, was inextricably connected to gendered behaviors. Boys were expected to be loud, tough, and active; girls were dainty, cuddly, and gentle. Children, especially boys, who did not display appropriate characteristics and interests needed correction, whether in the form of parental discipline or professional therapy.

On the other hand, feminist parents, scholars, and educators argued that traditional masculine and feminine roles were the result of social and cultural pressure, not biology. Second-wave feminists were particularly interested in challenging the sexist beliefs and structures they believed were responsible for women's lack of power and status. Friedan's *The Feminine Mystique,* in particular, was an indictment of cultural notions of femininity marketed as natural traits. In the public square this translated into protests and political activity. But for many this desire for equality resulted in a more personal, long-term goal: a new generation of men and women raised to be unrestricted by gender stereotypes. The answer, it seemed, lay not only with adults as they struggled to break out of their traditional roles, but also with children, especially the very youngest boys and girls. The solution to sexism seemed to be early intervention, in the form of "unisex child-rearing," a movement affecting even the youngest babies. The transfer of that newly coined term from pantsuits to parenting seems to signal a shift from the "frivolous" realm of trendy young adult fashion to the serious business of cultural transformation.

By the 1970s science and popular culture converged on a paradigm shift in parenting and education. What if femininity and masculinity were almost entirely nurtured? This would place the power for shaping children's gender and sexuality in the hands of parents and educators; medical professionals and mass media would play important supporting roles. This moment was a long time coming, beginning with the first child psychologists who had challenged the nineteenth-century view that masculinity and femininity were innate but undeveloped in babies, and that such traits naturally emerged as the child matured, without the need for coaxing or direction. G. Stanley Hall and others had argued instead that, like intelligence or musical talent, sex roles (as they were then called) were subject to good or bad influences, neglect or cultivation. Scientific evidence that masculinity and femininity were all or mostly learned behaviors would not have made the stakes any lower or the parents' task less important. In fact, as it turned out, believing that gender roles are mostly cultural only intensified those arguments over what masculinity and femininity should be.

The work of John Money in the 1950s and '60s not only introduced the modern concept of gender but also popularized the belief that in the process of identity formation, biological sex was subordinate to gender—that is, the cultural expressions associated with sex. At that time the leading expert in the treatment of intersex children (those born with ambiguous genitals), Money separated the acquisition of gender identity into biological and social processes. The former, he argued, began at conception and proceeded through five stages before birth. Studies in the late 1950s had established the effects of fetal hormones on brain development, a phenomenon popularly referred to as "brain sex." At birth the external genitalia identify the baby as a boy or girl, but then gender socialization takes over and becomes the more powerful influence.[9]

Before the reader gets too enthusiastic about his findings, I need to point out that Money has now been so discredited that his name serves as a warning for researcher hubris. Most of his fame rested on *Man and Woman, Boy and Girl*, a widely used college textbook coauthored with Anke Ehrhardt.[10] Besides introducing and elucidating the very useful concepts of gender identity and gender roles to a generation of college students, Money and Ehrhardt's book is best known for the story of John/Joan, an infant boy whose circumcision went terribly awry, leaving him with an irreparably damaged penis. The solution was surgical reassignment, conducted when the child was about a year and a half old, along with follow-up therapy and hormone treatments that Money claimed produced a well-adjusted girl. The fact that "Joan" had an identical twin brother gave additional weight to Money's claim to have successfully created female gender identity in someone born male. In addition to this famous case, Money also published widely on his "successes" with hermaphrodite (intersex) babies, who were usually transformed into girls through surgery and hormones, accompanied by behavioral therapy.

In the decades since Money's peak influence, follow-up studies of his patients have cast a huge shadow over these claims. Not only were they often unhappy with their female bodies, but as adults his patients rejected the feminine cultural patterns foisted on them. The feminized twin on whose story Money had built this reputation eventually chose surgical reversal of the operation and wrote his own story, *As Nature Made Him: The Boy Who Was Raised as a Girl*. Sadly, he eventually committed suicide in 2004 at the age of thirty-nine.[11] In the meantime, despite the unhappy outcome of Money's work, surgeries on intersex infants have continued to be common practice. Overwhelmingly, these babies are still recreated as females, because male-to-female surgery is generally easier than the reverse. This represents an extreme, rare effect of Money's work, but his work also helped propel acceptance of the belief that gender identity is socially constructed. In fact the roles of nature and nurture in human development are still controversial.

For scholars the distinction between biological sex and the expressions, behaviors, and personality characteristics associated with biological sex served a very useful purpose, seemingly isolating the sociocultural aspects of human behavior from the presumably more universal biological traits. Biological sex was a given, nearly immutable; socially constructed gender was a dependent variable, subject to not only influence by social interactions and media but also, potentially, intervention by parents, teachers, and therapists. Separating the two forces also conformed to the trend for academic specialization. Geneticists, endocrinologists, and other life scientists could focus on the physical (sex), leaving gender to the social scientists. Behavioral scientists began to scrutinize how we acquire gender in early childhood, including patterns of nurturing and education. These investigations were driven not only by scientific curiosity but also by popular demand for definitive answers. The feminist movement and the sexual revolution had opened a Pandora's box of questions and confusion about the most basic elements of human identity.

The same year that Money and Ehrhardt published their textbook, one of the most iconic fictional works of the unisex era appeared: Lois Gould's short story "X: A Fabulous Child's Story," a tale of an "Xperiment" in gender-free child raising. It was published in *Ms.* in 1972 and was expanded into an illustrated children's book in 1978.[12] In the story a baby, named simply X, is born to two parents who have agreed to keep its sex a secret as part of a huge, expensive scientific experiment. They are given a thick handbook to help them navigate future problems from how to play with X to dealing with boys' and girls' bathrooms at school.

The challenges grow larger and thornier when X enters the gendered world of school. Although the boys and girls initially share their parents' discomfort and insist on X's acting like one sex or another, they eventually envy and then imitate its freedom in dress and play. Finally the angry parents of the other children demand that X be examined physically and mentally by a team of experts.

> If X's test showed it was a boy, it would have to start obeying all the boys' rules. If it proved to be a girl, X would have to obey all the girls' rules.
>
> And if X turned out to be some kind of mixed-up misfit, then X must be Xpelled from school. Immediately! And a new rule must be passed, so that no little Xes would ever come to school again.

Of course, X turns out to be the "least mixed-up child" ever examined by the experts. X knows what it is, and "by the time X's sex matters, it won't be a secret anymore." Happy ending![13]

In an instance of science imitating art, "X: A Fabulous Child's Story" inspired a series of real-life studies that explored the relationship between an infant's sex (real or assumed) and the child's interactions with adults. The earliest published study was 1975's "Baby X: The Effect of Gender Labels on Adult Responses to Infants," by Carol Seavy, Phyllis Katz, and Sue Rosenberg Zalk. In the experiment a baby dressed in a yellow jumpsuit was presented to adult subjects with instructions to play with the baby, choosing a football, a rag doll, or a flexible plastic ring. The technician running the study was under instructions to give no clues as to the sex of the baby. Subsequent studies became progressively complex. Sometimes the baby's assumed sex was the variable, with the same infant given different names (Beth or Adam) and dressed in pink or blue, accordingly.[14] Other studies explored when and how well children learned gender stereotypes or how adults' use of these clues may or may not reveal their own beliefs about sex, gender, and appropriate behavior. Baby X research even trickled down to elementary school science fairs; two sixth-graders from my suburban Maryland neighborhood entered a project based on a trip to the local mall with a baby they dressed first in boys' clothes and then girls' and then recorded shoppers' responses to each variation.

What we've learned from all of these studies is that children understand and can apply gender stereotypes well before they reach their third birthday. These studies also confirmed the belief that adults routinely look for and use gender clues in their social interactions with babies and toddlers, unconsciously communicating gender stereotypes at the same time. These "Baby X" studies, combined with the emerging narratives in popular works such as the children's version of "X,"[15] *William's Doll, Free to Be... You and Me,* and *Sesame Street,* helped reinforce the feminist message that gender stereotyping was harmful to children.

One of the more subtle themes in Gould's story is the unequal value of feminine and masculine traits. Given that her essential message is that children should be free of stereotyped behaviors and treatment, she was surprisingly dismissive of some feminine markers. For example, the *Official Instruction Manual* mentioned in the story offers the following directions for interacting with their new baby: "plenty of bouncing and cuddling, both. X ought to be strong and sweet and active. *Forget about dainty altogether*" (emphasis in the original). This ambivalence, if not hostility, toward femininity is an important part of the cultural climate of the early 1970s.

Gould also draws a picture of clothing and toy stores that is not entirely accurate. In the story the parents are faced with a highly gender-binary landscape that sounds more like 2012 than 1972, with sharply distinctive boy and girl sections in the store. In reality, clothing and playthings for babies and toddlers a generation ago included many more neutral options than are available today. So X is provided not with neutral things that actually existed at the time, but instead a selectively androgynous blend of "blue pajamas in the Boys' Department and cheerful flowered underwear in the Girls' Department." In reality a baby in 1972 could have worn both blue pajamas and underwear in a floral print (Sears' Winnie-the-Pooh nursery print had Pooh, Eeyore, Piglet, and flowers), and they would have been considered neutral! Gould also invents fantastic, gender-bending toys and books, such as a boy doll that cries "Pa-Pa." X's favorite doll is a robot programmed to bake brownies and clean the kitchen. When the other children decide that X is not weird, but cool, the message they get is that by playing with both boys' and girls' stuff, X is "having twice as much fun as we are."

Finally, when the children decide to go to X's house to play, they are all shown in identical red-checked overalls. "X: A Fabulous Child's Story" tells us that some stereotypically feminine traits (daintiness) are undesirable, that children naturally desire both "boys'" and "girls'" things, and that the ultimate form of gender neutrality is uniformity with a masculine tilt. The X model of a "gender-neutral" world was masculine, like most of the unisex trend, with occasional touches of femininity to help boys be more nurturing and expressive. This aligns with much of the feminist opinion about dress in the late 1960s and '70s, which cast traditional women's clothing as limiting, objectifying, and disempowering while portraying men's clothing, especially pants, as symbolically empowering rather than just more practical.

This fictional child and its scientific counterparts provided support and evidence for the cultural and social origins of gender roles, framing the "nature or nurture" debate in a manner that has provoked discussion in living rooms and conference rooms ever since. Evidence of this discussion can be found in popular magazines, often drawing on emerging (and contradictory) scientific opinion. A lengthy article in *Newsweek* in 1974 asked "Do Children Need Sex 'Roles'?" and offered pro and con opinions from the psychiatric community.[16] Psychiatrists advocating traditional gender roles argued that children were the victims of "militant women's liberationists, overachieving fathers and . . . androgynous youth culture," and warned that unisex child raising would lead to more sexually aggressive girls and more passive boys. Such a reversal would also result in a greater incidence of homosexuality, they hinted, clearly based on antiquated notions of the "causes" of same-sex attraction and the continuing belief that it was a mental illness, despite the recent change in the American Psychological Association's (APA) official position. On the side of ungendered parenting were professionals who charged that the profession had long been in error when trying to adjust people to "the cultural status quo" rather than question the status quo itself. They also came armed with clinical experience and scientific research: psychologist Jeanne Humphrey Block offered evidence from her prizewinning research that adults who are raised to assume traditional roles are less satisfied with themselves. If the cultural roles were unhealthy or damaging—and subject to change—why not change them? The battling experts did agree on one point: it was fine to give baseball mitts to little girls and dolls to boys in early childhood, as long as it wasn't part of an agenda to "destroy the child's basic biological identity," but children needed to arrive at a stable gender identity by the time they started school.[17]

The elephant in the room in many of these discussions was homosexuality, specifically the treatment of boys who exhibited signs of femininity. Not surprisingly, the scholarly literature addressed these issues much more directly than the popular books and articles, although *Psychology Today* and similar popular science magazines occasionally helped bring these studies to the larger audience. Reporting on the work of the Gender Identity Project at the University of California at Los Angeles in 1979, *Psychology Today* asked, "Does a boy have the right to be effeminate?" The clinical psychologists at UCLA had published an article on their work in helping "gender-disturbed" children (mostly effeminate boys, since being a tomboy created fewer social problems for girls) learn more androgynous gestures and speech. In this article, as in the *Newsweek* piece, the clinicians were pitted against the more theoretical psychologists, who opposed these interventions, which they felt sent negative messages to the boys about themselves and amounted to efforts to cure or prevent homosexuality. Ever since the 1973 APA reclassification of homosexuality, treating it in children was bound to be controversial. The UCLA team defended their work as not being aimed at preventing homosexuality, but helping children fit into their social environment. Once more the argument boiled down to whether the person or the culture needed to be fixed.[18]

By the late 1970s claims that gender was almost entirely a matter of nurture were being taken seriously by a wider public, but with surprising results. Useful as the concept of gender as separable from sex is, it introduced a messy new variable into popular notions about sex and sexuality. The idea that gendered behaviors are entirely cultural could be used by both feminists and antifeminists. For many conservatives and antifeminists, biological essentialism (biology is destiny) was replaced by cultural chauvinism: yes, gender roles are cultural, but the traditional (Western, Judeo-Christian, middle-class—take your pick) cultural norms are superior and should be preserved. If gender could be taught that still begged the question of which gender rules should be passed along to the young.

The most progressive parenting literature frequently advocated "unisex child raising," applying the fashion term in a brand-new way. Unisex child raising included encouraging children to play with a variety of toys, modeling gender-free roles as adults by switching chores (Daddy cooks, Mommy mows the lawn), and choosing neutral clothing and hairstyles for the whole family. Public education also took a decidedly liberal position on gender stereotyping, promoting curricula and resources including a widespread adoption of *Free to Be . . . You and Me* for primary grades. A two-year study of gender stereotype "interventions" at a variety of grade levels convinced Marcia Guttentag and Helen Bray that undoing cultural training was possible, and they clearly believed that it was desirable. They were hardly radical in their advocacy; their goal was to "expand job and human opportunities" for boys and girls.[19] Yet it is easy to see how this agenda would have seemed offensive and even threatening to parents and educators who believed in the moral rightness of traditional cultural norms.

For children's clothing, unisex essentially meant more a wider range of colors, styles, and decoration for boys; fewer very feminine styles for girls; and more neutral choices for all. On the surface this was identical to trends for teenagers and adults, but the difference is in the effect. From tot lot to retirement we are engaged in a continual process of adjusting our appearance according to our inner sense of self and the accepted patterns of identity expression. Children engage in the process at the same time they are first acquiring identity, which, I suspect, makes a huge difference.

Children's fashions of the early 1970s demand our attention with their bright colors and gender-defying styling. In some of these old pictures it really is impossible to tell the boys from the girls. For young children not yet in school, unisex fashions combined more neutral styles and a trickling down of adult fashions. As with clothing for newborns, pastels were rejected in girls' clothing in favor of earth tones and bright primary colors. But a broader and deeper view reveals patterns that continued to follow old, established rules. Some of the "paradigm shifts" turned out to be mere fads. In the end unisex children's fashion enjoyed a very brief popularity and somehow also ushered in an era when juvenile styles from babyhood on were more gendered than they had been in the early 1960s.

Girls' clothing, beginning in the mid-1970s, began to regain feminine details that had been briefly discarded: ruffles, lace, puffed sleeves, and pastels. Yes, girls could wear pants to school, but pants were no longer perceived as exclusively masculine, and girls' styles featured the same dainty and fussy details as girls' dresses did. Consumers, parents and girls alike, who preferred plainer, more tailored styles found fewer and fewer options beginning in the mid-1980s. The plain T-shirts, overalls, and pajamas for children that once occupied several pages in the Sears catalog were reduced first to just a page or two and then to nothing except for a few yellow or green outfits for newborns. Boys' brief flirtation with color and pattern ended along with the peacock revolution, replaced by athletic styles, the preppy look, and camouflage. This time not even the tiniest babies escaped gender labeling; prenatal ultrasounds made it possible for parents to furnish them with a completely gendered environment from the very start. It was as if a switch had been pulled and gender ambiguity in babies disappeared completely.

Of course for most children born after the mid-1980s this hyper-gendered world was traditional—the way things had always been. Although it is clear that our cultural landscape is subject to change, we tend to see the world we knew at four or five as the way it always was, even when we learn it was not. A little girl born in the late '60s probably grew up wearing pants to school. Even if she learns that for generations this had been absolutely forbidden, she will never share the sense of rebellion and defiance her mother experienced when she wore jeans or a pantsuit in 1970. This sense of history colors what adults perceive as traditional, even when that "tradition" dates only to their infancy. They'll look back at the clothing of their childhood and reassess those fashions through the lens of their own personal tastes and experiences. One woman may look at her grade-school class picture and feel nostalgia for plaid dresses; another remembers only cold knees. The boy with the gender-free wardrobe in the early 1970s may later recall the embarrassment of being called a girl; another may miss the bright colors and patterns.

Unisex fashion played out differently for children than for grown-ups. On adult bodies unisex clothing can accentuate physical differences, creating a pleasant sexual tension. Babies and preadolescent children often don't look masculine or feminine, and dressing them in ambiguous clothing produces social discomfort. In a culture where "boy or girl?" determines our mode of address and interaction, an encounter with the unknown is fraught with anxiety for the onlooker. For children between three and six—old enough to know their own sex but not yet secure in its permanence—being mistaken for the wrong sex can be embarrassing or even frightening.

While the battle over the proper roles for men and women raged in the popular media throughout the 1970s, parents were left to clothe and raise their children with no clear agreement and confusing advice from the "experts." The only common theme in the advice literature was the assertion that the stakes were very high; children's future mental health and happiness were at stake. One thing is clear: people on both sides of the controversy seemed to agree on the tremendous power of the gender-shaping abilities of clothing. Feminist writers argued that traditional gendered clothing would make children repressed, rebellious, and unable to function in the new egalitarian society. More conservative voices warned that blurring the distinction between the sexes would confuse children, possibly even steer them into homosexuality.[20]

Future historians tracing the emergence of the American "culture wars" may not bother to look at children's clothing, but they should. A longitudinal study of two hundred "conventional and unconventional" families beginning in 1974 identified a cluster of attitudes and behaviors in a subset of unconventional households the researchers labeled as "pronaturalism"—a preference for natural/organic food and other materials, emotionally expressive men, low-conflict parent-child relationships—that set them apart from, and often at odds with, more conventional parents.[21] For a brief time in the 1970s, pronaturalist parents found their beliefs positively portrayed in the media and supported by public education and policy, or at least not deprecated. This changed with the emergence of the modern conservative movement and the "moral majority," which dominated both culture and politics in the 1980s.

While the multitudes of clinical studies offered no satisfactory answer to the question of why some people are homosexual while others are not, parents attempting gender-free child rearing found their efforts resisted by their own children. Even advocates of nonsexist child rearing noted the stubborn persistence of sexist behaviors and beliefs. Consistent with their own conviction that gender was a product of nurture, they tended to place the blame on media and consumer culture, dismissing the possibility that daughters' rejection of trucks and longing for frilly dresses had any basis in biology.[22] But many parents, faced with rebellion, felt like Jesse Ellison's mother, quoted in a 2010 article: "We all thought that the differences had to do with how you were brought up in a sexist culture, and if you gave children the same chances, it would equalize. . . . It took a while to think, 'Maybe men and women really are different from each other, and they're both equally valuable.'"[23]

In a 1981 journal article researcher Penny Burge reported that in her survey most parents supported nontraditional sex-role attitudes and practices.[24] But this does not represent every parent. Just because *Free to Be . . . You and Me* won awards and sold millions of records, books, and videotapes does not mean its message won universal approval. A parent who read *Psychology Today, Ms., Parents, McCall's,* or *Good Housekeeping*—or who even talked with other parents—would likely be familiar with the arguments for nonsexist child raising and unisex clothing but not necessarily persuaded by them. Feminists used the cultural construction of gender to push back on the claim that women had a natural inclination toward home and family. Conservative parents generally rejected unisex child raising along with other elements of feminist ideology, while less ideologically driven parents simply found gender-free clothing less appealing. Both categories of parents certainly had access to clothing choices other than gender-free throughout the era. Sears might not offer pastel toddler clothing, but specialty stores did, and in the 1970s many women still knew how to sew, which gave them even more options. And popular culture is complex and often contradictory: at the same time that girls were being encouraged to wear simple, modern styles, the television series *Little House on the Prairie* (1974–1982) and the nation's bicentennial celebrations popularized and romanticized versions of historical girls' dresses and women's traditional roles.

Nonsexist child rearing, and with it unisex clothing for children, was supposed to transform our culture by limiting children's exposure to stereotypes and preventing their acquisition of limited gender roles. Firm in their belief that gendered behaviors stemmed from nurture, not nature, progressive parents and educators launched a movement to reprogram boys and girls from birth to be completely free to express their "natural" selves. Much to their surprise, for many children their "natural selves" fell short of the egalitarian ideal. Unfortunately, all we have today with which to judge the success or failure of the unisex movement is anecdotes and subsequent history.

The anecdotes tell of failure after failure. My own son (born in 1986), as a toddler, used to bite his slice of cheese into the shape of a gun. Girls rejected trains and trucks and demanded Barbie dolls and nail polish. The stories go on and on. Are these behaviors really evidence that gender-free child rearing is a wasted effort, or do they suggest that gender is more complicated than originally thought? From the highly gendered vantage point of the early twenty-first-century children's clothing department, kids' unisex styles of the 1970s seem just a small blip in the steady transformation of infants and toddler clothing from ungendered to a nearly complete masculine/feminine binary. Yet that brief period has had lasting effects, including some unsettled issues that still vex us.

Not everyone follows fashion trends, but it is safe to say that unisex clothing options represented a controversial issue that thoughtful parents could not help but be aware of, even if they chose to disagree. Most of the unfinished business of unisex childrearing settled on the children of the 1970s, not their parents. Children, too, remember the clothing and their own reactions and preferences, and even if they rejected the gender ambiguity of the fashions, they absorbed the egalitarian messages of the unisex movement. Young women in the late 1980s and 1990s expressed a desire to "have it all," not just in terms of career and family but also in terms of feeling pride in feeling female. This was not a simple matter to translate into actions. For example, no parents thought about sexual assertiveness when they encouraged their daughters to be less "dainty," but by the late 1980s the popular media was bemoaning the sexualization of girls in their early teens. Was this the result of feminist influence and a sexually permissive culture, or an expression of young adolescent girls' real nature, unencumbered by "old-fashioned" notions of feminine delicacy?

Table 4.1. Birth Cohort of First-time Parents, 1980–1990

	Birth Cohort	Age in 1975	% 1980 Births	% 1985 Births	% 1990 Births
Mother	1961–1975	0–14	<1	43	71
	1946–1960	15–29	79	56	29
Father	1961–1975	0–14	0	24	53
	1946–1960	15–29	82	71	47

Source: U.S. Census Bureau, "1951–1994 Statistical Abstracts,"
http://www.census.gov/prod/www/abs/statab1951-1994.htm.

One possible explanation for this shift is demographics. Between 1980 and 1990 the majority proportion of births to first-time parents shifted from baby boomers (b. 1946–1964) to Generation Xers (b. 1965–1982). This generational perspective matters because of the huge difference between being a twenty-three-year-old choosing gender-bending clothing for herself or himself in 1975 and having unisex clothing selected for you as a three-year-old. This suggests that the children of the '70s became parents who were likely to prefer gendered clothing for their own offspring.

Even more striking, as the children of the 1970s became parents, they demanded even more stereotyped clothing and toys for their offspring than had existed in their childhood. Superficially, the explanatory pendulum seemed to have swung back toward "nature," because this gender revival was justified as satisfying children's innate preferences, with the anecdotal unisex failures providing the necessary proof. Yet the same parents placed no limits on their daughters' ambitions; like their mothers, young girls seemed destined to have it all: girly clothes, spa parties, and soccer—with pink uniforms. Add to this equation the advent of prenatal testing that revealed the baby's sex months before birth. Knowing only that fact about their unborn child, new parents seemed eager to embrace "traditional" gender in their preferences for clothing and nursery décor. Many of my baby boom sisters were horrified.

Something even more troubling has shown up in girls' clothing since the revival of feminine designs: women's clothing of the 1960s that essentially conflates femininity, youth, and sexual attractiveness has trickled down to girls' clothing, first for young teens, then to the 7–14 size range, and eventually even younger. It is not so jarring to see skimpy clothes and flirty models in the Juniors section; it seems completely consistent with the spirit of fashion trends since the 1960s. But seeing seven-year-olds in bikinis, posing like beach bunnies, while in the same spirit, seems inappropriate to many adults. The modern controversies over sexy dressing in child pageants and the KGOY (kids getting older younger) trend have their roots in the sexual and gender revolutions of the 1960s.

Part of the appeal of adult unisex fashion was the sexy contrast between the wearer and the clothes, which actually called attention to the male or female body. A grown man in a brilliant pink sports coat can still appear very masculine, even with a long haircut, because his voice, body shape, and gestures also convey gender. If he sported sideburns and other facial hair, the contradiction between "feminine" clothing and "masculine" physique actually created the desired tension and novelty. Similarly, women in pants appearing in popular humor were usually depicted as more attractive because of the way that trousers emphasized their curves. Ironically, unisex fashions for adults did not really blur the differences between men and women, but instead highlighted them.

One significant tie to previous patterns was a continued distinction between clothing for very young children and adult clothing. Toddler boys enjoyed a greater range of colors and patterns than older boys and men, and toddler girl fashions were shorter and more whimsically decorated than those for older girls and women. Above the toddler age range, however, age markers were blurred. It was not just existing gender rules that broke down during the 1960s; older conventions about what was age-appropriate also crumbled. What had once been clear distinctions according to age became a much looser and more permeable set of options. One sign was a more juvenile turn to teenagers' casual clothing, which became more colorful and playful. Minidresses on young women made them look like little girls, and the men's hairstyles and collarless jackets popularized by the Beatles were strongly reminiscent of toddler boys' classic Eton suits and long bangs. Through most of the 1960s unisex design was seen more in toddler clothing than in infants' wear as adult styles mimicked children's, which in turn reflected prevailing adult trends. This mutual influence resulted in adult clothing that was youthful and androgynous and children's clothing that looked "sophisticated" because of its resemblance to adult fashions.

This trend prompted considerable discussion in the style press. Fashion writers and cultural critics noted the "little girl" trend for women's clothing with some confusion. Was it asexual because it was immature, or was it super-sexy because of a "Lolita" effect, mimicking schoolgirl-themed pornography? There was no attention at the time to the implications for little girls wearing the same styles, but from a twenty-first-century vantage point, one can see the first outlines of early childhood sexualization in the baby doll dresses of young women.

It is worth considering that the relationship between girls' play clothes and fashions for teens and adult women was not simply one of trickling down, but was also a result of "carrying over" childhood clothing as girls grew to women. For example, jeans and overalls had been part of girls' playtime wardrobes for decades, and teenagers had been exchanging their skirts for dungarees after school since the 1940s. As rules of dress etiquette were discarded in the early '60s—no more hats or white gloves—and lifestyles became more laid-back, jeans and other casual trouser styles increased in popularity among young adults. Or to look at it from a different perspective, children who had grown up in jeans and T-shirts in postwar America saw no reason to stop wearing them just because they had outgrown the playground.

In recent years scholars and popular authors have once more challenged the notion that masculinity and femininity are innate; they are also attempting to highlight the roles of media and consumer culture in defining and promulgating gender stereotypes. Despite their efforts, however, the issue seems no closer to being settled than it ever was. Every few months there is a new story about a boy who dresses like a girl, a girl who dresses like a boy, or a boy who likes pink nail polish that sets off a new round of claims, counterclaims, and controversy.[25] Around the globe, parents attempting to raise ungendered children make the headlines, and their stories echo the messages of the unisex era.[26] Nearly always the public reaction is mostly reminiscent of the adults in "X: A Fabulous Child's Story": anger, derision, and warnings of future confusion. But they also have their defenders, many of them parents of the same generation: the ones who grew up highly gendered in the 1980s and who are rejecting the binary and looking for new alternatives.

So is gender identity an effect of nature or nurture? Science tells us that the foundations for sexual behavior are laid down before we are born and also that human variation is vast and complex. Knowing that most boys behave in a particular way does not tell you how your son will behave, nor will it explain why your daughter might prefer Barbies or Transformers. The dominant professional advice for parents of gender-fluid or gender-creative children is to watch and wait; sometimes it's a phase and sometimes it isn't, and interventions with the goal of "correction" do more harm than good. History tells us that children can wear dresses or pants, and can wear pink or blue or both together, but that strongly gendered or gender-free clothing has an unpredictable effect, most of it not evident until they are grown. The clearest answer, for now, to the age-old question is nature *and* nurture, sympathetically, unpredictably.

Litigating the Revolution

5

ashion has had a legal side for centuries. Powerful rulers once set limits on who could or could not wear certain finery and decreed that colors, badges, or hats be used to set certain groups of people apart as "others"—Jews, for example, who were required to wear yellow badges or pointed hats in parts of thirteenth-century Europe.[1] The umbrella term for these edicts is "sumptuary laws"; one of my favorites, from medieval Spain, begins with "the king may wear anything he wishes." Sumptuary laws reveal a great deal about a society—for example, which goods are highly valued (and therefore reserved for the élites) and also which groups may be considered a threat to the status quo. Amid the social turbulence of the Renaissance, wealthy merchants and their wives were often singled out as needing to be reminded of their inferiority to their high-born betters. Economist Thorstein Veblen observed in 1899 that in modern capitalism, wealth could be freely displayed by nearly everyone who has it, as a sign of socioeconomic superiority. But we still face restrictions in the form of dress codes, usually in schools or in the workplace, that attempt to enforce a uniform appearance or suppress potentially disruptive elements. These modern regulations have elements of social class (public schools with uniform dress codes tend to be in poorer districts), race (local ordinances against "saggy pants"), or gender (laws against cross-dressing and public indecency, dress codes that enforce gender stereotypes). Sumptuary laws don't come from out of the blue: they are a reaction by the powerful to undesirable behavior from their "inferiors." The rampant and dramatic changes in gender expression that emerged in the 1960s met with just such resistance, leading in some cases to the courtroom and sometimes even to prison. The litigious heat generated by long hair, short skirts, and women in pants is strong evidence that these were far from trivial issues for the parties involved. The fact that we are still arguing about the same principles, though in different clothing, is part of the ongoing legacy of the 1960s.

In nearly every case the defendants in these legal cases were what young people at the time would have labeled "the Establishment": school administrations, employers, or the military. The plaintiffs were arguing from their less powerful positions as students, employees, or simply as individuals (men, women, minors, people of color). Each of these variables carries with it distinct arguments on the part of both the plaintiffs and defendants. Although the prohibition of pants for women and long hair for men is often mentioned in tandem, the two situations could not have been more different. Court cases involving male plaintiffs dominate the legal record. There were seventy-eight court decisions at the state level or higher about long hair in the United States between 1965 and 1978, compared with just six cases about girls or women wearing trousers. Long-haired boys and men experienced harassment and even violence, while women and girls wearing slacks or jeans might just be turned away from a restaurant or sent home from school to change outfits. Between the first court case concerning pants, in 1969, to the last, in 1973, trousers for women went from being a novelty to a wardrobe staple with a minimum of public outrage.

Chronologically, the legal record begins in 1964 with lawsuits involving minors challenging school dress codes: first longhaired boys and later both boys and girls with a more extensive list of complaints. In the 1970s there was an increase in the number of cases brought by adults concerning workplace restrictions. The legal arguments on both sides shifted over time as well.

For men and boys perhaps the most contentious and visible aspect of unisex fashion concerned not clothing, but hair. The British Invasion in popular music deserves much of the credit for the early trend toward longer hair for men. The long hair craze swept the United Kingdom before it arrived on American shores, propelled at first by the Beatles and soon after by scruffier groups like the Rolling Stones. None had originated the style; art school students such as John Lennon, Paul McCartney, and

Mick Jagger had been sporting long hair for some time. The unisex effect was accentuated when British girls began adopting the same styles in the summer of 1964, either in imitation of the rock stars or to present a "his and hers" appearance when they were out with their boyfriends. There were skirmishes over long hair in schools, but overall the public reaction in the U.K. was nonchalant, with most people considering it as just another adolescent fad. Noting that long hair used to be associated with the upper class and close-cropped hair with the middle and lower class, adolescent psychologist Derek Miller pointed out that British teens were just bored and trying to stand out and that long hair was preferable to juvenile delinquency.[2] Mick Jagger of the Rolling Stones detected the moral panic behind some of the criticism: "They seem to have a sort of personal anxiety because we are getting away with something they never dared to do. It's a personal, sexual, vain thing. They've been taught that being masculine means looking clean cropped and ugly."[3]

Beginning in 1963, newspapers in the United States reported numerous instances of boys, some as young as nine, being barred from school for having long hair. Most of these confrontations ended with a quick trim. In a parochial school in New Hampshire, the administrator actually loaded eighteen students on a school bus and delivered them to a local barber. A smaller group of students defied the rules and ended up facing school or district hearings. The well-publicized story of fifteen-year-old Edward T. Kores Jr. of Westbrook, Connecticut, ended with Kores transferring to a private school after he lost his appeal to the state education commission. His father, a carpenter, at first vowed to "fight this in the court," but the family eventually decided against that course of action.[4]

The trouble escalated in fall 1964 when boys started showing up at school with a summer's growth of hair. It would seem that most school systems were caught unaware, without a true dress code, just vague guidelines about neatness. Newspaper accounts of similar events started popping up across the country. Most cases were resolved with a quick trip to the barber or brushing the boy's bangs off his forehead. But eventually a few ended up in local courts. Perhaps the significant detail to note about these cases is that because the boys were minors they had to have the support of their parents in order to take it to the legal level.

The number of hair resisters who took the next step—suing the schools in state-level courts—was smaller still. The earliest such case involving hair was *Leonard v. School Committee of Attleboro* (Massachusetts), which began with the first day of classes on September 9, 1964, and went all the way to the state supreme court, which upheld the school's right to dictate the appearance of students. George Leonard, already a professional musician performing under the name Georgie Porgie, had argued that the school did not have a written dress code and that his long hair was vital to his career, but the court ruled that the principal had the authority to tell Leonard to get a haircut and to expel him if he refused. When he attended an Attleboro High School all-class reunion in 2013, he was greeted as a celebrity; to his classmates and the younger students at the school, he had been a hero.[5] To some fans of freedom of expression, he still is: his entry at the Rhode Island Music Hall of Fame website claims, "Every kid who sports long hair, pink hair or a shaved head, or wears a nose ring, a tattoo or makeup, owes his right to do so to" the Pawtucket-born Leonard.[6] Georgie Porgie and his band appeared at least once with the Cape Cod garage band the Barbarians, who recorded the 1965 hit "Are You a Boy or Are You a Girl," the unofficial anthem of the long hair cause.

> Are you a boy
> Or are you a girl
> With your long blonde hair
> You look like a girl (yeah)
>
> You may be a boy
> You look like a girl
>
> You're either a girl
> Or you come from Liverpool
> (Yeah, Liverpool)
> You can dog like a female monkey
> But you swim like a stone
> (Yeah, a rolling stone)
>
> You may be a boy (hey)
> You look like a girl (hey)

You're always wearing skin tight
Pants and boys wear pants
But in your skin tight pants
You look like a girl[7]

Signs that this was a more serious issue appeared almost immediately. The New York Civil Liberties Union went to the defense of high school boys with long hair in 1966, releasing a statement saying that dress codes disapproving of hairstyles were violating constitutional guarantees by punishing "nonconformity and expression of individuality." That same year the American Civil Liberties Union (ACLU) wrote letters and memoranda to principals in three Philadelphia-area high schools asking them to rescind bans against hairstyles on the grounds that public schools have no authority to impose such regulations. The boys in two of the schools had directly appealed to the ACLU for help.[8] In 1968 the ACLU issued recommendations regarding the academic freedom of secondary-school students and teachers. The twenty-two-page policy statement was six years in the making and included the following student rights:

> To organize political groups, hold assemblies and demonstrations, wear buttons and armbands with slogans as long as these do not disrupt classes or the peace of the school

> To receive formal hearings, written charges, and a right to appeal any serious violation conduct or charge

> To dress or wear one's hair as one pleases and to attend school while married or pregnant unless these things "in fact" disrupt the educational process

> To publish and distribute student materials without prohibitions on content unless they "clearly and imminently" disrupt or are libelous

The authors of the statement argued that school administrators had often erred on the side of the need for order rather than the need for freedom in establishing and enforcing school rules. Titled "Academic Freedom in the Secondary Schools," the statement was distributed in booklet form to all major education associations and available from all state ACLU affiliates.[9]

Dress code cases were working their way through the courts just as quickly, often with the assistance of ACLU attorneys. The first such case reached the U.S. Supreme Court in 1966, but the court refused to hear it. Three adult male students from the Richmond Professional Institute (RPI; now Virginia Commonwealth University) had brought the case, which involved an administrator requiring them to shave their facial hair and get haircuts before they could register for classes. The plaintiffs—Norman Thomas Marshall, Robert D. Shoffner, and Salvatore Federico—claimed RPI was denying them the rights of self-expression and to be left alone and insisted that the consequence, being barred from registration, was cruel and unusual punishment. The circuit court judge had ruled against them, finding the rule "reasonable and in no sense arbitrary" and necessary for the "preservation of discipline."[10]

School administrators in many states had followed this case, as evidenced by the official comment about it from the High School Principals Association in New York: "The court statement to the effect that the question is one to be determined by common sense rather than by courts and [that] schools obviously have the authority to make rules on the matter express the views which we hope will now be adopted by our own superintendent of schools."[11] This last comment was a poke at Dr. Bernard Donovan, superintendent of schools in New York City, who, in the view of the principals association, had not only failed to support principals' efforts to nip longhaired defiance in the bud but had also interfered with local authorities by stepping in on a case involving two students at Forest Hills High School in Queens.[12] The sixteen-year-olds had been confined to the dean's office during the school day for two weeks, and the New York branch of the ACLU had lodged a protest with the New York State superintendent of schools, who had not yet responded. Donovan had ordered principal Paul Balser to let the boys attend classes in the meantime, and the result was an immediate avalanche of protest from teachers and the parents' association. Students interviewed by the *New York Times* had different views, however, ranging from disinterested ("It's just a fad") to defiant ("I don't think they had the authority to tell you to get a haircut"). In an article in *New York State Education* (the teachers association journal), Donovan had condemned "punitive action" in dress code cases, giving the example of one principal who was standing at the school's door with scissors, trimming hair. The tempest swiftly escalated, as the High School Principals Association sent a defiant letter to Donovan saying that in the absence of a policy from his office, they would construe his actions as applying only to Forest Hills High School. In the meantime they intended to "continue to maintain the kind of safety, dress and appearance regulations that will make our students presentable, teachable and employable."[13] In this and in similar cases all across the country, the Supreme Court's refusal to render a decision seems to have to complicated the question and only keyed up the controversy.

Not everyone over the age of eighteen agreed with dress code defenders. A sharp-eyed reader responded to the principals' statement with a letter to the editor of the *New York Times* that expressed the opposing view, one held by many parents and teachers: "I and some others interested in education and in doing things the American Way have discussed the situation in your city as elsewhere and have felt that Dr. Donovan rather than those principals which, given such exhibitions of their 'up the down staircase' mentalities, has acted to preserve common sense."[14] "Up the down staircase" is a reference to a best-selling memoir of a first-year teacher's experiences in a New York City school overseen by an overzealous administrative assistant the author calls "Admiral Ass." The battle lines in the culture wars were taking shape.

Most school and workplace conflicts over appearance were resolved without going to court, of course. A principal might warn dozens of long-haired boys that they faced suspension, and all or most would head to the barbershop, albeit reluctantly. Only a small minority of students, and their parents, chose to challenge dress codes legally. Still, the result was that nearly eighty such cases moved through the nation's courtrooms between 1965 and 1978, thirty-five resolved at the federal district level and twenty at the appellate level, landing in every federal circuit except the second. Eleven such cases applied to the U.S. Supreme Court, but all were denied certiorari, with the result that the varying judgments in the lower courts established the legal precedent in each state.

There were seventy-three long hair cases from schools or colleges decided by the courts between 1965 and 1978, (there were also workplace cases, which will be discussed separately); two-thirds of those were decided between 1970 and 1972. Frustratingly for all concerned, however, there was no clear trend in the decisions (see table 1). By the mid-1970s dress code fatigue was setting in. Some schools gave up. Teachers complained that dress code enforcement itself was more disruptive than long hair or girls wearing slacks. In some cases coaches and sponsors of extracurricular activities tried to make short hair a requirement for boys' participation, but those rules, too, often proved controversial and, in the long run, unenforceable. In the end neither side won the legal battle, yet both claimed a sort of victory. Long hair cases fell off because long hairstyles became widely acceptable in mainstream culture, which was a kind of vindication for the advocates of the more liberal position. But the Supreme Court had clearly left the authority for dress codes with the states and the local school systems, so a great variety of rules persisted and dress code controversies have never completely subsided. A map of the states where dress codes were upheld in the majority of cases neatly overlays the maps of opinion on many other cultural issues. At the extremes the states within the jurisdiction of the Fifth Circuit (Alabama, Florida, Georgia, Louisiana, Mississippi, and Texas) upheld the schools' position in twelve out of fourteen cases. In contrast, the Second Circuit (Vermont, Connecticut, and New York) had only three dress code cases between 1965 and 1978 and ruled in favor of the students every time.

Plaintiffs in the long hair cases of the 1960s claimed that school dress codes violated their constitutional rights, citing the First and Fourteenth Amendments most frequently. Their First Amendment argument was that one's appearance was protected speech. Dress codes that applied differently to students and adults, or to girls and boys, violated the Equal Protection Clause of the Fourteenth Amendment. Other cases pointed to protections of the Third, Fourth, Fifth, Sixth, Eighth, Ninth, and Tenth Amendments. There appears to be no consistent pattern of the success or failure of these various arguments over the entire period, but students and their families found encouragement in the case of *Tinker v. Des Moines Independent Community School District* (1969), where the Supreme Court had ruled 7–2 that minor students enjoyed constitutional protec-

Table 5.1. Court Decisions in School Long Hair Cases, 1965–1978

Year	Decisions	Dress Code Defeated	Dress Code Upheld
1965	1	0	1
1966	1	0	1
1968	1	0	1
1969	5	4	1
1970	15	7	8
1971	21	7	14
1972	12	7	5
1973	7	5	2
1974	2	2	0
1975	2	1	1
1976	3	2	1
1977	2	1	1
1978	1	0	1
Total	**73**	**36**	**37**

tions, including First Amendment rights.[15] However, the Tinker case involved the banning of black armbands, which students wore to protest the Vietnam War, not school dress codes. Justice Abe Fortas, writing the majority opinion, was careful and clear to point out: "The problem posed by the present case does not relate to regulation of the length of skirts or the type of clothing, to hair style, or deportment." His use of the phrase "the present case" left open the possibility that such regulations might also face a constitutional test. Justice Hugo Black, in his dissent, worried that "if the time has come when pupils of state-supported schools, kindergartens, grammar schools, or high schools, can defy and flout orders of school officials to keep their minds on their own schoolwork, it is the beginning of a new revolutionary era of permissiveness in this country fostered by the judiciary."

Tinker v. Des Moines did not open the door to riots in the schools, but it did open the floodgates on dress code cases. Students, their families, and attorneys saw an opportunity to broaden the narrow ruling, and administrators and school boards saw in the majority opinion some additional justification for school rules. The justices had agreed that freedom of speech was not unlimited and could be restricted out of concern for public safety or serious disruption. With this clearly in mind, dress code defenders increasingly cited the need to avoid "disruption" in their schools as a reason why outlandish or unusual hairstyles and clothing should be banned. The nature of these alleged disruptions ranged from amusing to disturbing. Teachers testified that the longhaired students distracted their classmates by "primping" or "flipping their hair." There were also numerous accounts of violent encounters between "shorthairs" and "longhairs," which are similar to the forced haircut story that surfaced during the 2012 presidential campaign, in which a teenage Mitt Romney and a few friends had pinned down a longhaired classmate and cut his hair.[16] In nearly all of the examples of violent disruption, the shorthaired students were the aggressors and the schools had failed to discipline students who harassed longhaired classmates. In a few cases they found that teachers had initiated the harassment by singling out longhaired students for criticism. Rather than punishing the harassed students, one judge noted, "We are inclined to think that faculty leadership in promoting and enforcing an attitude of tolerance rather than one of suppression or derision would obviate the relatively minor disruptions which have occurred."[17]

It was not just the rationales in the court decisions that were confusing the issue: the many defendants, plaintiffs, and witnesses expressed the multitude of reactions people experienced with regard to long hair. The courts also raised the question of whether the rules themselves were a source of disruption:

> It is contended that disruption is caused by the very fact of disobedience to a school rule, whatever the content of the rule may be. If so, this consideration lends no support to the necessity for, or the rationality of, the rule itself. If the rule itself is unnecessary, those who promulgate it must accept the consequences of its violation.[18]

> There is some uncertainty in our minds as to whether problems of behavior and discipline necessitated the dress code or whether the enforcement of the dress code merely contributed to the problems of behavior and discipline.[19]

This belief was underscored in *Independent School District v. Swanson* (1976) by the testimony an administrator from neighboring district who testified that his own district had abandoned dress codes because enforcement efforts had reduced schools to a "police state," which was disruptive to education.[20]

Another argument that was popular with the school boards was the connection between long hair and other negative behaviors. The problem was that there was not always a correlation—some of the longhaired students were honor students or star athletes—and even when a longhaired student was chronically absent or tardy or had poor grades, there was no guarantee that a haircut would resolve the issue. Arguments based on hygiene or safety were quickly knocked down, because girls also had long hair and were allowed to participate in labs and sports as long as they took sensible precautions. If girls could tie their hair back around Bunsen burners, so could boys.

By the early 1970s the outcome of any particular case depended on the language of the dress restrictions themselves and the testimony of witnesses, not on case law and precedent. Some of the dress codes were laughably vague; at a time when fashions were changing so rapidly, what exactly differentiated "extreme" from "conventional" hairstyles? When the offending haircut of a high school student was shorter than that worn by teachers from his own school, judges were quick to take note.[21]

The most common counterargument advanced by the schools was also the most difficult to support with actual evidence: that long hair was associated with delinquency or antisocial behavior. The testimony of dozens of administrators in these cases comprises a composite stereotype of "longhairs" that grew weaker as long hair became more common, less unkempt, and more acceptable to the wider public. The judge in Thomas Breen's case expressed his skepticism of the claims of the principal regarding the meaning of long hair on boys:

> In apparent seriousness he testifies: that "extreme hair styling" on boys especially "symbolizes something that I feel is not in the best interests of good citizenship"; that "whenever I see a longhaired youngster he is usually leading a riot, he has gotten through committing a crime, he

is a dope addict or some such thing"; that "anyone who wears abnormally long hair, to the decent citizenry, immediately reflects a symbol that we feel is trying to disrupt everything we are trying to build up and by we I mean God-fearing Americans"; that the students at his high school share his opinion "that long hair symbolizes revolution, crime, and dope addiction"; that in his opinion "wearing long hair is un-American" in this day and age; and that its symbolism renders long hair a distraction.[22]

School superintendent Dr. Raymond O. Shelton of Hillsborough (Florida) County Schools testified that in his experience "there is a direct relationship between appearance, an extreme deviant appearance, and conduct, and behavior." He also believed studies had shown that such persons tended to underachieve, although he was unable to cite any such studies.[23] In the case of *Howell v. Wolf,* in Marietta, Georgia (1971), administrators reported a lengthy list of undesirable traits associated with long hair:

> [Unkempt boys] generally contributed to disruptive activities in the school, were constantly tardy and had a greater percentage of absenteeism than other students. They were generally poorer students and were not well prepared for classroom work. They often combed and shook their hair in class and would play "peek-a-boo" through the long hair hanging over their face, all of which was disruptive to other students and teachers. They would gather as a group in one corner of the class, talk among themselves and often sleep. They had even eaten candy and popcorn and consumed soft drinks during class.[24]

In *Lambert v. Marushi* teacher Charles Cassell offered his opinion that long hair and unusual dress made students appear "arrogant and overbearing." Like many others with similar opinions, he was unable to cite an instance where long hair had actually been a disruption, other than occasional clashes between students, which were usually initiated by shorthaired boys.[25]

U.S. District Court Judge James B. Parsons, in his opinion siding with David Miller in his refusal to conform to school hair rules, points out,

It must be made clear from the outset that this is not a case involving a revolutionary type young man, who by bizarre attire, filth of body and clothes, obscene language and subversive-like organizational activity, seeks to wage war against the established institutions of the community or nation. It is not a case involving youth commonly referred to as "beatniks" or "hippies" or "yippies." It is simply a case of a seventeen year old boy wearing hair substantially longer than that permitted by the school's regulations.[26]

While the first few media reports attempted to cast long hair cases in schools as light, trivial news stories, the number of cases and the rhetoric used on both sides reveals that serious ideological differences were involved. These differences only deepened as the controversy spread and escalated. For the longhaired boys and their allies, the right to have long hair was just one front on the struggle for individual expression. The issue wasn't a trivial matter of hair and clothes, but the right to self-expression or to live one's private life as one pleased. It was no small matter to take a school system to court, not to mention moving up the chain of the judicial system. The plaintiffs deeply believed that they were in the right, that their personal choice of grooming and dress were protected by the Constitution, and that the school administration thus had no authority to dictate their appearance or to discriminate against people whose appearance they did not like. The defendants in these cases were equally convinced that longhaired students presented a dangerous defiance, a threat of anarchy.

Just as school regulations initially made no reference to boys' hair length, trousers had often been absent from lists of prohibitions for girls. Both trends caught the authorities unaware. In the case of girls' clothing there had been rules about skirt length and dress styles, which were interpreted later to mean proscribing pants when girls began to demand to be allowed to wear them. By the late 1960s pants were added to the list of explicitly forbidden items in most school systems. The language in the dress code for the Laurel Highlands School District in western Pennsylvania was typical in its vagueness:

Neat and conventional skirts and sweaters, skirts and blouses, or school dresses are required. Hemlines should not be too short, nor clothing too tight. Slacks and shorts are not to be worn unless specifically permitted for special occasions. Attractive hair styles, appropriate makeup, and a minimum of jewelry are suggested.[27]

It is no coincidence that the earliest court cases related to female students' wearing pants date to 1969, when miniskirts had reached their shortest length. Several of the dress codes specified skirt lengths that seem rather short if the objective was modesty: four inches above the knee (*Miller v. Gillis*, 1969), mid-thigh (*Carter v. Hodges*, 1970), and six inches above the knee (*Wallace v. Ford*, 1972). As was pointed out in every case, trousers could not possibly be considered more distracting or immodest than a miniskirt; in one instance the dress code had been modified just before the school year began because no skirts or dresses long enough to meet the requirement could be found in the local stores. Faced with a choice between immodesty and informality, informality won.

As the 1970s wore on, dress codes became more detailed and, not surprisingly, more difficult to enforce. Rather than simply allowing girls to wear pants and leaving the specific style up to them, some school systems found that if they allowed culottes (a divided skirt), a girl would show up in a jumpsuit with wide legs, arguing that it was no different from long culottes. The Perryville, Arkansas, school district agreed to permit jeans made for girls on the condition that if they had a front zipper it must be concealed by a tunic or square-tailed blouse. This particular school district admitted to having difficulty interpreting its own dress code, having sent girls home for wearing a midi-skirt (six inches below the knee), a knickers suit (a suit with knee-length gathered trousers), and a jumpsuit while admitting the outfits had caused no classroom disruption and were not immodest in any way.

The Civil Rights Act of 1964 was written to guarantee access to education, employment, and public accommodation and is associated in most Americans' minds with the end of racial segregation and discrimination. So what does it have to do with white boys wearing long hair? At first not very much. But with the help of the ACLU, attorneys for the plaintiffs in long hair cases made the connection almost immediately, arguing that

Which is more modest, dress or pants? (Circa 1970). Butterick B5817.
Image courtesy of the McCall Pattern Company, 2014.

minors—a group not explicitly included in the law—had the same civil
rights as adults. The basic question, appearing over and over in the case
law, was whether schools have the authority to limit the rights of minor
students (in the 1960s the age of majority was twenty-one, explaining
why a few of these cases included college dress codes).

The school systems first justified dress codes by simply asserting their
authority to set institutional rules, and for a few years that argument was

successful. But beginning in 1969 attorneys for the students began to cite *Griswold v. Connecticut* (the landmark Supreme Court case that established the "right to privacy") to counter the schools' "because I said so" argument. The first case to connect *Griswold* and appearance made its argument in this manner:

> The right of privacy is a fundamental personal right, emanating from the totality of the constitutional scheme under which we live. The hairstyle of a person falls within the right of privacy which protects his beliefs, thoughts, emotions and sensations, and the board of education has no legal ground to proscribe the hairstyle of a pupil when the board interferes with his right to self-expression in the styling of his hair. His right to style his hair as he pleases falls within the penumbra of the constitution which protects his right of privacy and his right to be free from intrusion by the government.[28]

Judging from their dogged pursuit of the issue, the ACLU clearly also believed that dress codes violated the First Amendment by limiting a students' freedom of expression. In several cases local ACLU attorneys contacted students who had been suspended from school for dress code violations, offering their support soon after the stories appeared in the papers. Within a year or two long hair had made the transition from a popular teen fad to an iconic emblem of rebellion, nonconformity, and protest. Journalist Daniel Zwerdling, then a sophomore at the University of Michigan, noted the shift in meaning in a very prescient editorial published in November 1968. Arguing that the attention to hair and appearance was diverting attention from more serious issues, he pointed out that most young men grow long hair and beards, "imagining what the pretty girl in class will say," not as a political statement. The overreaction of authority figures only served to create the very defiance they imagined when they saw the long hair and beards. At a time when the United States was waging both a Cold War against the spread of communism and a real war purportedly to defend democracy in Southeast Asia, the establishment's reaction also exposed the hypocrisy of "railing against totalitarianism and insisting on conformity."[29] From my vantage point in the early twenty-first century, 1968 seems to be an excellent candidate for the year that long hair went from minor irritant to "freak flag." The evening news was scary; against the backdrop of an escalating Vietnam War and attempted revolution in Czechoslovakia against the Soviet Union, student protest culture had spread from Europe to major universities in the United States. The emerging Black Power movement, impatient with slow progress and obstructionism in resolving inequality, made whites uneasy and opened a generation gap in African American homes. When Martin Luther King Jr. and Robert F. Kennedy were assassinated within months of each other, it seemed the year could not get worse, but it was only half over. The riots following the King assassination and the violent confrontations between police and demonstrators outside the Democratic National Convention in August helped "law and order" candidate Richard M. Nixon win the presidency. Small wonder that any tendency to nonconformity, including looking like a hippie or a Black Panther (even superficially), was perceived with alarm and greeted with hostility.

Workplace dress code cases were far less numerous than school cases and appeared later. Between 1971 and 1979 there were twenty-nine rulings on dress codes in the workplace, all but three concerning men's hair or facial hair. Unlike the even split in the school-related decisions, the courts ruled in favor of the employer twice as often as the worker when it came to workplace decisions. One striking aspect of these conflicts is class: most of the employees were lower-level clerical, service, or blue-collar workers.

Many of the long hair cases in workplaces came directly from the passage of Title VII of the Civil Rights Act of 1964, which banned discrimination in employment. Section 703(a) of the act provides:

> It shall be an unlawful employment practice for an employer—
>
> (1) to fail or refuse to hire or to discharge any individual with respect to his compensation, terms, conditions, or privileges of employment because of an individual's race, color, religion, sex, or national origin; or
>
> (2) to limit, segregate, or classify his employees or applicants for employment in any way which would deprive or tend to deprive any individual of employment opportunities or otherwise adversely affect his status as an employee, because of such individual's race, color, religion, sex, or national origin.[30]

The plaintiffs in these cases argued that restrictions on men's hair length or women's wearing slacks were a form of sex discrimination. This ended up being a surprisingly thorny issue, since employers had always seen the need to impose grooming standards either for safety or other reasons, but now found themselves having to reconsider those standards in a more inclusive workplace.

It is deliciously ironic that all of this fuss was created over sex discrimination as a result of Title VII. Sex as a prohibited criteria for employment practice was added by Southern Democrats as a "poison pill" designed to block the passage of the act—unsuccessfully, as it turned out. In many of the sex discrimination cases where it was alleged that a person's appearance had led to not being hired, the court relied on the regulations developed by the Equal Employment Opportunity Commission (EEOC) to help them navigate exceptions. The problem lay in the meaning of the words "bona fide occupational qualification," or BFOQ, meaning skills or attributes that are not considered illegal hiring standards if they are a legitimate requirement of the job. (For example, the ability to lift fifty pounds is a BFOQ for a furniture mover but not for a bank teller.) The EEOC recommends that the BFOQ exception be applied narrowly and that it be used to specifically prohibit a refusal to hire based on stereotyped characterizations of the sexes, or because the preferences of coworkers, employers, clients, or customers favor one sex or another. Probably the most prominent case of this was in the 1972 Fifth Circuit Court decision on *Diaz v. Pan American World Airways Inc.* The airline had refused to hire male flight attendants, claiming their customers preferred females. The airline attempted to justify the restriction because the airplane cabin was a "unique environment in which the psychological needs of the passengers are better attended to by females." Pan American lost.[31]

There's an interesting relationship between business dress codes and the public. In *Fagan v. National Cash Register* (1973) the court noted that the company's grooming policy had been initiated because of specific customer complaints about the personal appearance of employees. Just as employers could require that employees wear certain uniforms and had the right to package their products and services in the most attractive way possible, the court reasoned, they should also have the right to "package" their employees through the use of dress standards.[32] So in *Diaz v. Pan American,* while the airline could not discriminate against male applicants for the job of flight attendant even if females might be more appealing to the traveling public, the court did not say that stewards and stewardesses would have to be "packaged" by dressing alike. Requiring all flight attendants to wear skirts and have shoulder-length hair would not meet the standards of a BFOQ.

As with the school cases, the plaintiffs in workplace dress code cases sincerely believed that barring men from wearing long hair and women from wearing slacks were forms of discrimination based on sex. Where the courts agreed, they relied on the EEOC guidelines and held the employers to a fairly strict standard in determining if the dress code distinctions reflected a "bona fide occupational qualification." In *Willingham v. Macon Telegraph Publishing Co.* (1975), a male employee was fired for his failure to get a haircut. He was processing food, and workplace policy required male employees to wear hats and females to wear hairnets. When Willingham's hair grew too long to be covered by the hat, he asked if he could wear a hairnet. His request was denied, and he was subsequently fired because he wasn't abiding by the dress code. The court found that the regulation was not purely for sanitation purposes, since contamination could be prevented by having men's hair contained within a hairnet, so the insistence that men wear hats instead of hairnets was based on grounds other than sanitation. Decision for the plaintiff.[33]

In the case of *Donohue v. Shoe Corporation of America* (1972), a shoe store salesman was held to have been discriminated against on the basis of sex because he was fired for having long hair when his employers did not have the same requirements for saleswomen. The court was fairly strong in condemning the discrimination based on hair length, arguing the following:

> In our society we too often form opinions of people on the basis of skin color, religion, national origin, style of dress, hair length, and other superficial features. The tendency to stereotype people is at the root of some of the social ills that afflict the country and in adopting the Civil Rights Act of 1964, Congress intended to attack the stereotyped characterizations of the people would be judged by their intrinsic worth.[34]

In *Aros v. McDonnell Douglas Corporation* (1972), the court ruled similarly, saying, "The issue of long hair on men tends to arouse the passions of many in our society today. In that regard the issue is no different from the issues of race, color, religion, national origin, and equal employment rights for women."[35]

Opposing arguments often engaged in thought experiments that revealed much about the attorneys' attitudes. For example,

> [If] an employer required all employees to wear their hair in ponytail style, or required all employees to wear dresses, it could not be said that different standards were being applied to men and women. It seems obvious, however, that such requirements would discriminate in operation against male applicants and so would be prohibited. This illustration emphasizes the fact that Title VII should not logically be viewed to require males and females to be governed by identical appearance codes.[36]

Other judges ruled that if the plaintiff says his way of dressing is "expressing himself" or "doing his own thing," then style of dress and grooming is an extension of his personality, which they separated from gender identity. Put this way, the rule would have nothing to do with sexual bias, and "refusing to hire a longhaired male is merely avoiding a personality conflict between employer and applicant."[37] Employers were well within their rights, most of the courts agreed, in establishing dress codes to enforce a pleasing, uniform appearance as long as the rules did not prevent a class of people (men, women, African Americans) from being able to gain employment.

The evolution of the civil rights movement into the Black Power movement in the late 1960s further complicated questions of gender-appropriate grooming by intersecting them with expressions of racial identity. The popularity of the Afro hairstyle had little impact at the high school level, since the dress codes usually defined the proper hair length in terms of where it reached around the ears and collar. The Afro style made a much bigger stir in the military, though only very briefly. In 1969 airman August Doyle was court-martialed for disobeying an order to cut his Afro and was sentenced to three months of hard labor, fined sixty dollars a month during that time, and demoted. By the time he was released, however, the regulations had been relaxed.[38] African American women opting for Afros also experienced criticism and discrimination, as in the case of stewardess Deborah Renwick, who thought her three-inch natural style conformed to the United Air Lines requirement for short hair. The airline grounded her, and she agreed to trim her hair to just two inches, but she was still dismissed. Eventually, like Airman Doyle, she won: outraged black leaders and professionals organized a boycott and she sued the airline for a million dollars. United Air Lines backed off, offered to rehire her with back pay and a cash settlement, and agreed to revise its grooming guidelines to be more inclusive.[39]

The cases involving African American plaintiffs offer particularly rich insights into interaction between gender and other factors as cultural constructions and social realities. Since the 1970s the case law involving dress codes has been disproportionately dominated by attempts by school or workplace authorities to control the appearance of people of color or members of minority religions. Few as they are, the very earliest cases reveal the constriction of available options for racial and other minorities and the increasing likelihood that their transgressions will be punished more severely.

The complete text of Title IX of the Education Amendments Act of 1972 reads,

> No person in the United States shall, on the basis of sex, be excluded from participation in, be denied the benefits of or be subjected to discrimination under any education program or activity receiving Federal financial assistance.[40]

The passage of Title IX is largely remembered today for improving access to sports for girls and women. But Title IX was also used, along with the Fourteenth Amendment, to support boys' claims that regulations on hair length discriminated against them by treating them differently from girls. Many of these cases were decided by the Civil Rights Division of the Department of Health, Education, and Welfare (HEW) and later the Department of Education rather than through the courts. The first court case to be decided on this basis was *Jacobs v. Benedict* (1972) in the Ohio

Appellate Court. The sex discrimination argument essentially eliminated the "safety" defense for banning long hair on male students. It is clear
from some of the testimony that the authorities had initially thought that
requiring boys to wear hairnets or to tie their hair in ponytails would
shame them into getting haircuts, only to find, to their chagrin, the boys
had no objection to those accommodations.[41] But the Title IX argument
was not always persuasive, especially in more conservative courts; in
Trent v. Perritt the Fifth District Court reasoned that the law and the proposed HEW guidelines about gender discrimination that were being cir-
culated did "not require that the recipient erase all differences" between
boys and girls, and that requiring boys—but not girls—to have short hair
was not discriminatory.[42] In the long run the arguments against long hair
were defeated indirectly; because Title IX opened home economics and
shop classes to all students, the real requirements of safety and sanitation prevailed. In these settings all longhaired students regardless of sex
needed to keep their hair under control by any means, including ponytails, hairnets, or bobby pins.

The military academies offered a different challenge under Title IX,
because their dress codes—uniform clothing and grooming standards—
were originally designed only for men. When the U.S. Military Academy at West Point admitted the first women in 1975, there was a flurry
of attention in the press as to what they would wear and how their hair
would be cut. The academy's administration had worried publicly that
women would not fit in, being unprepared for the discipline or the tough
standards of West Point. But once the female students were accepted,
the school held a fashion show to show how the classic uniform would
be adapted. Their hair would be a short bob, not completely shorn, and
women cadets would be issued purses. (This was necessary because the
women's uniform had six fewer pockets than the male version.) They
would also wear bras, the school reported reassuringly. Instead of the
tailcoat, the dress uniform jacket was modified to be straight in the back
and worn with a knee-length skirt, not trousers.[43]

Title IX did have an impact on athletic clothing; predictably, it was
quite different for boys and girls. For male student athletes it could be
used to battle team dress codes requiring short hair and conserva-

tive dress. Uniformity and discipline were especially valued by athletic coaches, who were often the last holdouts, requiring athletes in football, tennis, and other sports to adhere to restrictive dress codes even when the rest of the students at the school were exempt. There was a rash of coach resignations in the early 1970s at both the high school and college level, with some coaches taking a dim view of the schools overriding their authority. The athletic director at a San Francisco–area high school predicted darkly, "This is the beginning of the end of all athletics."[44] Having so many professional and Olympic athletes dress contrary to school standards was also a blow to these restrictions. In every sport, students could point to examples of outstanding athletes with long hair, mustaches, and flashy personal wardrobes.

The situation for female athletes had been so appalling before Title IX that the immediate effects were not so much in terms of style as simple access. Even at wealthy schools, girls' teams made do with old uniforms while the boys' teams got new ones every year. Many girls' sports did not have uniforms at all, much less warm-up suits and team footwear. Instead, they wore the same one-piece gym suits used for physical education. By requiring that teams have equal access to funding, Title IX ensured that girls' and women's teams were properly equipped for the first time. This had a ripple effect in the active sportswear market in the years and decades to come, as the number of women who had played sports in school jumped into the millions, many of them continuing to participate and complete long after graduation.

The legal battles prove two things: personal decisions about appearance are far from trivial matters, and the establishment dearly wanted to control the emerging culture. The role of gender norms in the long hair controversy was very different for men and women. The court decisions tended to skitter around the direct question of gender roles, preferring instead to emphasize the schools' demand for order and discipline. Even this emphasis was gendered: the testimony of the authorities expressed a conviction that conformity and submission to rules is especially necessary for boys and young men. The dress codes themselves reinforced this distinction. Girls' dress codes placed a premium on modesty; boys' regulations were more likely to mention "conventional" standards. The

Perryville, Arkansas, administrator in *Wallace v. Ford* testified that the objective of the codes was to prevent girls from wearing "revealing or seductive" clothing and boys from wearing "bizarre" clothing.[45] West Point admissions officer Col. Manley Rogers was concerned that newly admitted female cadets were not ready for the rigors of the academy because, "You tell a 12-year-old boy about the need for discipline and tough training and he will understand; the girls have not been conditioned in that way."[46]

For boys and men the dominant expectation was that males, especially those in subordinate positions, should respect and follow authority. Aspersions on their masculinity, such as the common suggestion that "you can't tell boys from the girls," were patently false but nevertheless used as a method of coercion and control, in an attempt to shame a shaggy-haired boy into compliance. My own reaction to hearing the phrase was amusement: it marked the commentator as an uncool, unhip square. My male peers were similarly unimpressed. When science teachers required them to wear hairnets in labs, the boys shrugged and donned the hairnets. At the restaurant where I worked after college, the male servers—all members of the same rock band—complied with regulations by wearing matching shorthair wigs and thought the whole fuss was pretty amusing.

There were clearly times when disapproval escalated to physical violence. Anti–long hair sentiment seems to have run especially high among football players, who appeared regularly as the antagonists in harassment and forced-haircut anecdotes. How much of this was the result of locker room and sideline rhetoric that accused boys of being "sissies" or "faggots" if they did not meet expectations? A North Shore Junior High School football coach, in an article in the Texas High School Coaches Association magazine, said that coaches should ban "individuals that look like females," noting that long hair is "the sign of a sissy."[47] It took high-profile examples to counter these stereotypes; Olympic swimmer Mark Spitz is credited with breaking the long hair barrier for many athletes, probably in part because of the popularity of his door-size poster among young women. While the shorthair establishment tried to frame the issue as masculinity versus effeminacy, young men reframed it as "new man versus old man."

NPG.80.328
Mark Spitz

Olympic swimmer Mark Spitz, 1972.
National Portrait Gallery, Smithsonian Institution/Art Resource, New York.

Girls who violated dress codes were usually just sent home to change or actually given a change of clothes to wear, but they seldom faced suspension or expulsion, even for repeated violations. Boys were threatened with more serious consequences. It could be argued that clothes were easier to change than hair, but the disparity in the number of legal cases and the severity of the punishments suggest that the real underlying issue was resistance to authority. One measure of the importance of conformity and submission to authority in postwar masculinity is the narrow range of styles available to men and boys. The institutional reaction to nonconformity, as seen in the dozens of hair cases, is even more powerful evidence.

Besides concerns about female modesty and male compliance, the main objection to both male and female fashions of the late 1960s was that they were too casual. That was clearly the problem with girls wearing pants to school or women wearing them in the workplace. It was also the objection raised to jeans in general. The same rising tide that eliminated hats and white gloves had also swept away the barriers between clothing for work and leisure. The sense that the social fabric was loosening elicited different reactions from different people. Some found the new standards not just more comfortable but a sign of greater individual freedom of expression and thought. To others it marked the decline of civility and social standards that had provided a different kind of "comfort"—the assurance that stems from a society regulated by clear rules and standards.

Note that I resisted the temptation to associate these perspectives with particular age groups. If this had been a truly generational battle, there would be no culture wars today. The baby boomers would have won simply by outliving the opposition. But the many examples of conflict, even violent confrontation, between shorthaired and longhaired students suggest otherwise. Adults who defended men's right to wear long hair found themselves characterized as either heroes or traitors. Consider the case of new headmaster Robert Thomason at Horace Mann, an all-male private school in New York, who announced the suspension of the dress code to a standing ovation from the 545 students at a school assembly, but then faced opposition from parents and alumni.[48]

In the end all of the Sturm und Drang over appearance ended in a stalemate, on the national level. The U.S. Supreme Court refused to hear dress code challenges again and again, in 1968 (*Ferrell v. Dallas*), 1969 (*Breen v. Kahl*), 1970 (*Jackson v. Dorrier*), 1971 (*Swanquist v. Livingston, King v. Saddleback*), 1972 (*Olff v. East, Freeman v. Flake*), and 1973 (*Lansdale v. Tyler, Karr v. Schmidt, New Rider v. Board*).[49] The most eloquent defender of the civil libertarian side came from Justice William O. Douglas, who dissented from the denial of certiorari in nearly every case and thought the court should have heard the cases. Writing in his 1968 *Ferrell v. Dallas* opinion that a nation founded on the Declaration of Independence should allow "idiosyncrasies to flourish, especially when they concern the image of one's personality and his philosophy toward government and his fellow man," Douglas added,

> Municipalities furnish many services to their inhabitants, and I have supposed that it would be an invidious discrimination to withhold fire protection, police protection, garbage collection, health protection and the like merely because a person was an offbeat, nonconformist when it came to hairdo and dress as well as to diet, race, religion, or his views on Vietnam.[50]

In his 1971 *Freeman v. Flake* dissent, Justice Douglas noted, "Eight circuits have passed on the question. On widely disparate rationales, four have upheld school hair regulations . . . and four have struck them down," which he believed to be a compelling reason why the Supreme Court should take up the case.[51] Instead, the highest court let the widely divergent case law in each circuit set the precedent for their respective regions. Across the nation people on both sides believed they had won when in fact the basic conflict between personal expression and community standards has never been resolved.

The Culture Wars, Then and Now

6

It has been over fifty years since the confluence of youth culture, sexual revolution, and civil rights activism set the culture wars in motion. Judging by the present state of affairs, it may be another half century before the many questions raised in the 1960s are finally resolved. I wrote the bulk of this book in 2013, a year punctuated with important fiftieth-anniversary observations. The year 1963 was a watershed. It was the year that brought us the Beatles, *The Feminine Mystique,* the Great March on Washington, and the Kennedy assassination. The teenagers of 1963 are in their sixties now but still arguing about many of the same contentious issues that have occupied us since junior high. Commentators originally attributed the rifts in our society to the perennial conflict between youth and age, but the generation gap has faded with the passing of our own grandparents and parents. To paraphrase Pogo, we have met the culture warriors and they are us.

In the preceding chapters I have described the major battlegrounds as revealed through dress. In this chapter I use the same lens to examine what our current gender controversies and quandaries owe to the unfinished business of the sexual revolution. Finally, I ponder what may lie ahead.

The civil rights battles of the 1960s were not new nor were they just about race. They were the result of struggles dating back to the earliest years of European colonization. The ideal of equality, articulated in the Declaration of Independence, has a long, contentious history of claims by different classes, races, and nationalities, believers, and nonbelievers. Our country's history has been one of gradual expansion of civil rights, though not without tensions, resistance, and conflict. It also includes women, gays, lesbians, and, most recently, transpeople. To claim that the principles of equality and civil rights cannot be linked to sex, gender, or sexuality, particularly since the 1960s, is disingenuous and false.

The rise of second-wave feminism was certainly connected to the larger civil rights movement, sometimes in solidarity but frequently in tension fueled by the perspectives and agendas of women of different races and classes. Mix in the sexual revolution, timed to coincide with the adolescence of a demographic wave of unprecedented size and affluence, and the stage was set for cultural upheaval. Beginning in the mid-1960s all of the questions and tensions surrounding gender and sexuality were played out among factions that may seem to have been well defined. Closer examination reveals that individuals within those factions varied considerably, and movement between positions was more fluid, especially in the beginning. Dress continues to be a valuable lens for making identity-based conflict visible, because it is so intimately tied to our public and private selves. Fashion provides a means of keeping up with kaleidoscopic change. This project has focused on gender identities and expression, but there is also endless opportunity for other researchers to use the same approach to examine race, age, and other dimensions of difference and connection.

In our consumer society the marketplace is where most of us must go to literally materialize our lives. Clothing and accessory manufacturers can't provide every possible variation or every color in the visible spectrum. They restrict themselves to their own best guesses as to what will profit them. Whether we feel comfortable or uncomfortable in current trends depends on how well we fit the composite customer in the manufacturer's imagination. Advertising and branding are designed to help us envision ourselves as that imaginary consumer. If you experience no friction between your desires and the ideal lifestyles depicted in popular media, you are likely to be satisfied with the available options. If you do not see yourself in the glossy ads or share in the fantasies they promote, you are more inclined to notice the places where our culture chafes. In the late 1960s and early 1970s the instability and variety of popular styles meant consumers had an unprecedented opportunity to match their outsides to their insides, or their lifestyles to their lives. This may have been exhilarating to young consumers, who were eager to try on new looks and identities, but manufacturers and retailers were less happy. From season to season they gambled on trends ranging from Nehru jackets and turtle-necks to polyester double knits and designer jeans. Some of these inno-vations reflected permanent changes in cultural patterns; others turned out to be short-lived fads. The fads, particularly the most popular ones, should no more be dismissed as trivial than should major shifts such as the acceptance of trousers for women or the mainstreaming of jeans. All of them represented possibilities that seemed plausible to someone, at some point.

The sexual revolution and the women's liberation movement affected people of all ages across the spectrums of gender identity and sexual ori-entation. After all, so much of the way sex and gender are conceived and expressed in our culture is in terms of relationships between opposites or complements. Without a commonly understood gender binary, there can be no unisex or androgyny. Advocates for cultural change recognize this, and so do those who oppose any alteration in traditional gender roles or sexual mores.

In the battle between second-wave feminists and antifeminists in the 1970s, the conservatives were by far more organized and, ultimately, more successful, slowing down the political and economic progress that were the primary goals of second-wave feminism. If there was a moment when the wind shifted, it was at the November 1977 National Women's Confer-ence in Houston. Gloria Steinem claimed that the gathering would be a constitutional convention for American women, a setting for consolidat-ing their demands for political and economic equality. The conference program lists the group's demands, including steps to move women into positions of power and influence. The conference also planned to recom-mend that the federal government assume a major role in providing "bias-free nonsexist quality child care."[1] That was what was *supposed* to happen. Instead, antifeminists took over the nominating process for the Houston conference. Conservative leader Phyllis Schlafly organized busloads of women opposed to the ERA who registered on voting day, elected a con-servative delegation, and then left. By the time everyone got to Houston, antifeminist women controlled about 20 percent of the seats at the con-

ference. Throughout the three-day conference there were pro-family rallies across the city attracting attention and distracting from the business
of the meeting. "Houston will finish off the women's movement," Schlafly
said. "It will show them off for the radical anti-family pro-lesbian people
they are."[2] While it was not the end of the women's movement, the 1977
conference marked the high mark of progress on many feminist initia-
tives. They were able to win a three-year extension of the deadline for ratification of the ERA but not much else, and the ERA failed to reach ratification by 1982. As sociologist Philip Cohen has pointed out, the growth in
women's employment rates stalled in the 1990s, especially those of married women with young children.[3]

But Schlafly and antifeminist conservatives were not alone in their ob-
jections to the direction of cultural change. There were fissures and factions within the women's movement as well. Although right-wing pundits
have been depicting feminists as a single bloc for years, feminists from
the very beginning varied widely in their interests and arguments and did
not agree on objective or tactics. Cultural feminists, for example, sought
to elevate what they perceived as women's unique capacities. For cultural
feminists the problem with the gender binary was the power structure,
not the categories. It was possible to embrace motherhood and equality;
women in power would bring a "feminine essence" to balance masculine
tendencies. Liberal feminists emphasized political and legal reform such
as reproductive and abortion rights, while radical feminists argued that
significant change required changes to the root of the problem, identified as oppressive patriarchal social structures. Many black feminists
objected to the assumption that race could be disentangled from gender
and class and criticized much of the liberal and cultural feminist agendas as narrow and elitist.[4] Between internal and external criticism of the
women's movement, it is not surprising that progress has been slow over
the past fifty years. Examining the fashions of the 1960s and '70s provides
some insight into what the larger public was experiencing beyond the activists on the front lines.

For at least the past two and a half centuries, men's and women's clothing has been growing farther apart visually, even as women gained access
to higher education and the franchise. Though baby and toddler clothing

lagged behind this slow wave of gendering, even this last category of dress has divided more and more sharply into masculine and feminine styles. Scholars have been trying to explain this trend for more than a century from dozens of disciplinary perspectives. Until we are locked in one room and forced to arrive at a unified theory of gender expression, there won't be a definitive answer to why clothing styles persist in being gendered as male or female, even in the face of increasing economic, social, and political equality. For now, here is my best attempt: this pattern parallels the rise of individualism and of a culture that ties identity to consumption. Sex is one of our most basic identifiers, and until just recently it has been understood as a very clear binary. This pattern extended to individuals whose appearance or behavior did not fit into either category, who were commonly described in binary terms (effeminate gays, mannish lesbians, "shemales," and so on), and were considered at best abnormal and at worst immoral. Mainstream fashion reflected that underlying model and served as a vehicle for expressing one's individuality within well-established rules for masculinity or femininity, as appropriate—that is, until the 1960s.

Consider again the environmental science concept of punctuated equilibrium, which posits an evolutionary process of periods of dramatic change followed by periods of recovery, allowing for ecological adjustment. I believe the cultural equivalent of punctuated equilibrium is evident in the 1960s and '70s. After a short, anxious period of dizzying change around 1966–1969, the early 1970s ushered in a revival of classic styling, nostalgic escapism, and a superficial truce in the gender wars. For some there was a sense that progress had been made; women were making gains in the workplace, sports, and higher education, and gays and lesbians were living more open lives, especially in politically liberal parts of the country. But in more conservative quarters, those who were uncomfortable or hostile to gender equity and gay rights, sensing that progress had been stretched to the limit, continued their efforts to organize resistance and rebuild barriers. The study of dress since the late 1970s suggests that the tide of liberation was receding, and until just recently there were signs that we have settled back into a more gendered and restrictive status quo. Rather than see this pattern as cyclical, I see it as evidence that we are still working through the questions raised fifty years ago as individuals and as a society.

Adults now in their forties, who were children during the early years of the gender revolution, have played an important role in the gendering of children's clothing in the 1980s and 1990s. Raised on *Free to Be . . . You and Me* and *William's Doll*, these older Generation Xers traded their own neutral fashions in a nostalgic return to "classic" styles as they entered adolescence and then adulthood in the late 1970s and early '80s. As they became parents they began to influence baby clothing. Between 1980 and 1990 the proportion of births to first-time parents shifted from baby boomers and Generation Xers; the availability of neutral styles for infants plummeted between 1984 and 1986 and has stayed low until very recently.[5] The 1970s girl who had worn plain corduroy overalls over a striped turtleneck grew up dressing her own daughter in pastels and ruffles and adding a stretchy headband to the outfit when they went to the mall, just to make sure everyone knew the baby was female. Hair ribbons and barrettes for infants took the children's accessories industry by storm in 1988, signaling the end of unisex in infants' clothing.[6] Across a cross-section of retailers from mass-market catalogs to designer boutiques, infant clothing departments offered more gender-specific styles and fewer neutral options. Even in newborn sizes boys' clothing was not simply blue, but was blue with masculine motifs such as trucks or footballs, and the last traditional "baby" elements, such as round collars and smocking, were eliminated from infant and toddler boys' fashions.

How did this happen? As I explained in chapter 4, it may have initially been a reaction to the experience of wearing unisex styles as children, especially for children whose gender identity was still taking shape or who felt more keenly the deprivation of gendered clothing and toys. (Whether the loudest cries for weapons or Barbies came from tots with strong or weak gender identities, I will leave to the psychologists.) Certainly the connection between cultural environment and gender identity development is far from being understood. When girls began to wear pants to school in the 1970s, there were studies suggesting that girls who wore pants were more active during recess than girls who wore skirts or dresses. Later research introduced a wrinkle: girls who wore pants were perceived by their peers as more active, even when they weren't.[7] The relationship between highly feminized play clothes and girls' freedom to romp and get dirty is still unclear, but we do know that gendered clothing is an effective vehicle for encouraging stereotyped expectations. The more children's clothing has branched into distinctly masculine and feminine styles, and the fewer neutral options there are, the easier it is to attach those same labels to children, even when they are just a few weeks old. This may make it even more challenging for today's young parents and teachers to avoid essentializing children, because gender stereotypes might seem more natural to them.

The sharp gendering of children's clothing has created friction for children who do not fit easily into pink and blue boxes. Every few months there is a new story about a boy who dresses like a girl, a girl who dresses like a boy, or a boy who likes pink nail polish, setting off a new round of claims, counterclaims, and controversy. Many of these stories are told by their parents in clear efforts to challenge prevailing gender norms and to reach out to other parents in similar circumstances. Blogger Sarah Hoffman explained, "I started writing about my son because I don't think there is anything wrong with being a pink boy. I think being pink is just a natural variation of being a human being. I wanted to let other parents, doctors, teachers, and families of pink boys know that there are other pink boys out there—boys who struggle with the same sorts of things, with families who strive to support them in all their sparkly glory."[8]

This is in sharp contrast to the generations of "gender-nonconforming" children, mostly boys, who were quietly taken to therapists. Psychologists and social workers themselves have disagreed in their approach to these children, with some taking the relatively new approach of supporting kids wanting to live openly as members of the opposite sex. Others encourage kids to discard their more pronounced behaviors, explore new interests, and embrace the gender associated with their biological sex. Many therapists take the middle ground by accepting a boy's desire to wear dresses and saying it's fine for him to do so at home, but strongly discouraging him from wearing them to school, where he might encounter unpleasant responses or even bullying.

At the center of the issue is the connection, still not yet completely understood, between gender identity and adult sexual orientation. "I think parents are very worried and confused and there isn't clear-cut advice," says Ellen Perrin, chief of developmental-behavioral pediatrics at the Floating Hospital for Children at Tufts Medical Center in Boston. "It's a complex issue."[9] Parents wonder if their child will someday want sexual reassignment surgery; the answer is probably not. According to years of study, most gender-variant children (between 85 and 90 percent) grow up quite content with their biological sex. Will gender-variant children grow up gay? For boys that is more likely, though still not a sure thing. In contrast only about one-third of gender-variant girls later identify as lesbian or bisexual.[10]

But it's not just parents of gender-variant kids who are trying to break out of the binary. Around the globe, parents are once more attempting to raise ungendered children, and their stories echo the messages of the unisex era. Nearly always there is a loud negative reaction from critics who see them as foolish, misguided, or even abusive. But with every one of these stories, the ranks of defenders increase, many of them children of the 1980s looking for alternatives to highly gendered clothing and toys for their own offspring. As I write this in 2013, there is not only more resistance, including more parents choosing not to know their unborn baby's sex, but there are also more neutral clothing options on the market. Most of the alternatives come from online retailers, many of them small businesses, not the mass merchants of children's fashion. Consumers are also pushing back against gendered toys and books—and winning. When thirteen-year-old McKenna Pope organized a Change.org petition to ask Hasbro for a ungendered version of the classic Easy-Bake Oven, the manufacturer unveiled plans for a black and silver version.[11]

Mainstream women's fashions today show little evidence of the unisex era. The clothing changes that accompanied the women's movement beyond the acceptance of pants were subtle, not revolutionary, and the resilience of beauty culture and "traditional" feminine styling has puzzled many gender scholars. In 1977 John T. Molloy's *Dress for Success for Women* offered a means by which women could secure their places in business and politics. Some of his advice seems antiquated today—his warnings that pants-wearing women might be too threatening to male bosses, for example. But overall Molloy was suggesting only that women pay attention to the rules that men had learned to observe in the workplace: focus on the job, not on the clothes. The themes in his advice for women were little different from his recommendations for men: invest in well-made clothing in classic styles that will last for years; save the flash and fun for leisure. Women's business styles followed the Molloy prescription through the early 1980s and then drifted into familiar old territory. The conflict between women's desire to be taken seriously as students, workers, and athletes and the importance of an attractive appearance was never completely resolved. They followed the current trends in silhouette and skirt length. They incorporated softer fabrics and this season's colors. Suits lost their importance when dresses made a comeback, and the simple blazer suit took a backseat to trendy cuts and fabrics.

Of the three primary strands of advice for women in the early 1960s—from Friedan, Brown, and Andelin—Helen Gurley Brown's vision of sexual liberation seemed to have gained the most traction, as women's clothing, even in the workplace, has continued to focus on physical attraction as the most important element in femininity. The other two philosophies—feminism and antifeminism—have been battling each other for dominance for fifty years, leaving the marketplace clear for what I'll call "cosmofeminism," in honor of Helen Gurley Brown's longtime leadership of *Cosmopolitan*. From an entrepreneurial standpoint, cosmofeminism was the likeliest vehicle for business success. Many second-wave feminists were hostile to fashion, when they considered it at all. Although the stereotypes of hairy-legged, frumpy "women's libbers" are both unfair and false, the truth is that the movement didn't lend itself to commodification, nor did it wish to do so. *Ms.* magazine was no handmaiden to commerce, having refused advertising its publishers considered "insulting or harmful to women" for its first fifteen years and being essentially ad-free since 1991. The conservative antifeminist movement also focused more on political action than on fashion and beauty and, consequently, has had little direct influence on fashion. Ironically, both of these forces helped propel the popularity of cosmofeminist dressing for women and girls, though probably inadvertently. New generations of feminists have reclaimed makeup and high heels along with other feminine elements once rejected by their mothers and grandmothers. In 2013 the *Financial Times* reported that "feminism is back in fashion," quoting current *Cosmopolitan* editor Joanna Coles as an example of the trend: "Probably the most feminist thing I have in my own closet this season are Tamara Mellon's genius, sexy, hugely practical legging boots, which pull on in one easy movement. . . . Women want fashion to keep up with the speed of their lives."[12] Coles, born in that banner year 1963, has not only claimed that *Cosmopolitan* is "deeply feminist" but also that it has done more for women's rights than feminist academics.[13]

Conservative antifeminists see gendered clothing as a natural expression of innate and essential differences between men and women. Although Helen Andelin died in 2009, *Fascinating Womanhood*'s legacy lives on in local club chapters, online classes, and even a Facebook group. The rise of conservative religion has complicated the advice given as observant Christian, Jewish, and Muslim women struggle to balance the demands of modesty and femininity in a consumer culture where sexiness seems so essential in female fashions. In fact concern about the conflation of "feminine" and "sexy" is one point of agreement across the feminist-antifeminist spectrum, especially as it affects girls.

Compared to the fashions of the 1950s and early 1960s, today's clothing for women, including girls in their teens and even younger, is more revealing and more focused on sexual attraction (or objectification, if you prefer). Cleavage, once relegated to beach, ballroom, and boudoir, is visible in classroom and office settings. Dresses and skirts are almost always above the kneecap (sometimes way above), and it is difficult to find women's shorts that are longer than mid-thigh (which probably explains the popularity of cropped pants and capris). To many women the implicit cultural message that they should want to be sexually attractive in every waking moment and every social situation is oppressive. This is felt particularly by women who don't "measure up," by virtue of age, body size, or other media-influenced ideals, who may see images of themselves only in "before" pictures in ads or in reality makeover shows.

I believe that the sexualization of femininity is also connected to the phenomenon of early feminization of girls. It probably wasn't the fathers who first embraced a return to gendered baby clothes in the mid-1980s; it was the same mothers who were buying "romantic" dresses and ruffly blouses for themselves. The Walt Disney Company may have commercialized the princess dress in the late 1990s, but the homemade versions its former chairman Andy Mooney saw at *Disney on Ice* performances inspired the idea.[14] This hyper-gendering of little girls' clothing associated "girly" femininity (ruffles, pastels, flowers, and the rest of the lexicon of softness) with being a little girl, with the result that girls grow out of it and into—well, what?

One vital aspect of children's gender identity in a media-rich consumer culture is that the boys and girls start to influence the market at a very young age. At four and five little girls may clamor for pink and glitter so ardently that parents mistake their demands for innate needs. When their princess enters third or fourth grade and rejects pink, girly styles as "babyish," the parents find themselves fighting a battle over clothing that is too sexy for an eight-year-old. Blogger Suzette Waters observed that her nine-year-old daughter, Anna, left "pink behind" and traded it for blue, purple, and black.[15] According to child development literature, this is a clear sign that Anna had mastered the concept of "gender permanence" and no longer needed to adhere to stereotyped clothing and toys in order to maintain a stable gender identity. The once beloved symbols of femininity looked childish instead, and Anna wanted a more grown-up look.

This phenomenon has attracted a great deal of attention in the last decade, especially since the American Psychological Association published the report of its task force on sexualization of girls in 2010.[16] The report documents the expansion of sexualized media since the 1980s as it reached younger and younger girls and details the already observed consequences, including "cognitive functioning, physical and mental health, sexuality and attitudes and beliefs." As I was writing this chapter, the performance of twenty-year-old Miley Cyrus on the 2013 *MTV Video Music Awards* show had Twitter all atwitter and occupied nearly every talk show and blogger for a week, despite looming crises in Syria and the media coverage of the fiftieth anniversary of the March on Washington. By the time you are reading this, I have no doubt that more young stars have committed more outrage, but this episode stands out for the way that all of the trends converged in a single location. Miley Cyrus had been a child actor in the classic wholesome Disney mode, first packaged for consumption in 2006 at the age of thirteen as "Hannah Montana," in the TV series of the same name aimed at younger girls who had outgrown princesses. Replacing fairy-tale fantasy with a story line about a teenager who leads a secret life as a pop star, Disney launched a line of items, including clothes, bedding, luggage, makeup, and toys through mass-market retailers across the country.[17] The clothing featured the pop star side of the character's persona, and because Cyrus's character was modeled on existing images of (adult) female performers, it soon drew criticism from some parents, who felt that the look was too mature for Hannah Montana's young fans.

What happened when Miley outgrew teen pop fashion may have been disturbing, but it wasn't surprising. Compare her experience with other post-1970s celebrities such as Drew Barrymore, Britney Spears, or Lindsay Lohan. Their trajectory from cutie pie to cheesecake parallels the blurring of size-age boundaries in girls', teens', and women's clothing. This relationship between celebrity and consumer culture has been around for some time, although the particulars have changed. For stars of an earlier generation the pattern was prolonged childhood, an abbreviated adolescence, and early domesticity, as seen with Shirley Temple, Judy Garland, and Elizabeth Taylor, all of whom married before they turned twenty.

The youth-driven fashions of the 1960s had long ago erased the boundary between young adults and teens in women's fashions, and a similar transformation eliminated the distinction between tweens and teens between the late 1970s and the early 1990s. Combine that with the reassignment of more modest expressions of femininity to girls under the age of seven and women over fifty, and what's left is sexualization for everyone else. The APA identified half of the problem—sex-saturated media that broadcast an image of women as objects of desire and sexual violence (and often cast women of color as actively seeking those attentions)—but missed the more insidious piece of consumer culture that primes toddlers and preschoolers for sexualization by initiating them into a world of femininity that they are destined to outgrow within a few years. When four-year-old girls want everything pink and glittery, it's nature, but when they're eight and they want flirty, it's the media's fault? That's having your cake and eating it too.

In addition to the hypersexualization of women's fashion, we also see evidence of visions of equality and femininity dating back to the 1960s, which offered new choices in nearly every facet of women's lives. But these choices were neither equally available nor equally valued, resulting not only in the well-known "mommy wars" between women working outside the home and stay-at-home mothers but also in the marginalization of women who do what they must because they have no choice. Women and girls of all ages are subject to a beauty culture that may be different from that of the 1950s and early 1960s, but it is no less problematic. Despite fifty years of modern feminism, an analysis of Google searches revealed that parents were twice as likely to seek ways to help their daughters to lose weight than to look for similar advice for their sons, despite the fact that the proportion of overweight girls and boys is essentially similar.[18]

John T. Molloy is still dispensing advice, and his opinions on clothing for career women who aspire to leadership positions has changed only slightly. He now endorses pantsuits, and his reasons are revealing: "The suit remains the uniform for women executives but today it is as likely to be a pantsuit as a traditional skirted model. The pantsuit was made a legitimate executive uniform by Hillary Clinton and today pants are being worn by women because the skirts that are being shown are not appropriate for business."[19]

What about masculinity? What do today's fashions reveal about how the gender revolution affected men and boys? Once the peacock fever had passed, they too reverted to older patterns. Still, some deep and permanent changes did emerge from the chaos of the 1970s. Men benefited more than women had in the loosening of occasion-specific rules for dress and today enjoy are greater range of options than they did during the 1950s. Although the unstructured leisure suit in its pastel polyester incarnation went out of style, other, less revolutionary casual styles moved into the workplace. Even in a conservative fashion culture like the federal government, sport coats are more common today than suits. The Washington, D.C., Metro during summertime rush hours is filled with men in shirt sleeves and tie; they wear no jacket at all, or they leave one at the office "just in case." "Casual Friday" has evolved into a weeklong affair labeled "business casual." Men's leisure clothing is colorful and expressive, even if what they are expressing is no more than love for their local football team. The men's grooming industry has flourished since the appearance of the first unisex salons in the late 1960s, even reviving the humble barbershop. Of course, the twenty-first-century version is not so humble; it's an upscale exercise in nostalgia for "a time when barbershops provided real men a place where they shared common values, where they could relax, and where they could enjoy meaningful conversation with old friends and new acquaintances."[20]

The popular award-winning series *Mad Men* has focused attention on the 1960s and the experiences of men and women as they navigated their ways through a culture in transition. Through this series, post-boomer viewers have learned about the 1960s from a completely different angle from the stereotyped "flower power" and civil rights lenses. This has revived interest in the look of the period, but even the most ardent fan of the show just wants to look like Don Draper, not behave like him:

> On the outside, Don is successful, rich and married with children. But in reality he is a deserter, a drunk, an adulterer and, to be frank, pretty fucked up.[21]
>
> Draper then serves as not role model but as a warning.[22]

With the advantage of hindsight and history, viewers know that the masculine culture of *Mad Men* is headed for challenging times. The irony is that we still may not be able to predict where Don Draper will be in the twenty-first century, other than retired or dead. Men's lives took so many different directions in the late 1960s that a man in his early forties in 1968 could not begin to fathom what the future held. Even with today's look-alike fashions, a time-traveling Don Draper would find himself in a strange new world fifty years later.

One important distinction, though less visible, between clothing for men and women is the pace and magnitude of fashion changes from season to season and from year to year for business and formal dress. Men's clothing for the office has been reduced to classic styles and a limited range of colors and fabrics for generations. They rent most of their formal wear, which is also only lightly touched by fashion. Why so many women have been so reluctant to relinquish fashionable clothing, particularly in the workplace, is a puzzle, and the answer is complicated. Part of the explanation may lie at the intersection of feminism, antifeminism, and cosmofeminism, in the territory sometimes called "having it all." Part of it may be a side effect of the gains won by the women's rights movement. The fortieth anniversary of Title IX was celebrated at the governmental level and by many women in sports. But it is telling that in writing about the occasion *Washington Post* columnist Valerie Strauss felt compelled to dispel several myths about how Title IX had hurt male athletes and men's sports. This is perhaps the most pernicious accusation of the women's movement: that the advancement of women has come at the expense of men. This echoes the antifeminist counterarguments of Helen Andelin in *True Womanhood:* "One of the greatest threats to a man's position . . . is when his wife earnestly pursues a career. The dedication and drive required for success tends to push the man into the background."[23] Dialing back on the power suits, or even compensating with styles that convey softness and seduction, may have been a way to relieve this tension. British journalist Caitlin Moran, author of *How to Be a Woman*, wrote in 2012: "When we imagine the fully emancipated 21st-century woman, we are apt to think of some toned, immaculately dressed overachiever, leading a Fortune 500 company while bringing up bilingual twins. And that's what simultaneously stresses women out to the point of living on a Pinot Grigio drip, and terrifies insecure men. This idea of perfect, sexy, superhuman lady-titans, winning at everything. That's what scuppers moves toward gender equality."[24]

For all the privilege associated with being male in our culture, comments like these bring to mind the Freudian-influenced concept of fragile masculinity, vulnerable to "corruption" in early childhood. Much of stereotypical male behavior may be aggressive, but their clothing is defensive. The traditional suit is going strong, still shielding men's bodies from view and still deflecting ridicule through conservative cut and color. It is easy to see that it may have been premature in the 1970s for women to dress too much like their male co-workers. It also may have been too soon to ask them to relinquish fashion as a marker of femininity.

The role of queer fashion professionals—designers, models, journalists, and curators—is significant. In the 1960s gay male designers could challenge prevailing gender norms through their designs, but just up to point. Today's more accepting climate has made it possible for them to be much more open personally and creatively, which in turn has brought discussions of gender expression to the forefront once more. Whether it is transgender runway models or lines of ready-to-wear clothing expressly for butch lesbians and androgynous straight women, the market is responding to the demand for options. Less evident but even more important has been the steady erosion of the visual stereotypes of gays and lesbians; the news coverage of same-sex weddings has exposed the general public to the range of body types, hairstyles, and clothing in the LGBTQ population, in all its glorious ordinariness.

I also have a hunch that the popularity of cosplay (dressing up as a character from a book, film, or computer game) is part of an emerging sense that all clothing is costume. (Or, in the words of RuPaul, "We're born naked, and the rest is drag.") This is more true with feminine dress than masculine clothing, as there is still a lingering tendency to think of menswear as "just clothes." The extent to which femininity had become a performance by the early twenty-first century is best illustrated by the popularity of makeover reality shows, from TLC's *What Not to Wear* (2003–2013) to *RuPaul's Drag U* (2010–2013) on Logo. The latter is the most fascinating for any student of gender. A competitive makeover show, it featured three "biological women" who were coached to discover their inner divas by three drag queens. In this, as in all makeover shows, the underlying message was not only that femininity is a learned behavior but also that women who have not acquired it are missing a vital aspect of themselves. On *Drag U* this message extended to lesbians as well as straight women, resulting in a truly mind-bending episode featuring a trio of self-described "butch" students learning how to walk in four-inch heels from their gay male coaches.

One of the reasons I wanted to write about unisex fashions is that they seemed emblematic of a very complicated—and unfinished—conversation about sex, gender, and sexuality. Perhaps the crowning achievement of the conservative movement has been the creation of a stereotype of the 1960s and '70s as self-indulgent and aimless—just a bunch of free-love hippies waving protest signs and getting high. That is certainly one way to trivialize the yearnings of millions of people for lives of their own choosing. Many of us who grew up in the 1960s have mixed feelings about that era, though mine are more positive than Senator Santorum's. The conversation now comprises so many voices that it may seem there will be no end to the chaos. But I am hopeful that a multitude of voices is exactly what is needed to resolve the conflicts generated by social and cultural categories. As feminist activist and social critic Naomi Wolf wrote, "Underlying all of these movements is the democratic ideal from the 1970s that asserts: No one person has the natural right to suppress, silence or dominate any other person, simply because of where both are situated in society."[25]

Perhaps we are just halfway through a century-long conflict that will be a footnote in our great-great-grandchildren's history books. We still have a long way to go before pink is just a color again, female athletes can wear their hair long or short without arousing speculation about their sexuality, and men can trade their khaki trousers for cotton skirts on humid summer days—without having to shave their legs. In the meantime, we need to listen to one another in order to grasp the consequences of the individual freedom we claim to prize so highly. We already know enough about the origins of beauty culture and fat shaming; we need to understand the outcomes they produce in real people's lives.

Perhaps "clothes make the man" after all. In an exercise in aspirational dressing, consider the possibilities if our wardrobes reflected the full range of choices available to each of us. Imagine that we dressed to express our inner selves and our locations not as fixed but as flexible. Imagine a consumer culture so responsive that no one felt excluded or shamed.

While male-female relationships may be a driver in shaping gender roles, they're unlikely to be the entire story. An important part of the interplay between existing and emerging gender roles for women has taken place among women. For every liberated, pants-wearing, makeup-rejecting woman in the 1960s, there was another women the same age who still dreamed of *being* Miss America rather than picketing her. Women do not dress just to attract men; lesbians certainly do not. Historically, blue- and pink-collar workers have tried to remind their upper-class sisters in the women's movement that they want "bread and roses"—the right to beauty in their lives, not just economic security. Women enforce and influence women's appearance perhaps even more strongly than men do, especially when they are young.

We are living at a time when individual expression is far more possible than ever imagined, through social media, blogging, self-publishing, and myriad other platforms. We can choose to listen or ignore the voices of others, but we cannot make them go away. Their very diversity challenges our attempts to sort them into categories, so perhaps we should stop trying. Consider, for example, the use of stereotypes in clothing to mark homosexuality as "the other." Fashion journalist Clara Pierre commented optimistically in 1976 that unisex clothing and the sexual revolution had reduced fears of sexual ambivalence and "clothes no longer have to perform the duty of [sexual] differentiation and can relax into just being clothes."[26] Her celebration was premature, but when a popular reality show can feature straight men being re-fashioned by five "queer" guys, change is in the air.[27]

A more open climate for discussing issues of gender identity and expression has paralleled shifting public opinion on gay rights and marriage equality, issues that are far from being settled. Is gender identity a matter of nature or nurture? Science tells us that the foundations for sexual behavior are laid down before we are born, but also that human variation is vast and complex. Perhaps, in addition to making the mistake of assuming a binary model, we have been asking the wrong questions about gender all along. As long as gender was envisioned as separate paths stemming from biological starting points, it made sense to ask how the paths were laid down or why some individuals strayed from the paths. Now it's time to consider the consequences of cultural norms, not their origins.

Knowing that most boys behave in a particular way does not tell you how your son will behave, nor will it explain why your daughter might prefer Barbies or Transformers. History tells us that children can wear dresses or pants, and that both girls and boys can wear pink or blue, but that strongly gendered or gender-free clothing has an unpredictable effect, most of it not evident until they are grown. The effect of either/or constructs when status differences are involved can be insidious. If men are expected to be sexually aggressive while women are passive, the results are a double standard for sexually active men and women, overemphasis on women's appearance, homophobia, and a rape culture. When "princess boys" adopt stereotypical signifiers of femininity, such behavior can be defended as an indication that they are performing their authentic selves. When "girly-girls" embrace the same signifiers, does it make sense to criticize them for adopting an artificial construction imposed by consumer culture? These and other contradictions are signs that our basic assumptions need to be revisited.

We are still untangling the complicated relationships between sex, gender, and sexuality. One way to begin is to let go of worldviews that no longer fit scientific facts. The binary model of sex, particularly the notion of male and female as opposites, needs to join the flat earth and the geocentric universe in the discarded theory bin. I feel a twinge of sympathy for demographers who will have to come up with new boxes on forms to accommodate evolving notions of gender, but they already have had some practice adjusting to changes in how we see race, so they will probably be fine.

The fashions of the 1960s and '70s are the manifestation of attempts to solve the problems of gender inequality all at once, driven by the impatience of youth, within the context of emerging—and incomplete— understanding of the biological and cultural complexities responsible for that inequality. It now seems inevitable that efforts to modify or supplement the existing binary model with androgyny, ambiguity, or the ungendered unity of futuristic unisex would falter and fail in the short run. The binary model itself, however, is showing clear signs of fatigue.

My distrust and skepticism for categories has been growing throughout this project. In real life there are many alternatives to a binary construction of gender; the Bem model was just the beginning. Because it still relies on sorting personality traits into "masculine," "feminine," or "neutral," it hangs on a skeleton of binary gender stereotypes. The malleability of these categories reveals their artificiality; it is quite visible in baby clothing, where the definition of "neutral clothing" has shifted from white dresses to green coveralls in less than a century. The categories are also interdependent; what makes a garment masculine is its lack of femininity.

The possibilities for ridding ourselves of this binary view of gender boil down to two choices: no gender categories, or a finite (but yet undetermined) set of gender categories. Since the late 1970s new scholarship challenged the essentialism that stems from binary models of sex and gender. Third-wave feminism began by shifting the focus from gender to examining how individuals represent intersections of numerous identities, including sexuality, race, class, and ability. Although biology is important, it is not destiny. Forty years of gender research using multidimensional instruments such as the BSRI indicate that the correlation between biological sex and masculinity or femininity is weaker now than it once was.[28] Feminist biologist Anne Fausto-Sterling argues that not only is biological sex not binary but also the act of determining a child's sex, based only on visible markers, is culturally constructed.[29] Judith Butler, coming from a completely different direction—feminist rhetoric and literary studies—arrives at a similar conclusion: our definitions of sex are themselves culturally gendered, and basing our search for identity on these shifting "facts" sets us on fruitless, circular paths.[30]

There are suggestions that gender binary thinking has reached its limit, especially in the last market it touched: children's clothing. Even while juvenile clothing has become more gendered than ever before, it has also become a site of growing parental discontent and resistance. The push back against early sexualization of girls is one sign of dissatisfaction with the double standard that stems from the gender binary. Another sign is the revolt against pink, princess culture and the lack of neutral or even nuanced options. As infants grow into toddlers, they become active participants in the gender binary fashion show, much to the amusement, chagrin, or dismay of their parents. For many boys and girls this participation is enthusiastically embraced. These are the girls who insist on wearing nothing but pink and prefer dresses to any form of pants and the boys who clamor for buzz cuts and ubiquitous sports imagery. But what about the others? What about tomboys, the little girls who in earlier decades could have worn plain girls' styles or their brother's hand-me-downs without appearing out of the mainstream? What about boys who feel out of place in hypermasculine clothing and are drawn to softer colors and fabrics, but for whom the English language has no positive term? What about the one person in one hundred classified as "intersex," whose body differs from standard male or female, or those whose inner sense of identity may not conform to the gender chosen for them at birth by their parents? Clearly one consequence of a strong gender binary in children's clothing is the lack of expressive options for children's fluid identities, especially for children who are chafed by stereotyped, binary images of masculinity and femininity. As the categories have tightened, squeezing out neutral options, a growing number of adults have realized that children who don't fit the binary suffer real distress. Increasingly their response is not to "fix" their children, through training, punishment, or therapy, but to argue for cultural change.

This is a beginning, but we are still years, if not decades, from resolving all of the issues raised by the sexual revolution. Change will come, because so much of what happened fifty years ago cannot be undone. Civil rights can be undone, but not un-thought. Oral contraceptives will not be un-invented, nor abortions prevented, by making them illegal or difficult to obtain. In the words of Unitarian minister Theodore Parker, made famous by civil rights leader Martin Luther King Jr., I do believe that "the moral arc of the universe is long, but it bends toward justice."[31] In this case my vision of justice includes freeing ourselves from the assumptions and stereotypes that are the logical byproducts of outmoded categories. I have no idea what you or I, or our children and grandchildren, will be wearing when that day comes, but I like to imagine that it will be a perfect fit.

It isn't just our clothing that will fit; we will fit—within our communities and even standing in a crowd of strangers. Culture is the inarticulate shaping of rules and boundaries, signaling belonging and exclusion within a society and determining the rewards for fitting in and the consequences for nonconformity. If we desire a society of individuals, each empowered to achieve their full potential, we need to produce a culture that recognizes human diversity, offers options, and respects choices. We began to move in that direction with the questions of the 1960s; some of the answers were visible in the fashions of the period. Looking closely, we can also detect the confusion and conflict that began fifty years ago and continue unresolved. We may still have a long way to go, but I share the optimism of Frank Zappa:

> There will come a time when everybody who is lonely
> will be free to sing and dance and love.

> There will come a time when every evil that we know
> will be an evil that we can rise above.

> Who cares if hair is long or short or sprayed or partly grayed?
> We know that hair ain't where it's at.

> There will come a time when you won't even be ashamed if you are fat.[32]

 *Notes*

Introduction

1. Santorum quoted in Charles M. Blow, "Santorum." The original speech is archived on the Oxford Center for Religion and Public Life website at http://www.ocrpl.org/?p=96.

2. Dolan, "Fox's Elisabeth Hasselbeck."

3. Paoletti, *Pink and Blue.*

4. Justice Winter, Massie v. Henry, February 2, 1972.

5. For intersectionality in women's fashion, Maxine Leeds Craig, *Ain't I a Beauty Queen?* includes a thorough discussion of the relationship between black beauty culture, feminism, and the civil rights movement. Stylist Lloyd Boston (*Men of Color: Fashion, History, Fundamentals*) offers a detailed history of African American men's fashions and their role in men's fashions since World War II. Monica Miller's *Slaves to Fashion* employs an intersectional lens in her historical study of black men's use of elite fashions to perform both race and gender.

1. Movers, Shakers, and Boomers

1. Roberts, "Old Grad Returns," 303.

2. Horowitz, "Mitt Romney's Prep School Classmates Recall Pranks."

3. Bentley, "For the Right to Wear Our Hair Long."

4. Goodson, "Next Generation Brand."

5. Coupland, *Generation X.*

6. Kimmel, "Real Man Redux," 48.

7. Kagan and Lunde quoted in Adams, "Male & Female: Differences between Them."

8. Benedek and Adelson quoted in ibid.

9. Kagan and Symonds quoted in ibid.

10. Wyden, "When Both Wear the Pants."

11. I am indebted to Dr. Susan-Marie Stedman, a scientist at NOAA, for this insight.

12. Miller, *Slaves to Fashion.*

13. "Harry Hay Interview."

14. Lobenthal, *Radical Rags,* 139.

15. Faure, *Rudi Gernreich*, 23.

16. Kazin, "The Young: The Party of Hope," 122.

17. Vanderbilt quoted in Lobenthal, *Radical Rags*, 132.

18. Ibid., 132.

19. Bullough, *Science in the Bedroom.*

20. Constantinople, "Masculinity-Femininity"; Bem, "Measurement of Psychological Androgyny."

2. Feminism and Femininity

1. Smith and Greig, *Women in Pants.*

2. Fairchild, *Fashionable Savages*, 87.

3. Audsley, *Bowling for Women*, 11; emphasis added.

4. Fairchild, *Fashionable Savages*, 177.

5. Pierre, *Looking Good*, 137.

6. "Hem and the Haw," *Newsweek*, 80.

7. Bradley, *Husband-Coached Childbirth*, 240.

8. Heidrich, Berg, and Bergman, "Clothing Factors and Vaginitis."

9. "Beauty Bulletin," *Vogue*, 127.

10. Ibid., 146.

11. Torres quoted in Fairchild, *Fashionable Savages*, 88.

12. Bender, "New Fashions Are Sad Blow to 'Older' Set," 20.

13. Farrell-Beck, *Uplift: The Bra in America*, 147.

14. Fiegel, *Dream a Little Dream of Me*, 157.

15. Ibid., 217.

16. Ollove, "1960s Siren."

17. Fiegel, *Dream a Little Dream of Me*, 176.

18. Ibid. 157; Ollove, "1960s Siren."

19. Klemesrud, "Day for Plump, Motherly Models," 38.

20. Milinaire and Troy, *Cheap Chic.*

21. "Personality Types and the Clothes That Go with Them," *Seventeen*, August 1965.

22. *Seventeen*, June 1965, 22.

23. Pierre, *Looking Good*, 138.

24. Davidson, "Foremothers"; "Women Who Are Cute When They Are Mad," 81.

25. "What If . . . Gloria Steinem Were Miss America?," 132.

26. Gilder, *Sexual Suicide*, 7.

27. Von Furstenberg, *Diane: A Signature Life*, 55.

28. Molloy, *Dress for Success for Women.*

29. Molloy, *Dress for Success.*

30. Molloy, *Dress for Success for Women*, 72.

31. Laver quoted in Taylor, "Women Perplex Fashion Historian."

3. The Peacock Revolution

1. The term "peacock revolution" appeared in Frazier's *Esquire* columns in 1968 but was originally coined by consumer psychology icon Ernest Dichter in 1965. Haye et al., *Handbook of Fashion Studies,* 193.

2. Nicholson, "Men's Clothes," 38.

3. Dearborn, *Psychology of Clothing,* 59.

4. Nystrom, *Economics of Fashion,* 71–78.

5. Babl, "Compensatory Masculine Responding," 252–257.

6. Grambs and Waetjen, *Sex, Does It Make a Difference?,* 115; emphasis in original.

7. Lobenthal, *Radical Rags,* 140.

8. Conekin, "Fashioning the Playboy," 454.

9. Lobenthal, *Radical Rags,* 139.

10. Kendall, "Men's Fashions," 174.

11. Bender quoted in Lobenthal, *Radical Rags,* 134.

12. Fish quoted in ibid., 157.

13. Green, "Modified Mod," 149.

14. Lobenthal, *Radical Rags,* 149.

15. John Rogers, donation cover letter, 1980, Fashion Archives and Museum, Shippensburg University, PA.

16. "Bill Blass," Voguepedia.

17. Ephron, "Man in the Bill Blass Suit," 330.

18. "Suited for City Squiring," *Playboy,* 135.

19. Lobenthal, *Radical Rags,* 39.

20. Ibid., 153.

21. Gernreich quoted in ibid., 39.

22. Taylor, "Men's Fashions in the 1960's," 62.

23. Priore, "Joe Pepitone."

24. Palmer quoted in Bennett-England, *Dress Optional,* 37.

25. Green, "Back to Campus," September 1965, 140–142.

26. Green, "Back to Campus," September 1966, 179.

27. Both ads appear in *Playboy,* September 1966.

28. Hentoff, "Youth—the Oppressed Majority," 136.

29. Green, "Back to Campus," September 1967, 179.

30. Green, "Back to Campus," September 1968, 159.

31. Green, "Back to Campus," September 1969, 276.

32. *Bonnie and Clyde,* directed by Arthur Penn. Warner Bros.–Seven Arts and Tatira-Hiller Productions, 1967.

33. Bennett-England, *Dress Optional,* 151.

34. Faure, *Rudi Gernreich: A Retrospective.*

35. Johnston, "What Will Happen to the Gray Flannel Suit?"

36. Taylor, "Hair Grooming Goes Unisex," 38.

37. Phalon, "Long-Hair Trend Thinning Barber Ranks," 20.

38. "Setting Your Own Style," 61–88.

39. "Resort Fashion Report," 104.

40. Aletti, "Discotheque Rock '73," 60.

41. Miller, *Slaves to Fashion*.

42. Bennett-England, *Dress Optional*.

43. Lynes, "What Revolution in Men's Clothes?," 26.

44. *A Queer History of Fashion: From the Closet to the Catwalk*.

45. Cole, *Don We Now Our Gay Apparel*.

46. *Hair: The American Tribal Love-Rock Musical* (1967) and *Oh! Calcutta!* (1969) debuted off-Broadway and then moved into major productions in New York and London. A pay television video version of *Oh! Calcutta!* (1971) was released to theaters in 1972, and a film version of *Hair*, directed by Miloš Forman, was released in 1979. *Bob and Carol and Ted and Alice* (1969) began as a feature film written and directed by Paul Mazursky and starring Natalie Wood, Robert Culp, Elliott Gould, and Dyan Cannon.

47. Pierre, *Looking Good*, 160.

48. Blazina, *Cultural Myth of Masculinity*.

4. Nature and/or Nurture?

1. Zolotow, *William's Doll*; Thomas, *Free to Be . . . You and Me*.

2. Cook, *Commodification of Childhood*.

3. "New Day Dawning at Sears," 44–45.

4. Paoletti, *Pink and Blue*.

5. Blank, *Straight: The Surprisingly Short History*.

6. Tanous, *Making Clothes for Your Little Girls*, 16.

7. "How to Sell Boys' Wear," 67–68.

8. "Spring 1974 Swatch Book," 16.

9. "Male and Female Differences," 43–44.

10. Money and Ehrhardt, *Man and Woman, Boy and Girl*

11. "Who Was David Reimer (also, Sadly, Known as 'John/Joan')?"; Colapinto, *As Nature Made Him*.

12. Gould, "X: A Fabulous Child's Story," 1972; Gould, *X: A Fabulous Child's Story*, 1978.

13. Gould, "X: A Fabulous Child's Story," 1998.

14. Seavey, Katz, and Zalk, "Baby X." 103–109.

15. Gould, *X: A Fabulous Child's Story*, 1978.

16. Woodward, "Do Children Need Sex Roles?," 79–80.

17. Ibid.

18. Horn, "Does a Boy Have the Right to Be Effeminate?," 34, 100–101.

19. Guttentag and Bray, *Undoing Sex Stereotypes*.

20. B. Rice, "The Power of a Frilly Apron: Coming of Age in Sodom and New Milford," *Psychology Today*, September 1975, 64–66.

21. Weisner and Eiduson, "Children of the 60's as Parents," 66.

22. Carmichael, *Non-Sexist Childraising.*

23. Ellison, "My Parents' Failed Experiment."

24. Burge, "Parental Child-Rearing Sex-Role Attitudes," 199.

25. Examples of this sort of news item abound and include Palmer, "Angelina Jolie Says"; "J. Crew Ad Showing Boy"; Fisher, "My Son, the Princess"; and Hoffman, "On Parenting a Boy Who Is Different."

26. "Boy or Girl?"

5. *Litigating the Revolution*

1. Ribeiro, *Dress and Morality*, and Robson, *Dressing Constitutionally*, both offer extensive descriptions of early sumptuary laws.

2. Derek Miller cited in Emerson, "British 'His and Her' Hairdos," 29.

3. Mick Jagger quoted in ibid.

4. "School Orders Boy," 44.

5. Rhodes, "Attleboro High Alums Come Together," *Sun Chronicle.*

6. Bellaire, "Story of Georgie Porgie."

7. Morris and Morris, "Are You a Boy or Are You a Girl."

8. "Legal Group Snips at School 'Rights.'"

9. "Students' Rights Stressed in Report."

10. "Supreme Court Lets Maryland Ruling Stand."

11. "High Court Bars Review of Ruling on Long Hair."

12. Buder, "Principals Score Long-Hair Ruling," 31.

13. "Now It's a Short Cut to Learning."

14. "Student Fashions."

15. Tinker v. Des Moines Independent Community School District (1969).

16. Horowitz, "Mitt Romney's Prep School Classmates."

17. Massie v. Henry (1972).

18. Cash v. Hoch (1970).

19. Blaine v. Board of Education (1972).

20. Independent School District v. Swanson (1976).

21. Massie v. Henry (1972).

22. Breen v. Kahl (1969).

23. Dawson v. Hillsborough (1971).

24. Howell v. Wolf (1971).

25. Lambert v. Marushi (1971).

26. Miller v. Gillis (1969).

27. Martin v. Davidson (1971).

28. Yoo v. Moynihan (1969).

29. Zwerdling, "Unshaven, Unshorn, and Unacceptable."
30. "Title VII of the Civil Rights Act of 1964."
31. Diaz v. Pan American World Airways, Inc. (1972).
32. Fagan v. National Cash Register Company (1973).
33. Willingham v. Macon Telegraph Publishing Co. (1975).
34. Donohue v. Shoe Corporation of America (1972).
35. Aros v. McDonnell Douglas Corporation (1972).
36. Golden, "Sex Discrimination and Hair-Length Requirements," 349.
37. Ibid., 350.
38. "Jailed Airman Finds Rules Have Changed," 10.
39. "Airline Stewardess Wins Right," 1.
40. "Title IX, Education Amendments of 1972."
41. Jacobs v. Benedict (1973).
42. Trent v. Perritt (1975).
43. Feron, "Fashion, If Not Tradition," 45.
44. Lipsyte, "Hair Again," 58.
45. Wallace v. Ford (1972).
46. Feron, "Fashion, If Not Tradition."
47. "Coaching Staff Resigns," 42.
48. "Horace Mann Boys," 1.
49. Johnson, "Constitution, the Courts, and Long Hair," 32.
50. "Hairy Case," 13.
51. Freeman v. Flake (1971).

6. The Culture Wars, Then and Now

1. Schulman, Seventies: The Great Shift, 186.
2. Ibid., 187.
3. Cohen, "Opting Out and Jumping In."
4. hooks, Feminist Theory.
5. Paoletti, Pink and Blue.
6. "Direction '88," D9.
7. Kaiser, Rudy, and Byfield, "Role of Clothing in Sex-Role Socialization."
8. Hoffman, "On Parenting a Boy Who Is Different."
9. Perrin quoted in Schoenberg, "When Kids Cross the Gender Divide."
10. Schoenberg, "When Kids Cross the Gender Divide."
11. Grinberg, "Hasbro to Unveil Black and Silver Easy-Bake Oven."
12. Coles quoted in Long, "Feminism Is Back in Fashion."
13. Sterne, "Joanna Coles: 'Cosmopolitan.'"
14. Orenstein, "What's Wrong with Cinderella?"
15. Waters, "Leaving the Pink Behind."
16. American Psychological Association, "Sexualization of Girls."

17. Tirella, "Hannah Montana Crowned."

18. Stephens-Davidowitz, "Google, Tell Me. Is My Son a Genius?"

19. Molloy, "Suits and Accessories."

20. "Kennedy's Barber Club Experience."

21. Staplehurst, "Don Draper Effect."

22. Baldoni, "'Mad Men': Learning from the Dark Side."

23. Andelin, *Fascinating Womanhood*, 118.

24. Moran, "Gender Equality."

25. Wolf, "Gender Equality."

26. Pierre, *Looking Good*, 160.

27. Referring to *Queer Eye for the Straight Guy* (2003–2007), Bravo.

28. Twenge, "Changes in Masculine and Feminine Traits," 5–6.

29. Fausto-Sterling, *Sexing the Body*.

30. Butler, *Gender Trouble*.

31. Parker, "Justice," 18.

32. Zappa, "Take Your Clothes Off When You Dance."

Bibliography

Legal Cases

Aros v. McDonnell Douglas Corporation, 348 F. Supp. 661 (C.D. Cal. 1972).

Blaine v. Board of Education, 210 Kan. 560 (1972).

Breen v. Kahl, 398 U.S. 937 (1969).

Cash v. Hoch, 309 F. Supp. 346 (W. D. Wis. 1970).

Dawson v. Hillsborough, 322 F. Supp. 286 (M.D. Fla. 1971).

Diaz v. Pan American World Airways, Inc., 348 F. Supp. 1083 (S.D. Fla. 1972).

Donohue v. Shoe Corporation of America, 337 F. Supp. 1357 (C.D. Cal. 1972).

Fagan v. National Cash Register Company, 157 U.S. App. D.C. 15 (1973).

Ferrell v. Dallas Independent School District, 393 U.S. 856 (1968).

Freeman v. Flake, 448 F. 2d 258, 10th Cir. (1971).

Howell v. Wolf, 331 F. Supp. 134 (N.D. Geo. 1971).

Independent School District v. Swanson, 553 P.2d 496 (Okla. 1976).

Jackson v. Dorrier, 400 U.S. 850 (1970).

Jacobs v. Benedict, 39 Ohio App. 2d 141 (1973).

Karr v. Schmidt, 401 U.S. 1201 (1973).

King v. Saddleback, 404 U.S. 979 (1971).

Lambert v Marushi, 322 F. Supp. 326 (S.D. West Va. 1971).

Lansdale v. Tyler, 411 U.S. 986 (1973).

Martin v. Davidson, 322 F. Supp. 318 (W. Penn. 1971).

Massie v. Henry, 455 F.2d 779 (4th Circuit 1972).

Miller v. Gillis, 315 F. Supp. 94 (N.D. Ill., E.D. 1969).

New Rider v. Board of Education, 414 U.S. 1097 (1973).

Olff v. East, 404 U.S. 1042 (1972).

Swanquist v. Livingston, 404 U.S. 983 (1971).

Tinker v. Des Moines Independent Community School District, 393 U.S. 503 (1969).

Trent v. Perritt, 391 F. Supp. 171, (S.D. Miss 1975).

Wallace v. Ford, 346 F. Supp. 156 (E.D. Ar-Kan W.D. 1972).

Willingham v. Macon Telegraph Publishing Co., 507 F.2d 1084 (5th Circuit. 1975).

Yoo v. Moynihan, 28 Conn. Supp. 375 (1969).

Published Sources

Adams, Virginia. Behavior: "Male & Female: Differences between Them." *Time,* March 20, 1972, 53–57.

"Airline Stewardess Wins Right to Wear Afro Hairdo." *Afro American,* September 19, 1970, 1.

Aletti, Vince. "Discotheque Rock '73: Paaaaarty!" *Rolling Stone,* September 13, 1973, 60–61.

American Psychological Association. "Sexualization of Girls." American Psychological Association. http://www.apa.org/pi/women/programs/girls.

Andelin, Helen. *Fascinating Womanhood.* Updated ed. New York: Bantam, 1990.

Audsley, Judy. *Bowling for Women.* New York: Sterling, 1964.

Babl, James D. "Compensatory Masculine Responding as a Function of Sex Role." *Journal of Consulting and Clinical Psychology* 47, no. 2 (1979): 252–257.

Baldoni, John. "'Mad Men': Learning from the Dark Side of Don Draper." *Forbes* online. April 30, 2013. http://www.forbes.com/sites/johnbaldoni/2013/04/30/mad-men-learning-from-the-dark-side-of-don-draper.

"Beauty Bulletin." *Vogue,* February 15, 1965, 121–124, 146–147.

Bellaire, Rick. "The Story of Georgie Porgie and the Cry Babies: Rhode Island's Original Rock 'n' Roll Rebels." *The Rhode Island Music Hall of Fame Historical Archive,* June 2011. http://www.ripopmusic.org/musical-artists/musicians/georgie-porgie.

Bem, Sandra L. "The Measurement of Psychological Androgyny." *Journal of Consulting and Clinical Psychology* 42, no. 2 (1974): 155–162.

Bender, Marylin. "New Fashions Are Sad Blow to 'Older' Set." *New York Times,* January 26, 1964.

Bennett-England, Rodney. *Dress Optional: The Revolution in Menswear.* Chester Springs, PA: Dufour, 1968.

Bentley, Eric. "For the Right to Wear Our Hair Long." *New York Times,* August 30, 1970, 69.

"Bill Blass." Voguepedia. *Vogue* online. http://www.vogue.com/voguepedia/Bill_Blass.

Birmingham, Frederic Alexander. *Esquire Fashion Guide for All Occasions.* New York: Harper and Row, 1962.

Blank, Hanne. *Straight: The Surprisingly Short History of Heterosexuality.* Boston: Beacon Press, 2012.

Blazina, Chris. *The Cultural Myth of Masculinity.* Westport, CT: Praeger, 2003.

Blow, Charles M. "Santorum and the Sexual Revolution." *New York Times,* March 2, 2012. http://www.nytimes.com/2012/03/03/opinion/blow-santorum-and-the-sexual-revolution.html.

Bonnie and Clyde. Directed by Arthur Penn. Warner Bros.–Seven Arts and Tatira-Hiller Productions, 1967.

Boston, Lloyd. *Men of Color Fashion, History, Fundamentals.* New York: Artisan, 1998.

"Boy or Girl? This 4-month-old is being raised genderless." http://shine.yahoo.com /parenting/boy-or-girl-this-4-month-old-is-being-raised-genderless-2487988 .html.

Bradley, Robert A. *Husband-Coached Childbirth*. 4th ed. Westminster, MD: Bantam Dell, 1996.

Brown, Helen Gurley. *Sex and the Single Girl*. New York: Bernard Geis Associates, 1962.

Buder, Leonard. "Principals Score Long-Hair Ruling." *New York Times,* October 15, 1966, 31.

Bullough, Vern L. *Science in the Bedroom: A History of Sex Research*. New York: Basic Books, 1994.

Burge, Penny Lee. "Parental Child-Rearing Sex-Role Attitudes Related to Social Issue Sex-Role Attitudes and Selected Demographic Variables." *Home Economics Research Journal* 9, no. 3 (March 1981): 193–199.

Butler, Judith. *Gender Trouble: Feminism and the Subversion of Identity*. New York: Routledge, 1999.

Carmichael, Carrie. *Non-Sexist Childraising*. Boston: Beacon Press, 1977.

"Coaching Staff Resigns in a Dispute over Hair." *New York Times,* December 12, 1970, 42.

Cohen, Philip N. "Opting Out and Jumping In." Family Inequality. August 14, 2013. http://familyinequality.wordpress.com/2013/08/14/opting-out-and-jumping-in.

Colapinto, John. *As Nature Made Him; The Boy Who Was Raised as a Girl*. New York: HarperCollins, 2000.

Cole, Shaun. *Don We Now Our Gay Apparel: Gay Men's Dress in the Twentieth Century*. Oxford: Berg, 2000.

Conekin, Becky. "Fashioning the Playboy: Messages of Style and Masculinity in the Pages of *Playboy* Magazine, 1953–1963." *Fashion Theory: The Journal of Dress, Body, and Culture* 4, no. 4 (2000): 447–466.

Constantinople, Anne. "Masculinity-Femininity: An Exception to a Famous Dictum?" *Psychological Bulletin* 80, no. 5 (1973): 389–407.

Cook, Daniel. *The Commodification of Childhood: The Children's Clothing Industry and the Rise of the Child Consumer*. Durham, NC: Duke University Press, 2004.

Coupland, Douglas. *Generation X: Tales for an Accelerated Culture*. New York: St. Martin's, 1991.

Craig, Maxine Leeds. *Ain't I a Beauty Queen?: Black Women, Beauty, and the Politics of Race*. Oxford: Oxford University Press, 2002.

Davidson, Sara. "Foremothers." *Esquire,* July 1973, 71–74.

Dearborn, George Van Ness. *The Psychology of Clothing*. Princeton, NJ: Psychological Review Company, 1918.

Direction '88. *Earnshaw's Infants, Girls, and Boys Wear Review,* February 1988, D9.

Dolan, Eric W. "Fox's Elisabeth Hasselbeck: Are Male-Wussifying Feminists a National Security Problem?" The Raw Story. January 17, 2014. http://www.rawstory

.com/rs/2014/01/17/foxs-elisabeth-hasselbeck-are-male-wussifying-feminists-a
-national-security-problem.

Ellison, Jesse. "My Parents' Failed Experiment in Gender Neutrality." *Newsweek,*
March 22, 2010. http://www.newsweek.com/my-parents-failed-experiment
-gender-neutrality-69487.

Emerson, Gloria. "British 'His and Her' Hairdos Blur 'Him-Her' Line." *New York
Times,* July 3, 1964.

Ephron, Nora. "The Man in the Bill Blass Suit." *New York Times Magazine,* December 8,
1968, 330.

Fairchild, John. *The Fashionable Savages.* Garden City, NY: Doubleday, 1965.

Farrell-Beck, Jane. *Uplift: The Bra in America.* Philadelphia: University of Pennsylvania
Press, 2002.

Faure, Jacques, ed. *Rudi Gernreich: A Retrospective, 1922–1985.* Los Angeles: Fashion
Group Foundation, 1985.

Fausto-Sterling, Anne. *Sexing the Body: Gender Politics and the Construction of Sexuality.* 1st ed. New York: Basic Books, 2000.

Feron, James. "Fashion, If Not Tradition, Ready for Women Cadets at West Point." *New
York Times,* November 20, 1975, 45.

Fiegel, Eddi. *Dream a Little Dream of Me: The Life of Cass Elliot.* Chicago: Chicago Review Press, 2008.

Fisher, Keri. "My Son, the Princess." Personal Essays. http://babble.com/little-boy
-pink-my-son-gives-girly-girls-a-run-for-their-taffeta/index2.aspx.

Friedan, Betty. *The Feminine Mystique.* New York: W. W. Norton, 1963.

"Gender Equality." *New York Times* online. November 30, 2012. http://www.nytimes
.com/2012/11/30/opinion/global/gender-equality.html.

Gilder, George F. *Sexual Suicide.* New York: Quadrangle, 1973.

Golden, H. Bruce. "Sex Discrimination and Hair-Length Requirements under Title
VII of the Civil Rights Act of 1964: The Long and Short of It." *Labor Law Journal*
25, no. 6 (1974): 336–351.

Goodson, Scott. "The Next Generation Brand." *Forbes* online. September 26, 2012.
http://www.forbes.com/sites/marketshare/2012/09/26/the-next-generation
-brand.

Gould, Lois. "X: A Fabulous Child's Story." *Ms.,* December 1972.

———. *X: A Fabulous Child's Story.* Illustrated by Jacqueline Chwast. New York:
Daughters Publishing, 1978.

———. "X: A Fabulous Child's Story." *Polare* 22, February 1998. http://www.gender
centre.org.au/resources/polare-archive/archived-articles/x-a-fabulous-childs
-story.htm.

Grambs, Jean Dresden, and Walter Bernhard Waetjen. *Sex, Does It Make a Difference?:
Sex Roles in the Modern World.* North Scituate, MA: Duxbury Press, 1975.

Green, Robert L. "Back to Campus." *Playboy,* September 1965.

———. "Back to Campus." *Playboy,* September 1966.

———. "Back to Campus." *Playboy,* September 1967.

———. "Back to Campus." *Playboy,* September 1968.

———. "Modified Mod." *Playboy,* September 1966.

Grinberg, Emanuella. "Hasbro to Unveil Black and Silver Easy-Bake Oven after Teen's Petition." CNN.com. December 18, 2012. http://www.cnn.com/2012/12/18 /living/hasbro-easy-bake-oven/index.html.

Guttentag, Marcia, and Helen Bray. *Undoing Sex Stereotypes.* New York: McGraw-Hill, 1976.

"Hairy Case." *New York Times,* October 20, 1968, 13.

"Harry Hay Interview." The Progressive. August 31, 1998. http://progressive.org /mag_cusachay.

Haye, Amy de la, Agnès Rocamora, Joanne Entwistle, Helen Thomas, Regina Root, and Sandy Black, eds. *The Handbook of Fashion Studies.* London: Bloomsbury Academic, 2013.

Heidrich, F. E., A. O. Berg, and J. J. Bergman. "Clothing Factors and Vaginitis." *Journal of Family Practice* 19, no. 4 (1984): 491–494.

"The Hem and the Haw." *Newsweek,* October 5, 1970, 80.

Hentoff, Nat. "Youth—the Oppressed Majority." *Playboy,* September 1967, 136–138.

"High Court Bars Review of Ruling on Long Hair." *New York Times,* November 12, 1966, 49.

Hoffman, Sarah. "On Parenting a Boy Who Is Different." http://www .sarahhoffmanwriter.com/sarah-hoffmans-blog.

hooks, bell. *Feminist Theory: From Margin to Center.* 2nd ed. Cambridge, MA: South End Press, 2000.

"Horace Mann Boys to Set Own Rules." *New York Times,* September 30, 1968, 1.

Horn, Jack C. "Does a Boy Have the Right to Be Effeminate?" *Psychology Today* 12 (April 1979), 34, 100–101.

Horowitz, Jason. "Mitt Romney's Prep School Classmates Recall Pranks, but Also Troubling Incidents." *Washington Post,* May 10, 2012. http://www.washingtonpost .com/politics/mitt-romneys-prep-school-classmates-recall-pranks-but-also -troubling-incidents/2012/05/10/gIQA3WOKFU_story_4.html.

"How to Sell Boys' Wear." *Earnshaw's Infants, Girls, and Boys Wear Review,* October 1978.

"Jailed Airman Finds Rules Have Changed." *Washington Afro-American,* March 3, 1970, 10.

"J. Crew Ad Showing Boy with Pink Nail Polish Sparks Debate on Gender Identity." FoxNews.com. April 11, 2011. http://www.foxnews.com/us/2011/04/11/jcrew-ad -showing-boy-pink-nail-polish-sparks-debate-gender-identity.

Johnson, T. Page. "The Constitution, the Courts, and Long Hair." *NASSP Bulletin,* 1973.

Johnston, Moira. "What Will Happen to the Gray Flannel Suit?" *Journal of Home Economics* 68, no. 8 (1972): 5–12.

Kaiser, S. B., M. Rudy, and P. Byfield. "The Role of Clothing in Sex-Role Socialization: Person Perceptions versus Overt Behavior." *Child Study Journal* 15 (1985): 83–97.

Kazin, Alfred. "The Young: The Party of Hope." *Vogue*, August 1, 1968, 122–123.

Kendall, Elaine. "Men's Fashions, Too, Reflect the Times." *New York Times*, August 2, 1964.

"The Kennedy's Barber Club Experience." http://www.kennedysbarberclub.com /kennedys-experience.

Kimmel, Michael S. "Real Man Redux." *Psychology Today*, July 1987, 48–52.

Klemesrud, Judy. "A Day for Plump, Motherly Models." *New York Times*, July 17, 1968, 38.

Laver, James. *Modesty in Dress: An Inquiry into the Fundamentals of Fashion.* London: Heinemann, 1969.

"Legal Group Snips at School 'Rights.'" *New York Times*, April 17, 1966, 36.

Lipsyte, Robert. "Hair Again." *New York Times*, April 16, 1970, 58.

Lobenthal, Joel. *Radical Rags: Fashions of the Sixties.* New York: Abbeville Press, 1990.

Long, Carola. "Feminism Is Back in Fashion." *Financial Times.* January 17, 2014. http:// www.ft.com/intl/cms/s/2/aa71a6bc-7de1-11e3-95dd-00144feabdc0.html#axzz2r8v BlolM.

Lynes, Russell. "What Revolution in Men's Clothes?" *Harper's,* May 1967, 26.

"Male and Female Differences." *Time,* March 20, 1972, 43–44.

Mazursky, Paul. *Bob and Carol and Ted and Alice.* Columbia Pictures, 1969.

Milinaire, Caterine, and Carol Troy. *Cheap Chic.* New York: Harmony Books, 1975.

Miller, Monica L. *Slaves to Fashion: Black Dandyism and the Styling of Black Diasporic Identity.* Durham, NC: Duke University Press, 2010.

Molloy, John T. *Dress for Success.* New York: Warner Books, 1975.

———. *Dress for Success for Women.* New York: Warner Books, 1977.

———. "Suits and Accessories." Dress for Success the Blog by John T. Molloy. May 20, 2013. http://www.thedressforsuccesscolumn.com/?p=539.

Money, John, and Anke Ehrhardt. *Man and Woman, Boy and Girl.* New York: New American Library/Mentor, 1972.

Moran, Caitlin. "Gender Equality." *New York Times* online. November 30, 2012. http:// www.nytimes.com/2012/11/30/opinion/global/gender-equality.html.

Morris, Ron, and Doug Morris. "Are You a Boy or Are You a Girl." EMI Music Publishing, 1964.

"A New Day Dawning at Sears." *Earnshaw's Infants, Girls and Boys Wear Review,* February 1988, 44–45, 48.

Nicholson, Harold. "Men's Clothes." *Small Talk,* 34–45. New York: Harcourt, Brace and Company, 1937.

"Now It's a Short Cut to Learning." *New York Times,* November 13, 1966, E9.

Nystrom, Paul H. *Economics of Fashion.* New York: Ronald Press, 1928.

Ollove, Michael. "1960s Siren: Baltimore's Cass Elliot Spoke to a Generation with Her Music, and Now Her Voice Is Being Heard Again." *Baltimore Sun,* May 4, 1997, 1E.

Orenstein, Peggy. "What's Wrong with Cinderella?" *New York Times Magazine,* December 24, 2006. http://www.nytimes.com/2006/12/24/magazine/24princess.t.html.

Palmer, Brian. "Angelina Jolie Says There's Nothing Wrong with Shiloh Wearing Neckties: Did Children Always Wear Gender-Specific Clothing?" *Slate,* n.d. http://www.slate.com/id/2260366.

Paoletti, Jo B.. *Pink and Blue: Telling the Boys from the Girls in America.* Bloomington: Indiana University Press, 2012.

Parker, Theodore. "Justice." In *Readings from Great Authors,* ed. John Haynes Holmes, Harvey Dee Brown, Helen Edmunds Redding, and Theodora Goldsmith, 17–18. New York: Dodd, Mead and Company, 1918.

"Personality Types and the Clothes That Go with Them." *Seventeen,* August 1965, 346–347.

Phalon, Richard. "Long-Hair Trend Thinning Barber Ranks." *New York Times,* December 31, 1970.

Pierre, Clara. *Looking Good: The Liberation of Fashion.* New York: Reader's Digest Press, 1976.

Pleck, Joseph H., and Jack Sawyer. *The Myth of Masculinity.* 1974; Cambridge: MIT Press, 1981.

Priore, Domenic. "Joe Pepitone: How to Be a Jock and Still Be Cool." *Examiner,* January 26, 2010. http://www.examiner.com/article/joe-pepitone-how-to-be-a-jock-and-still-be-cool.

"Princess Boys and Star Wars Girls." http://www.mamapedia.com/voices/princess-boys-and-star-wars-girls.

A Queer History of Fashion: From the Closet to the Catwalk. Museum at the Fashion Institute of Technology. September 13, 2013 through January 4, 2014. http://exhibitions.fitnyc.edu.

Ragni, Gerome, James Rado and Galt MacDermot. "Hair." April 29, 1968, New York: Biltmore Theater.

"Resort Fashion Report." *Esquire,* January 1974, 104.

Rhodes, George W. "Attleboro High Alums Come Together." *Sun Chronicle,* May 2013. http://www.thesunchronicle.com/devices/news/local_news/attleboro-high-alums-come-together/article_92ef6bc2-a64a-5792-9001-60b713c98b24.html?mode=jqm.

Ribeiro, Aileen. *Dress and Morality.* Oxford: Berg, 2003.

Rice, B. "The Power of a Frilly Apron: Coming of Age in Sodom and New Milford." *Psychology Today,* September 1975.

Roberts, Steven. "An Old Grad Returns to Bayonne High School for His Tenth Reunion and Finds He Is Old-Fashioned at Twenty-Seven." *New York Times,* December 6, 1970, 303.

Rogers, John. Donation cover letter, 1980. Fashion Archives and Museum at Shippens-
    burg University, Pennsylvania.
Robson, Ruthann. *Dressing Constitutionally: Hierarchy, Sexuality, and Democracy from
    Our Hairstyles to Our Shoes.* New York: Cambridge University Press, 2013.
Santorum, Rick. "The Press & People of Faith in Politics." Speech transcript. August
    2008. Oxford Centre for Religion and Public Life. http://www.ocrpl.org/?p=96.
Schoenberg, Nara. "When Kids Cross the Gender Divide." *Chicago Tribune,* August 17,
    2010. http://articles.chicagotribune.com/2010-08-17/features/sc-fam-0817
    -gender-issue-20100817_1_gender-variant-behavior-kids-cross-dresses.
"School Orders Boy: Brush Bangs Back and Go to Classes." *New York Times,* December
    17, 1964.
Schulman, Bruce J. *The Seventies: The Great Shift in American Culture, Society, and Poli-
    tics.* Cambridge, MA: Da Capo, 2002.
Seavy, Carol A., Phyllis A. Katz, and Sue Rosenberg Zalk. "Baby X: The Effect of Gen-
    der Labels on Adult Responses to Infants." *Sex Roles* 1 (1975), 103–109.
"Setting Your Own Style." *Gentleman's Quarterly,* Winter 1974–1975.
Smith, Catherine, and Cynthia Greig. *Women in Pants: Manly Maidens, Cowgirls, and
    Other Renegades.* New York: H. N. Abrams, 2003.
"Spring 1974 Swatch Book." *Earnshaw's Infants, Girls, and Boys Wear Review,* July 1973.
Staplehurst, Richard. "The Don Draper Effect." CALM: The Campaign against Living
    Miserably. June 19, 2013. http://www.thecalmzone.net/2013/06/dondraper.
Stephens-Davidowitz, Seth. "Google, Tell Me. Is My Son a Genius?" *New York Times*
    online. January 18, 2014. http://www.nytimes.com/2014/01/19/opinion/sunday
    /google-tell-me-is-my-son-a-genius.html.
Sterne, Peter. "Joanna Coles: 'Cosmopolitan' Is a 'Deeply Feminist' Magazine." Capital
    New York. December 3, 2013. http://www.capitalnewyork.com/article/media
    /2013/12/8536817/joanna-coles-cosmopolitan-deeply-feminist-magazine.
"Student Fashions." *New York Times,* November 27, 1966, 13.
"Students' Rights Stressed in Report." *New York Times,* October 2, 1968, 36.
"Suited for City Squiring." *Playboy,* September 1969, 135.
"Supreme Court Lets Maryland Ruling Stand." *Rome [Georgia] News-Tribune,* Novem-
    ber 14, 1966, 2.
Tanous, Helen Nicol. *Making Clothes for Your Little Girls.* Peoria, IL: Chas. A. Bennet
    Co., 1954.
Taylor, Angela. "Men's Fashions in the 1960's: The Peacock's Glory Was Regained."
    New York Times, December 15, 1969, 62.
———. "Hair Grooming Goes Unisex." *New York Times,* August 12, 1971, 38.
———. "Women Perplex Fashion Historian." *New York Times,* February 9, 1966, 42.
Thomas, Marlo, and Friends. *Free to Be . . . You and Me.* Bell Records, 1972.

Tirella, Joseph V. "Hannah Montana Crowned New Queen of 'Tween.'" U.S. Business, NBC News. February 8, 2008. http://www.nbcnews.com/id/23051344/ns /business-us_business/t/hannah-montana-crowned-new-queen-tween.

"Title VII of the Civil Rights Act of 1964." http://www.eeoc.gov/laws/statutes/titlevii .cfm.

"Title IX, Education Amendments of 1972." http://www.dol.gov/oasam/regs/statutes /titleix.htm.

Twenge, Jean M. "Changes in Masculine and Feminine Traits over Time: A Meta-Analysis." *Sex Roles* 36, no. 5–6 (March 1997): 305–325.

Tynan, Kenneth, and Jacques Levy. "Oh! Calcutta!" New York: Eden Theater, June 17, 1969.

U.S. Census Bureau. "1951–1994 Statistical Abstracts." http://www.census.gov/prod /www/abs/statab1951-1994.htm.

Von Furstenberg, Diane. *Diane: A Signature Life.* New York: Simon and Schuster, 1998.

Waters, Suzette. "Leaving the Pink Behind: Word from a Mother." http://www .columbiatribune.com/arts_life/family_life/blogs/word_from_a_mother /leaving-the-pink-behind/article_44aa42cb-5506-5970-ae5e-bbcc5b8f315a.html.

Weisner, Thomas S., and Bernice T. Eiduson. "The Children of the 60's as Parents." *Psychology Today,* January 1986.

"What If . . . Gloria Steinem Were Miss America?" *Esquire,* July 1973, 132.

"Who Was David Reimer (also, Sadly, Known as 'John/Joan')?" Intersex Society of North America. http://www.isna.org/faq/reimer.

Wolf, Naomi. "Gender Equality." *New York Times* online. November 30, 2012. http:// www.nytimes.com/2012/11/30/opinion/global/gender-equality.html.

"Women Who Are Cute When They Are Mad." *Esquire,* July 1973, 81–83, 302.

Woodward, K. L. "Do Children Need Sex Roles?" *Newsweek,* June 10, 1974.

Wyden, Barbara. "When Both Wear the Pants." *St. Petersburg Times,* March 1, 1970.

Zappa, Frank. "Take Your Clothes off When You Dance." Lyrics. 1961 (out of copyright). From the album *We're Only in It for the Money,* 1968.

Zolotow, Charlotte. *William's Doll.* New York: Harper and Row, 1972.

Zwerdling, Daniel. "Unshaven, Unshorn, and Unacceptable." *Today's Education* (November 1968): 23–24.

Index

Italicized page numbers refer to illustrations.

abortion, 1930s, 23–24
"Academic Freedom in the Secondary
    Schools" (ACLU), 127
active sportswear, 61
Adelson, Joseph, 25
advertising, 75, 78, 121
African American models, 86
African and Asian styles, 10, 29, 59, 86
Afro hairstyle, 142–143
age compression, 45
age distinctions, 100
AIDS, 90
A-line skirt, 41, 45
allies in older generations, 15, 17, 27, 75
alternative lives, 88
American Civil Liberties Union (ACLU),
    127–128, 136, 138
"American Costume," 39
American Dream, 50
American Psychological Association, 25,
    34, 112, 160
Amies, Hardy, 88
Andelin, Helen B., 36, 37, 41, 54, 159, 164
androgynous styles, 30
androgyny, 6, 33, 44
antifeminists, 152–153, 158
antiwar rallies, 17
appearance, behavior associated with,
    133–134
appropriation of minority or subcultural
    styles, 29

"Are You a Boy or Are You a Girl" (Bar-
    barians), 126–127
Aros v. McDonnell Douglas Corporation, 142
art school students, 124–125
artificial secondary sex characteristics,
    64–65
*As Nature Made Him: The Boy Who Was
    Raised as a Girl* (Colapinto), 108
Asian clothing, 29, 59
athletes, 74, 86, 144–145, 146, 147, 164
athletic clothing, 144–145
attractiveness, 12–13, 36

Babl, James, 65
baby boom generation, 9–10, 17–18, 21–23,
    27; "leading edge," 19, 53; memories,
    30–31
baby doll dresses, 121
baby dresses, 95, 97
"Baby X: The Effect of Gender Labels on
    Adult Responses to Infants" (Seavy,
    Katz, and Zalk), 110
Balser, Paul, 128
Barbarians, 126–127
barbershops, 11, 81–83, 163
bare legs, 40
baseball, 74
Beatles, 9, 20, 27, 52, 70, 124; hairstyle, 82
Beats, 88
beauty, "natural" vs. "artificial," 12, 32
behavioral psychology, 33, 109
bell-bottoms, 76
Bem, Sandra, 33

Bem Sex Role Inventory (BSRI), 33, 65, 168

Bender, Marylin, 44–45, 67

Benedek, Therese, 25

Bennett-England, Rodney, 79, 86–87

Bentley, Eric, 18

binary model of gender, 7, 94–95, 111, 118, 152–153, 154, 167–168

biological essentialism, 113

biological sex, 22–23, 25, 109

birth control, 1, 6, 17, 22–24

bisexuality, 22, 25, 90

Black, Hugo, 131

black armbands, 131

black feminists, 153

Black Power movement, 12, 16, 139, 142

Blank, Hanne, 95

Blass, Bill, 69, 72, 79

Block, Jeanne Humphrey, 112

Bloomer, Amelia, 39, 52

Bloomer dress, 39, 57

Bloomingdale's, 55

Blow, Charles, 1

Bob and Carol and Ted and Alice (1969), 22

bodies: ideal, female, 43–44; ideal, male, 70

Bold Look, 68

bona fide occupational qualification (BFOQ), 140, 141

Bonnie and Clyde (1967), 79

Bourdin, Guy, 55

boyfriend sweaters, 30

Bradley, Robert, 41

brain sex, 108

bras, 31, 46, 53, 55

Bray, Helen, 114

breadwinner role, 87–88

breeching, 39

Breen, Thomas (plaintiff), 133–134

British Invasion, 12, 124–125

British menswear, 66–67, 72

Brown, Helen Gurley, 10, 35, 36, 38, 158

Brylcreem ad, *80*

Bullough, Vern, 33

Burge, Penny, 117

Burr, Raymond, 89

Bush, George H. W., 20

business casual, 61

business suits, men's, 13, 15, 59; cultural Darwinist view, 64; lapel width and fit, 62, 70; origins, 62

business suits, women's, 56, 157–158

bustline, 42, 43

Butler, Judith, 169

caftans, *73, 74,* 81

"California Dreamin'" (Mamas and the Papas), 46–47

campus styles, 45

Cardin, Pierre, 6, 67, 69–70, 72, 88

Carnaby Street, 9, 10, 59

Cassell, Charles, 134

casual clothing, men's, 61, 66

casual Friday, 61, 163

Chambre Syndicale de la Haute Couture, 69

Chanel, Coco, 40

Cheap Chic (Milinaire and Troy), 52

children: "Baby X" studies, 110–111; failures of non-gendered child raising, 118, 119; feminization of girls, 45, 119–120, 159–162; gender roles, learned, 92; gender-nonconforming, 13, 95–96, 156–157, 169–170; homophobia and child raising, 113; non-gendered child raising, 10, 92, 107, 110–118, 157; "tomboyism," 95–96, 113; toys, 111, 157

children's clothing: accessories industry, 155; age distinctions, 100; for babies, 97–98; carrying over, 121; dressy clothes, 100, 102; girls buying boys' clothes, 103; mail order catalogs, 94; more gendered after early 1970s, 114–115; pink and blue, 96–97; play clothes, 98–100, *99, 101;* rules for, 105;

school clothes, 100; sexualization of, 119–121; for toddlers, 97, 98, 120; unisex, 100–104, *101, 102*. *See also* children's clothing, by era

children's clothing, by era: nineteenth century, 95–97; 1950s and early 1960s, 97; between 1962 and 1979, 100–105, *101, 102*; after early 1970s, 114–115; after mid-1970s, 105–106; after mid-1980s, 115

Civil Rights Act of 1964, 6, 12, 136–137, 139–140

civil rights movement, 1, 4, 16, 17, 150

civil rights movements, as efforts to include people, 26–27

classic clothing, revival of, 27–28, 53, 83–84, 90, 154–155

Clinton, Bill, 20

Clinton, Hillary, 162

Cohen, Philip, 153

Cold War, 138

Cole, Shaun, 89

Coles, Joanna, 158

college students, 75–76

colonization, 150

color palettes/colorways, 10, 104–105, 158

conflict in fashions, 32

Congress to Unite Women, 53

conservative movement, 116, 165–166

conservative women, 41

Constantinople, Anne, 33

consumer culture, 10, 27, 154; connection to others, 18; generational categories used, 20–21; preschoolers and, 93

Continental Look, 66

Cook, Daniel T., 93

Corby, Colleen, 45–46

corporate culture, 84

cosmetic surgery, 57

cosmetics, 52, 57

cosmetologists, 82

"*Cosmo* Girl," 10

cosmofeminism, 158

Cosmopolitan, 37, 44, 158, 159

cosplay, 165

Costume Society of America, 93

Coty Award, 72

counterculture, 1960s, 74

countermovements, 53–55

Coupland, Douglas, 20

couples motif, 78

Courrèges, André, 40, 42, 67

crocheting, 49, 78, *78*

cross-dressing, 30

cruel and unusual punishment, 128

culottes, 136

cultural chauvinism, 113

cultural feminists, 153

culture change, 15, *170–171*

culture wars, 1, 9, 13–14, 90, 150–171; acceptance of gender-nonconforming children, 156–157; binary model of gender and, 152–153, 154, 167–168; generation gap as opening, 17; legal cases and, 129

cutaways, 62

Cyrus, Miley, 160–161

dandyism, 86

Darwin, Charles, 27

Davidson, Sara, 54

Declaration of Independence, 26, 149, 150

democratic ideal, 166

Democratic National Convention (1968), 139

demographics, 20, 119, *119*

Department of Health, Education, and Welfare (HEW), 143, 144

Diamond, Milton, 33

diaper shirts, 97

Diaz v. Pan American World Airways Inc., 140–141

dieting, 46

Dior, Christian, 41

disco, 84, *85*

disillusionment, 50

Ditto brand jeans, 49–50

"Do Children Need Sex 'Roles'?" (*Newsweek*), 112

"do your own thing," 18–19, 32, 48, 51, 142

Donohue v. Shoe Corporation of America, 141

Donovan, Bernard, 128–129

"Don't Call Me Mama Anymore" (Elliot), 48

Douglas, William O., 149

Doyle, August (plaintiff), 142–143

drape suits, 66, 67

dress codes, 123–127; elements of social class in, 123; extracurricular activities, 130; school, 6, 28, 30, 123–130; team, 144–145; workplace, 129–130, 139–143

Dress for Success (Molloy), 56, 59, 84–85

Dress for Success for Women (Molloy), 56, 157–158

Dress Optional (Bennett-England), 79

Duke of Windsor, 81

Earnshaw's, 103

earth mother, 48

Eddie Bauer, 83

Edwardian elegance, 66

Ehrhardt, Anke, 108

Elliot, Cass, 10, 46–47

Ellison, Jesse, 117

employment, women and, 2, 6, 12

Enjoli perfume commercial, 52

Ephron, Nora, 54, 72

Equal Employment Opportunity Commission (EEOC), 140

Equal Protection Clause, Fourteenth Amendment, 130

equal protection under the law, 26

Equal Rights Amendment (ERA), 6, 54, 152–153

equality, 6, 39, 150

Erasmus, 106

Esquire, 54, 60, 68

Establishment, 124

event dressing, 52

evolutionary biology, 27

evolutionary/cyclical theories of fashion change, 64–65, 67, 154–155

exercise, 10, 43–44, 46

existential questions, 13–14

fads, study of, 152

Fagan v. National Cash Register, 140–141

Fairchild, John, 39–40

family styles, 78, 104

Fascinating Womanhood (Andelin), 36, 37, 38, 44, 159

fashion: as expression of convictions, 18; as superficial, 13, 17

fashion advice, in books, 37–38

Fashion Archives and Museum of Shippensburg University, 70–71

fashion designers, 6, 41–42, 50, 67–68; queer fashion professionals, 88, 165; Silent Generation, 20; women's, in menswear, 69

fashion industry, 8, 30

fashion studies, 2

Fashionable Savages, The (Fairchild), 39–40

fat bodies, 44; Cass Elliot's style, 46–48

Fausto-Sterling, Anne, 169

Federico, Salvatore (plaintiff), 128

Feminine Mystique, The (Friedan), 4, 10, 22, 24, 35; challenges to "nature" debate, 107; launches second-wave feminism, 36–37

femininity, 29, 35–58; changing notions of, 10; competing visions, 36; fear of, 63 hostility toward, 111–112; "man-tailored" clothing permitted, 30; resistance to stereotypes, 57; sexualization of girls, 159–162

feminism: backlash, 53–55; cosmofeminism, 158; femininity, view of, 111–112; first-wave, 38; second-wave, 16, 106–107, 151; third-wave, 169. *See also* women's liberation movement

Ferrell v. Dallas, 149

fetal hormones, 108

fibers and fabrics, 10, 32, 46, 59, 78, 103, 158

fictional characters, 87

First Amendment, 130, 138

first-time parents, 119, *119*

first-wave feminism, 38

Fish, Michael, 67–68, 69

flamboyance, 86

football players, 146

Forest Hills High School (Queens), 128–129

Fortas, Abe, 131

foundation garments, 46

Fourteenth Amendment, 130, 143

Frazier, George, 10, 59

Frederick's of Hollywood, 55

Free to Be . . . You and Me (Thomas), 7, 92, 111, 114, 117, 155

Freeman v. Flake, 149

French aristocracy, 18

Freud, Sigmund, 63, 87

Freudian psychology, 21, 62–63, 87, 95

Friedan, Betty, 4, 22, 23, 26, 35, 36–37, 50, 57

fur coats, 74, 86

futuristic vision, 32

Gap store, 49

Gatsby style, 81

gay liberation movement, 9, 10, 31, 59, 90, 165

gay men, fashion and, 88–89

gender: binary view of, 6–7, 94–95, 111, 118, 152–154, 157, 167–168; bipolar model, 33; sex conflated with, 3

gender identity, 14–15, 22–23, 108–109; children's clothes and, 94; civil rights movements linked with, 26–27

Gender Identity Project (University of California at Los Angeles), 113

gender mix-ups, 30, 115–116

gender permanence, 160

gender revolution, 22–25

gender roles, 10, 106, 145, 152, 166; learned, 11, 92; origins, 107, 112; psychological strain, 91; socially constructed, 7, 107–108, 112–113, 118. *See also* nature or nurture debate

gender rules, 27–30

gender studies, 2–3

gender-neutral, as masculine, 111–112

gender-nonconforming children, 13, 95–96, 122, 156–157, 169–170

"generally acceptable" forms of dress, 8

generation gap, 17, 49

Generation X, 20, 119, 155; memories of unisex era, 30–31

Generation X: Tales for an Accelerated Culture (Coupland), 20

generational categories, as advertising construct, 20–21

Gentleman's Quarterly (GQ) (magazine), 60, 83–84

Gernreich, Rudi, 4, 9, 31–32, 73–74, 88; predictions, 79, 81

Gilder, George, 54

girdles, 40, 46

girls' dresses, historical ,117

Godfather, The (1972), 81

Gould, Lois, 109–110, 111–112

Grambs, Jean, 65–66

granny length skirts, 52

gray flannel suit, 49, 59, 62, 81, 175n35
greasers, 66
Great Depression, 21, 24, 79
Great Gatsby, The (1974), 81
Greatest Generation, 19
Greece, ancient, 63
Green, Robert L., 67, 69, 74, 75, 76
Griswold v. Connecticut, 138
grooming industry, men's, 11, 82, 163. *See also* hair styles
Guttentag, Marcia, 114

hair styles: Afro, 142–143; Afros and braids, 12; children's, 103; long hair on men, 1, 2, 11–12; male, well-groomed, *80*, 81–82; men-only establishments, 83; unisex salons, 11, 81–83
hair-care products, 11, 81, 82, 163
Hall, G. Stanley, 96, 107
Hannah Montana, 161
Harrad Experiment, The (Rimmer), 22
Harvey of Carnaby Street, 75
"having it all," 164
Hay, Harry, 31
Hefner, Hugh, 17, 21, 67, 89
Heinlein, Robert, 22
hemlines, 10, 43, 52, 90, 136; midi-skirts, 41, 52, 136; miniskirts, 30, 40, 45, 136
Hentoff, Nat, 75
Hepburn, Katharine, 40
heteronormative advertising, 78
High School Principals Association (New York), 128–129
hippie styles, 69, 74
h.i.s. (advertiser), 75
"his 'n' hers" clothing, 30, 76–78, 77; for children, 104
"his 'n' hers" hairstyling, 82–83
Hoffman, Sarah, 156
Hollywood glamour, 47–48
Hollywood stars, 28

home-sewn clothing, 51, 78, 94, 117
homophobia, 10, 59, 61, 63, 87, 113
homosexuality, 21, 25, 113, 116; declassification of as mental disorder, 34, 113
How to Be a Woman (Moran), 164
Howell v. Wolf, 134
Hudson, Rock, 89
Husband-Coached Childbirth (Bradley), 41

identity formation, 107–108, 114
immaturity, male, 87
Independent School District v. Swanson, 133
individual rights, 17
individualism, 154
individuality, 65, 75, 135
"Inn Shop, The" 76
interactionism, 33
intersectionality, 169
intersex people, 25, 108–109, 170
investment dressing, 83
Italian-style trousers, 66
Ivy League style, 67, 74–75

J. C. Penney, 70, 76, 94
Jacobs v. Benedict, 143–144
Jaffe, Richard, 50
Jagger, Mick, 125
Jayson shirt company, 75
jeans, 3, 28, 30, 40, 49–50, 86, 100, 136, 148; for children, 97, 97, 100, 103, 121
jet-set avant-garde, 72
Journal of Home Economics, 81
jumpsuits, 44, 49, 51, 136
Junior sizes, 42–43, 44, 76, 102

Kagan, Jerome, 25, 26
Katz, Phyllis, 110
Kazin, Alfred, 32
Kelleher, Tim, 76
Kendall, Elaine, 67
Kennedy, Robert F., 139

Kent State, 17
kids getting older younger (KGOY), 45, 119–120
King, Martin Luther, Jr., 139, 170
King's Road line (Sears), 76
Kinsey, Alfred, 21
kipper ties, 68
knee breeches, 18
knickers suit, 136
Kores, Edward T., Jr., 125

L. L. Bean, 83
Ladies Circle Knitting and Crochet Guide, 77
"ladylike" image, 28–30, 40, 45, 102
Lambert v. Marushi, 134
Lands' End catalog, 90
Lane Bryant, 48
lapels, 62, 70
Lauren, Ralph, 68, 72, 79
Laver, James, 57, 67
legal cases, 6, 8, 11–13, 123–149, *131;* ACLU and, 127–128, 136, 138; African American plaintiffs, 142–143; constitutional rights, 130, 135; cruel and unusual punishment, 128; Fifth Circuit, 130; Forest Hills High School (Queens), 128–129; long hair on men, 1, 2, 124–135, *131;* males, focus on, 30, 124, 148; pants for women, 135–136; parental support for minors, 125, 129; school dress codes, 123–130; Second Circuit, 130; Title VII, 12, 139–142; Title IX, 6, 143–145; U.S. Supreme Court, 128–131, 138, 148–149; workplace dress codes, 129–130, 139–143
leisure styles, 40, 61, 81
leisure suit, 70, 79, 81, 162
"Lemon Frog Shop," 45–46
Leonard, George (Georgie Porgie), 126
Leonard v. School Committee of Attleboro, 126
lesbians, 38, 53, 165, 166

Levi's jeans, 49
LGBTQ (lesbian, gay, bisexual, transgender, queer) rights, 10, 165
liberal feminists, 153
licensing, 82
lifestyle, 18–19
lingerie, 55–56
"little girl" trend, 120–121
long hair on men, 11–12, 28; anti–long hair violence, 124, 146, 148; delinquency, allegations of, 133–134; legal cases, 1, 2, 124–135, *131;* stereotypes, 133–134
lounge suit/sack suit, 62
Lunde, Donald, 25
Lynes, Russell, 8, 88

Mad Men (2007–), 163
Mademoiselle, 52
madras plaids and paisleys, 78
magazines: men's, 21, 60, 64, 67, 72, 74–76; women's, 10, 19, 37, 42, 44, 51, 72, 76, 158, 159
"Male Liberation Festival," 24
Mamas and the Papas, 10, 46–48
Man and Woman, Boy and Girl (Money and Ehrhardt), 108–109
Mannes, Marya, 75
mannish clothing, 41
"man-tailored" clothing, 30
Marshall, Norman Thomas (plaintiff), 128
masculine mystique, 60, 64, 87–88
masculine signifiers, women's appropriation of, 51
masculinity, 24, 29–30; competing models, 60; as cultural artifact, 61, 63, 67; current fashions, 162; expressive forms, 29, 79; as fragile, 63–66, 164; in relation to femininity, 61; school-age boys, 65–66
masculinity, rules of, 29
Masters and Johnson studies, 17

Mattachine Society, 31
Maurice Rentner Ltd., 72
McLuhan, Marshall, 73
"Me Decade," 2
Mellon, Tamara, 158
Men and Masculinity (Pleck and
    Sawyer), 24
men of color, 84
men's movement, 24
menswear: African American clothing,
    29, 59; Asian clothing, 29, 59; British,
    66–67, 72; casual clothing, 61; Conti-
    nental styles, 67; decorative details, 59;
    fur coats, 74; gay men and, 88–89; "his
    'n' hers" clothing, 30, 76–78, 77; leisure
    suit, 70, 79, 81, 162; Mods and Rock-
    ers, 66–67, 69, 74; neckwear, 61, 66,
    67–70; peacock revolution, 6, 10, 59–91;
    Romantic revival, 10, 28–29, 59; Saville
    Row styles, 66, 67; sexiness, 86–87;
    women's fashion designers in, 69
micro-mini skirts, 52
midi-skirts, 41, 52, 136
Milinaire, Caterine, 52
Miller, David (plaintiff), 134–135
Miller, Derek, 125
Miller, Monica, 29, 86
miniskirts, 30, 40, 45, 136
Miss America pageant, 53, 54, 57, 166
Misses sizes, 42–43, 48, 102
Mods, 66–67, 69, 74
Molloy, John T., 56, 59, 84–85, 157–158;
    current advice, 162
moment dressing, 52
mommy wars, 162
Money, John, 22, 23, 25, 33, 107–109
Montgomery Ward, 84, 94, 99, 101
Moran, Caitlin, 164
morning coat, 62
movies, 79, 81
Mr. Fish, 68

Ms., 9, 158
Museum at the Fashion Institute of Tech-
    nology, 88
musicians, 9, 12, 46–48, 66, 86; Silent
    Generation, 20

Namath, Joe, 86
National Organization for Women, 53
National Women's Conference (1977),
    152–153
"natural" vs. "artificial" beauty, 12, 32,
    44, 46
nature or nurture debate, 8, 22, 33, 92–
    122; failures of non-gendered child rais-
    ing, 118, 119; introduction of nurture,
    95–96; parenting advice, 96; second-
    wave feminism and, 106–107. *See also*
    children; children's clothing; gender
    roles
nature plus nurture hypothesis, 95
Nazi edicts, 31
neckwear, 61, 66, 67–70
Nehru, Jawaharlal, 70
Nehru jacket, 70–72, 71, 74
neutral clothing, 30, 94–95; for babies
    and toddlers, 97; cost, 98; feminized
    versions of masculine styles, 103; nine-
    teenth century, 95–97. *See also* unisex
    clothing
New Look, 41
New York Civil Liberties Union, 127
New York Times, 16, 52
"Newport Look," 81
Nicholson, Harold, 65
Nixon, Richard M., 16, 139
"no-bra bra," 31, 46
nostalgia, 2, 6, 55, 68, 79, 81
nurses, dress codes for, 40

office styles, 56
older women, 44–45

"-ologies," 33
O'Neill, George, 22
O'Neill, Nena, 22
Open Marriage (Nena and George), 22

pageants, 120
paisley, 78
Palmer, Jim, 86
Palmer, Mark, 74
pants, for children, 97, *97*, 99, 100, 103, 121
pants, for women, 6, 8, 10, 12, 13, 28, 38–39;
    cut and style, 40; legal cases, 135–136;
    peer perceptions, 155–156; rules for,
    39–40; as subversive, 39. *See also* jeans
pantsuits, 28, 40, 45
panty girdles, 40, 46
pantyhose, 40–41, 42, 46
parenting, 107; ambivalence and anxiety,
    11, 12; demographic changes, 119, *119. See*
    also children
Parker, Theodore, 170
Parsons, James B., 134–135
patterns, 42, 43, 51–52, 73, 78, *102*, 137; con-
    servative, 83
peacock revolution, 6, 10, 59–91; back-
    ground for, 64–68; on college cam-
    puses, 74–76; gay men and, 88–89;
    rejection of masculine mystique,
    60–64; sexual attractiveness, 73–74,
    86–87; unisex clothing, 76, *77*, 78. *See*
    also menswear
Penn, Arthur, 79
Penthouse, 60
Pepitone, Joe, 74
Pepsi ads, 19
Perrin, Ellen, 157
personality dressing, 52, 79
Peters, Nick, 83
Phillips, Michelle, 47
photographs, *4, 5*
Pierre, Clara, 52, 89–90, 167

Pill, the (oral contraceptives), 22, 23–24,
    44, 50
pink, as symbol of femininity, 104
Pink and Blue: Telling the Boys from the
    Girls in America (Paoletti), 7, 94
pink boys, 156
pinkification, 97
plaids, 78
plastic surgery, 44
playboy, 87, 89
Playboy, 16, 21, 60, 67, 72; "Back to Cam-
    pus" issue, 1969, 75–76; college issues,
    84; generation gap and, 75–76; sartorial
    conservatism, 74–75
Pleck, Joseph, 24, 91
plus sizes, 48
Polo brand, 68
polyamory, 22
polyester double knits, 78
ponchos, crocheted, 49, 78, *78*
pop psychology, 63
Pope, McKenna, 157
pornography cases, 21
power suits, 56
premarital chastity, 50
prenatal testing, 115, 119
presidents, 19–20
preteens/young teens, 45–46
princess dress, 160
Profile du Monde, 47
proliferation of choice, 51–53
pronaturalism, 116
Psychology Today, 9
punctuated equilibrium, 27, 154

Quant, Mary, 42
queer fashion professionals, 165
Queer History of Fashion, A, 88

race-based legal cases, 142–143
racial identity, 12, 86

ready-to-wear clothing, 48, 69, 165
Reefer Madness (1936), 16
Renwick, Deborah (plaintiff), 143
restraint of women, 46
Richmond Professional Institute (RPI), 128
right to privacy, 138
Rimmer, Robert, 22
Roaring Twenties, 21
Roberts, Steven, 16
Rockers, 66
Roger, Manley, 146
Rolling Stone, 84
Rolling Stones, 124
Romantic revival, 10, 28–29, 59
Romney, Mitt, 16, 132
RuPaul, 165
RuPaul's Drag U (2010–2013), 165

Saint Laurent, Yves, 88
sandals, 58
Santorum, Rick, 1, 2, 3, 166
Saturday Night Fever (1977), 84
Saville Row styles, 66, 67
Sawyer, Jack, 24
Schlafly, Phyllis, 54, 152–153
school dress codes, 6, 28, 30, 123–130
scientific studies, 7, 9, 25–26; child psychology, 107
Sears catalog, 42, 42, 43, 44, 84, 94; children's clothing, 97; King's Road line, 76; "Lemon Frog Shop," 45–46; mod look for men, 76; neckwear, 68–69
Seavy, Carol, 110
second-wave feminism, 10, 16, 35–36, 106–107, 151; fissures in, 53, 153
self-expression, 13, 70, 73, 128, 135, 138
self-reflexivity, 14
separate sphere, 64
Sesame Street (1969–), 92, 111
Seventeen, 52, 76

sex, conflated with gender, 3
Sex and the Single Girl (Brown), 35, 36, 158; clothing chapter, 37–38
sex characteristics, 64–65
sex discrimination, 139–141
sex roles, 22, 107
sexiness, male, 86–87
sexology studies, 17
Sexual Behavior of the Human Female (Kinsey), 21
Sexual Behavior of the Human Male (Kinsey), 21
sexual orientation, 87, 95
sexual revolution, 1, 4, 13, 17–18, 21–22, 152
Sexual Suicide (Gilder), 54
sexuality: birth control and, 23–24; double standard, 24, 44, 50, 168; as learned, 95; male, and sexual orientation, 87
"sexy," definition, 73–74
sexy little dresses, 55
Shakespeare, William, 106
Shelton, Raymond O., 134
shifting erogenous zones, 67
shirt suits, 70
Shoffner, Robert D. (plaintiff), 128
Shrimpton, Jean, 72
"Sighs and Whispers" catalog, 55
Silent Generation, 19–20
"sissyish" boys, 95–96, 113
sizing systems, 42–44
skinny bodies, 44
skirt lengths, 41
slacks. *See* pants, for women
slavery, 86
slopers, 43
smooth line under clothes, 40, 46
socialites, 72
sodomy and public indecency laws, 25
sources, 8
Space: 1999 (1975–1977), 31, 51
specialty stores, 117

Spitz, Mark, 146, *147*

Spock, Benjamin, 17

sport coats, 162

sports clothing, 6

Stanton, Elizabeth Cady, 39, 53

Star Trek (1966–1969), 6, 51

stasis, 27

Steinem, Gloria, 54, 152

stereotypes, 7, 53–54, 57, 95; children and, 111–112, 121; gay men and, 89; long hair on men, 133–134; as "natural," 158

Sting, The (1973), 81

stockings, 40–41

STOP ERA movement, 54

Stranger in a Strange Land (Heinlein), 22

Strauss, Valerie, 164

streetwalkers, movie, 58

Streisand, Barbra, 48

"success suit," 56

summer of love, 69

sumptuary laws, 123

Symonds, Martin, 26

Syracuse University, 17

tailors, 62

Taylor, Angela, 82

teachers, dress codes for, 41

team dress codes, 144–145

Teddy Boys, 66

teenage models, 42

teenagers, 9, 21, 27. *See also* legal cases

teenagers, sexualization of, 118–120

teen-oriented fashions, 10, 42–44, 102; preteens/young teens, 45–46, 105; Youthquake, 10, 19, 42, 48. *See also* Junior sizes

third-wave feminism, 169

'30s-inspired clothing, 79

Thomason, Robert (headmaster), 148

thong bathing suit, 32

three-piece suit, 78

Tinker v. Des Moines Independent Community School District, 130–131

Title VII (Equal Employment Opportunity), 12, 139–142

Title IX (Equal Opportunity in Education), 6, 143–145, 164

"tomboyism," 95–96, 113

topless bathing suit, 4, 9, 31

Torres, Ruben, 44

toys, 111, 157

tradition, perception of, 115

Tree, Penelope, 72

Trent v. Perritt, 144

Troy, Carol, 52

True Womanhood (Andelin), 164

Turnbull and Asser, 68

turtlenecks, 30, 31, 54, 66, 70, 72, 76, 78

2001: A Space Odyssey (1968), 51

2012 presidential campaign, 1, 2, 3, 12

undergarments/underwear, 10, 39, 55–56, 86

understanding attributed to youth movement, 32, 51

unfinished business of unisex, 4, 8, 14, 53, 118, 150

unisex clothing, 2, 6; as controversial, 118; for entire family, 104–105; 1968 as year of, 31; origins, 30; peak in 1970s, 4; physical differences highlighted, 8, 32, 51, 115, 120, 153–154; as sexually attractive, 36. *See also* neutral clothing

"unisex society," 25–26

"up the down staircase," 129

U.S. Constitution, 26, 130, 135

U.S. Military Academy at West Point, 144

U.S. Supreme Court, 128–131, 138, 148–149

vaginal infections, 42–43

Van Runkle, Theodora, 79

Vanderbilt, Gloria, 32

variety of available styles, 10

Veblen, Thorstein, 123
vest suit, 78
vests, *102,* 103
Victorian-revival sensibility, 41
Victoria's Secret, 55–56
Vietnam, 16, 131, 139
Village People, 89
vintage sensuality, 55
virginity, technical, 50
Vogue, 10, 19, 43, 51, 72, 76
Von Furstenberg, Diane, 6, 28, 55
Vreeland, Diana, 10, 19

Waetjen, Walter, 65–66
Wallace v. Ford, 145
Walt Disney Company, 160
Washington, D.C., 162–163
Washington Post, 19
Waters, Suzette, 160
Western-style jeans, 100

William's Doll (Zolotow), 92, 111, 155
Willingham v. Macon Telegraph Publishing Co., 141
Wolf, Naomi, 166
women of color, 29
women's liberation movement, 1, 4, 152
Women's Wear Daily, 39, 55, 73
working class, 29, 66, 139
workplace dress codes, 129–130, 139–143
wrap dress, 55
Wyden, Barbara, 26

X: A Fabulous Child's Story (Gould), 13, 109–110, 111–112, 121

Youthquake, 10, 19, 42, 48

Zalk, Sue Rosenberg, 110
Zappa, Frank, 171
Zwerdling, Daniel, 138

Jo B. Paoletti is Associate Professor of American Studies at the University of Maryland. With degrees in apparel design and textiles from Syracuse University, the University of Rhode Island, and the University of Maryland, she has concentrated most of her research on two main questions: How does consumer culture shape gender identity? How does gender "identity work" influence consumer culture? This effort began with her 1980 dissertation, *Changes in the Masculine Image in the United States, 1880–1910,* and continues through *Pink and Blue: Telling the Boys from the Girls in America* (2012) and *Sex and Unisex: Fashion, Feminism, and the Sexual Revolution.* Her current projects include a "research memoir" about the intersection of age and gender. When she needs a respite from research, she enjoys long-distance train travel, experimenting with beer-food pairings, and the domestic arts.